Mead Dixon, 1978

PLAYING THE CARDS
THAT ARE DEALT

PLAYING THE CARDS THAT ARE DEALT

Mead Dixon, the Law, and Casino Gaming

University of Nevada
Oral History Program

FROM ORAL HISTORY INTERVIEWS WITH MEAD DIXON,
CONDUCTED BY KEN ADAMS,
A NARRATIVE COMPOSED BY R. T. KING

This project was supported by the William F. Harrah College of Hotel Administration and the Gaming Research Center at the University of Nevada, Las Vegas. This support was made possible through gifts from Verna Harrah, the wife of the late William F. Harrah, and from the Promus Companies, the parent company of Harrah's Casino Hotels, and from the Eddie and Peggy Jean Gambarana Endowment.

University of Nevada Oral History Program
Reno, Nevada 89557

Library of Congress Cataloging in Publication Data:

King, R. T. (Robert Thomas), 1944-
Playing the cards that are dealt : Mead Dixon, the law and casino gaming : from oral history interviews with Mead Dixon / conducted by Ken Adams, a narrative composed by R. T. King.
p.   cm.   Includes index.
ISBN 1-56475-365-4
1. Dixon, Mead, 1919-   . 2. Lawyers--Nevada--Biography.
3. Casinos--Law and legislation--Nevada--History. 4. Gamling--Nevada--History.   I. Adams, Ken, 1942-   . II. Dixon, Mead, 1919-   . III. Title.
KF373.D56K56   1992
340' .092--dc20
[B]   92-34676
                                                                CIP

Publication Staff:

Production Manager: Helen M. Blue
Senior Production Assistant: Linda J. Sommer
Production Assistants:
Verne W. Foster and Ann E. Dalbec

Contents

Introduction

NEVADA ENCOMPASSES OVER 150,000 square miles of spectacular basin and range–country in which water is precious, temperatures are extreme, and the wind is relentless. The region's environment may be harsh, but its mountains contain rich deposits of non-ferrous ores, and its climate permits a precarious agriculture. For almost a century after the emigrant trails were opened, Nevada's small population supported itself primarily through mining, ranching, and farming, the majority of its inhabitants dwelling in loosely scattered communities, taking maximum advantage of scarce natural resources; but following World War II Nevada rapidly evolved into one of the most urbanized states in the union. In 1992 over 90 percent of the state's citizens reside in the major metropolitan areas of Las Vegas and Reno, and they neither ranch nor mine. The rise of the casino gaming industry is behind this remarkable metamorphosis.

Nevada is unique among the states in having an economy driven principally by the take of gambling casinos and their related enterprises. This condition was slow to develop. The state's early prospectors and buckaroos lived by an uninhibited frontier ethos, and by the 1860s gambling establishments were an accepted part of the social and economic landscape of Nevada; they were not, however, a dominant feature, and in 1910 Progressive reformers succeeded in having gambling outlawed entirely in the state. Illegal gambling houses continued to operate without much interference from the authorities, but even when casino gaming was once again made legal in 1931, the activity remained principally a diversion that only incidentally had any economic impact. However, in the years following World War II casino gaming began to grow faster than all other segments of the economy combined. Riding its surge, Reno's population quintupled and Las Vegas's increased tenfold. At least since the 1950s, not only Nevada's economy, but its very identity have been shaped by the nature of casino gaming and its magnetic appeal to the American imagination. Like it or not (and the state is deeply divided on this issue), the Nevada of the late twentieth century is not just dominated by casino gaming, it is practically defined by the enterprise.

In *Playing the Cards That Are Dealt*, the reader will encounter forty years of casino gaming history as lived and observed by one of the industry's most respected figures. L. Mead Dixon began practicing law in Reno in 1950. He quickly became an important participant in the expansion of casino gaming in that community, at Lake Tahoe, and in Las Vegas. In 1957 Dixon became the principal attorney for William F. Harrah and his Harrah's Clubs, and by the late 1960s he was on the boards of directors of Harrah's, the Showboat and the Tropicana. Following Mr. Harrah's death, Dixon was named the executor of the Harrah estate; shortly thereafter he was elected chairman of the Harrah's board, from which position he accomplished the 1980 merger of Harrah's with Holiday Inns, Inc. As a member of the Holiday board of directors, Mr. Dixon was instrumental in the subsequent expansion of Harrah's and Holiday into Atlantic City, and after returning to the Showboat board following his retirement from Holiday, he also guided that company's successful expansion into Atlantic City. Mead Dixon is, clearly, very knowledgeable about the inner workings of some of the most important casino gaming enterprises in America, and he has an expert's understanding of the effects of change over time in the economic, political and regulatory environments in which casinos must operate.

The oral history interviewing from which this narrative is derived was done by Ken Adams, a former student of mine. Mr.

Adams began a career in casino gaming in 1969. From 1982 to 1990 he was the casino manager and then director of casino operations for the Comstock Hotel-Casino in Reno, before leaving to found a very successful casino management consulting firm. Adams is the publisher and co-editor of the *Nevada Gaming Almanac*, and as chairman of the Educational Advisory Committee for the University of Nevada, Reno's Center for Professional Development he was instrumental in creating a university-based gaming studies program. For the Dixon oral history, Adams brought to his research and interviewing not only an insider's familiarity with the important themes, but also a keen sense of history developed through education, extensive travel, and a remarkable (and still growing) personal library. Mr. Adams was extraordinarily well qualified to conduct the interviews on which this book is based, and I feel fortunate that we were able to secure his services.

It is the goal of the Oral History Program to explore in depth a variety of subjects that are important to understanding the twentieth century history of Nevada. The subjects emphasized in this book are the casino gaming industry and some of its more prominent figures. Thus, although included within is considerable information about Mead Dixon's life, this is not a life history: the preparation and interviewing that Ken Adams did were directed less toward learning about Dixon the man than learning *through* Dixon about certain aspects of casino gaming in mid to late century. Although the interviews were carefully planned and directed, as the months of interviewing and review unfolded Adams found himself following as often as leading, moving in unexpected directions that added texture and depth and fuller development to the record. This always happens in the best, most satisfying oral history encounters, and it is part of the allure of the method.

My supervision of the interviews was calculatedly historiographic. By this I mean that since Dixon and Adams would be producing a collaborative, creative interpretation of the past, I wanted that interpretation to be informed by the historical imagination. Once I was satisfied that Mr. Dixon had the memories, I asked Mr. Adams to try to bring them out in an organized fashion consistent with what I believe to be the strengths of the historical process. Adams's questions were designed to draw responses that would reveal change over time, causality, and sequential development (one thing leading to another) where they existed. We were also very much interested in Mr. Dixon's analysis of events and of the strengths, weaknesses and personalities of some of the many gaming figures, politicians and attorneys who are mentioned in the work. The product of all of this was thirty-two hours of tapes which resulted in 1,200 pages of verbatim transcription.

Notwithstanding the considerable planning and preparation that went into the interview, and Mr. Dixon's articulate and thoughtful responses to Adams's questions, the 1,200-page transcript is not easy to read and understand; in fact it is a trial. That is the norm in oral history exercises of this magnitude. Only in the particular, only within its discrete elements, is structure apparent in the original transcription, and lack of structure is not the only thing inhibiting accessibility to the information embedded within: Such is the dynamic of oral history interviewing that in a work of this size the verbatim transcription, taken as a whole, speaks with a voice that is almost unintelligible. Oral communication, when represented in print–stripped of gesture, inflection, tone, and other components that go unrecorded on tape, or for which there are no symbols on the keyboard–is encumbered by fractured syntax, false starts, repetition, and numerous other impediments to clear understanding of its intended meaning.

Unorganized, incoherent, and longer than a telephone book–clearly, the people interested in reading this would be few. I have tried to make that experience unnecessary. Although it has been composed to read as a first-person account by Mead Dixon, *Playing the Cards That Are Dealt* is not an oral history transcript: it is instead my interpretation of the work that Adams and Dixon created over months of interviewing, reviewing, and documentary research. This constructed narrative, as I call it, is an effort to make the fruits of oral history methodology coherent and accessible to the average reader. These are not Mead Dixon's words precisely as he spoke them, in the order in which he spoke them, but I have recreated his speech as faithfully as possible consistent with the aim of composing a readable volume from the elements of the interviews. In addition, Ken Adams's questions, which established the structure and elicited the detail of the work, have been subsumed into the narrative, and I have imposed a measure of chronological and topical order on the whole that was not always evident in the interviewing. (In this I had valuable assistance from Helen Blue, who did the first rough reorganization of the material.)

While I wished to compose a readable narrative, it was not my intent to polish Mead Dixon's story to a high shine, and *Playing the Cards That Are Dealt* reveals some of the problems inherent in working with what is available when it does not precisely fit the chosen form. The natural episodic structure of oral history is apparent in the occasional lack of smooth transition from subject to subject, and when this occurs it is indicated in the text by a break between paragraphs. The reader will also encounter at least two departures from conventional composition: when Mr. Dixon laughs in amusement or to express irony, I represent this with [laughter]; and ellipses are used not to indicate that material has been deleted, but that a statement has been interrupted or is incomplete . . . or there is a pause for dramatic effect.

Mead Dixon has read the finished manuscript in page proof form, and affirmed in writing that it accurately interprets the content of the interviews upon which it is based. Still, I hope that there will be some readers who are interested in examining the unaltered record. Copies of the tape recordings of the interviews, their transcriptions (with corrections noted), and extensive collateral material are in the archives of the Oral History Program of the University of Nevada, Reno. As with all such efforts, while I can vouch for the authenticity of *Playing the Cards That Are Dealt*, I do not claim that it is entirely free of error. It should be approached with the same caution that the prudent reader exercises when consulting government records, newspaper accounts, diaries, and other sources of historical information.

The Oral History Program and I are indebted to a number of people for the hard work and creativity that they contributed to this project. Chief among them is Mead Dixon, who, as the reader will learn in Chapter 14, was failing in health and experiencing considerable pain throughout the interview process. His courage, determination and endurance are truly exemplary. I owe him special thanks for the patience with which he reviewed my narrative and responded to my many requests for amplification, some of which may have seemed unreasonable . . . perhaps because they were.

Esther DeVries-Nielsen, Mr. Dixon's assistant, was very important to the success of the project, assisting us at every stage of the work. Mrs. DeVries-Nielsen devoted many hours to helping us research the chronology of events and the spelling of proper names; her meticulous proofreading of the manuscript resulted in a number of important corrections; and she was instrumental in the selection, acquisition and identification of photographs–all of this while remaining unfailingly cheerful, even under the pressure of looming deadlines. We are deeply appreciative.

Susan Jarvis, director of the Gaming Resource Center of the UNLV Library, recommended Mr. Dixon as a chronicler in our gaming history series, served as a very effective and supportive liaison with her campus and interested parties in Las Vegas (including potential external funders), and in general should be recognized as the principal initiator and facilitator of the project. Our thanks also to the staffs of the Reference, Special Collections, and Government Publications departments of the University of Nevada, Reno Library for research assistance, and to Cam Sutherland of the University of Nevada Press for technical advice in the design of the dust jacket.

David J. Christianson, dean of the William F. Harrah College of Hotel Administration and the Gaming Research Center at the University of Nevada, Las Vegas, personally put the support of his college behind this project, for which we are very grateful. As noted on the copyright page, this support was made possible through gifts from Verna Harrah, wife of the late William F. Harrah, and from the Promus Companies, the parent company of Harrah's Casino Hotels, and from the Eddie and Peggy Jean

Gambarana endowment. Our thanks to all for the contribution they have made to enriching the historical record of casino gaming in Nevada.

ROBERT THOMAS KING
Reno, Nevada
September, 1992

[1]

An Illinois Boyhood

I WAS BORN IN SPRINGFIELD, ILLINOIS, on September 9, 1919: nine, nine, one-nine-one-nine . . . but I never won a quarter on the four nines. [laughter]

The Dixon side of my family came from Dixon, Illinois, a small town on the Rock River about a hundred miles west of Chicago, which was named after my great-great-grandfather. In our family memory, the Dixons were relatively more celebrated than the Browns, my mother's side. The early John Dixon was born in New York from English stock, and he came to Illinois in the early 1830s. As a postman out of Springfield, carrying the mails up to the north, he came to Lee's Ferry, where he decided that running a ferry would be a hell of a lot better than carrying the mail; so he bought it and created the town of Dixon, which has a quasi-reputation for being where Abe Lincoln headquartered during the so-called Black Hawk War. In Dixon there is a statue of Abe as a young officer in the Illinois militia; and, of course, John Dixon is prominent as the founder of the town, and they made a big brass plaque to him, and those two are together.

My brother, John Brown Dixon, and my father and I are the only persons in the family that ever really escaped Dixon. All the rest seemed to enjoy living in a town that had their name on the water tank and on the jail, and it has its reputation as being the hometown of Ronald Reagan. My family was always involved in politics there, but Ronald Reagan's father, Jack Reagan, was *deeply* involved in politics. The Dixons were Democrats, and so were the Reagans until Ronald got to Hollywood and became a Republican, but any connection between the Reagans and the Dixons had long since been severed.

My mother's family was the Brown family from Mechanicsburg, Illinois, about fifteen miles east of Springfield. Dr. Josiah Brown was a physician and a surgeon in Mechanicsburg. The town is typical of small Illinois farm towns, and it's a wonder anyone could succeed, but apparently in their day Josiah and his wife Elvira were prominent enough to merit having their pictures painted. They did what was usual for people in the Middle West: they bought farmland, and they left it to their son—my grandfather, Zack Brown. But Zack didn't like to work. Grandmother eventually moved to Springfield and started a small subdivision and a boardinghouse near the state capitol, and Zack came off the farm and lived with her for about two years and died sometime in the early 1900s. Grandmother Brown lived until 1930.

My father, Louis Dixon, was born in 1873, and my mother, Emma Brown, in about 1886. I have never been told the date they were married, but it was probably during World War I. (I suppose they were married. They would have to have been, because I was legitimate—I suspect that was important in those days.) [laughter] My father lived until 1938 when he was sixty-five, and my mother lived until 1941. In my youth, we were reasonably prosperous, but beginning with the crash of 1929 we lived frugally because the Depression was a very real thing to us—it had the effect of wiping out all our financial resources and my father's employment. The result was that I started working at odd jobs at age fourteen, and it seems to me that I have never stopped working since!

My father's education did not go beyond the eighth grade, at which point he left school to work in a market. There, he acquired the ability to wrap packages with a deftness and skill that I admired. Sometime very early on, he decided to seek better opportunities than Dixon offered, and he went to Springfield, the state capital. About 1900 he became employed by the Court of Honor, which was a fraternal beneficiary society, typical

of its time. It was what Amos and Andy[1] would call a "buryin'
society"–you paid a dollar a month, or whatever the current dues
were, and you had a decent burial, which seemed to concern a
lot of people in those days. (If you joined the Court of Honor,
your survivors would also be assured of a certain amount of
money–I think a thousand dollars was the limit.) Every Saturday
night at the office they had a party so that the dues-paying
members would come to the Court of Honor. They had a piano,
a piccolo player, and a few other instruments and general
fraternalism. The number of members grew until the company in
1926 converted into a stock association and became a conventional life insurance company known as Springfield Life Insurance Company. That company lasted pretty well until the mid-
1930s, when it succumbed to the Depression and became the
Abraham Lincoln Life Insurance Company.

My father's career was primarily with the Court of Honor.
He was secretary of that company, and of Springfield Life; and
when they finally became Abe Lincoln Life, he was pretty well
through due to the changing ownership and the Depression and
so forth. Beginning in 1930 or 1931, he and the other people at
the company took substantial salary reductions. My dad's max
salary was fifteen thousand dollars a year . . . I know that. I
think it was reduced to somewhere around four thousand dollars
a year as a result of the crash. That lasted for a year or two, and
by 1932 or 1933 it was zero or nominal. He was gone, period!
From that time on, we had no money–just whatever we had
managed to rat-hole away as a family. But that wasn't unusual in
those days of bank closures, a very real depression, and hobo
jungles . . . people making chalk-marks on your driveway to
indicate whether you were good for a handout or not, people
looking for work . . . .

When I was born we were living at 620 Pasfield Avenue, and
then we moved to 211 South Glenwood Avenue, which was in a

---

[1] Amos and Andy was a comedy radio program, broadcast nationally from
1926 to 1960.

good, white-collar part of town. We had a nice big white house, two and a half stories tall, with a lovely back yard. (It remains a beautiful home today–old fashioned but beautiful.) But my mother insisted that we move in next to Grandmother, so in 1925 we left this nice neighborhood where I knew all the kids, and we moved to where the interurban railroad would go by and shake the house. Our house was near Chapman's Laundry, and nearby a fellow named Dagget was building a cheap garage which later became a saloon. It was a bad move. The people in the neighborhood were all of modest income or flat-assed broke; they worked in the coal mines or were unemployed. In effect, I had a working-class society of schoolmate friends who lived in our neighborhood, and we lived differently than they did.

Our family was literate, and reading was encouraged, so as a child I did a great deal of reading all of the time. I got special privileges down at the Lincoln Library, and could take out as many books as I wanted. The librarians were very nice to me: I learned how to use the Dewey decimal system. As a consequence of my upbringing, when I was in grade school I was substantially more familiar with the bigger world than my schoolmates. I thought I knew something about physics, and I thought I knew something about famous people, because I read and read and read! But I did *not* master any social skills.

In the early years we spent all of our summers up on the river, because it was so hot in Springfield. We had a place on the river in Havana, Illinois, and I learned a great deal about the river and swimming and mud flats and steamboats. I was a river rat, and, therefore, not a part of organized sports such as tennis or baseball or those things that existed in the city. So the combination of reading in the wintertime and being on the river in the summertime did not help me particularly in understanding social interaction with my peer group.

My family was very interested in the world and in politics and what was going on, and I always listened to the conversations. Like so many people, we ate at the kitchen table, and we had dinner at noon, which was the custom in the Middle West. Supper was the evening meal, and was always made up of things that were left over from prior meals. It was a way of keeping things from building up in the icebox until people threw them away, as they do today. After supper we would study, read, play games or talk a bit before bedtime.

We kids slept in the attic, and each kid had his own way of survival. I had a little crystal set that I created with some copper wires and so forth. I could listen to the crystal set under the covers, and no one would know that I was listening to it in the middle of the night. Our first family radio was quite an event. We tried several radios–big superheterodyne numbers, and things of that kind, with about eight dials and an indoor antenna. There were various kinds of speakers that you hung on the wall, and radios in those days ran off a six-volt battery. In 1925 or 1926, we were *finally* able to get a radio that would tune in a station, and Grandmother loved to come and listen. We got a station from Louisiana, I think. The announcer would rant and rave about our economic system and the cross we had to bear in the form of chain stores. [laughter] Sunday night became the big radio night, when we were all gathered around for Eddie Cantor and the Amos and Andy show. We would often have our Sunday evening supper around the radio, instead of at the kitchen table. We just ate sandwiches and that sort or thing, and we all listened to the radio together; that was kind of fun!

My father was an intelligent, hard-working and motivated person, and he was well liked–he liked people, and people liked him. He was a gentleman, but that didn't mean that he was a weak person–he had sufficient pride in his bearing that he carried himself well, yet he had a reasonably wide range of talents, and if you saw him in an old wooden boat rowing down the river, or if you saw him out in the woods hunting rabbits, or if you saw him duck hunting, he seemed to fit very well into each of those environments. When dressed for business he carried a platinum watch, which conferred more status than gold in those days, and he had the watch fob and the vest, so he fit into the business environment.

My father was interested in people. He did not draw lines, and he could get along just as well with the yardman, or with filling station attendants or garage men, as he could with an executive. When working at the insurance company as it was going broke, there were lots of mortgages outstanding, and he foreclosed on lots of properties. He had to deal with people who were losing their farms or their properties or their homes, and he often tried to find ways to keep them in possession if he could. I have been there by the hour when he either met with them or talked with them by telephone, and I recall him buying and selling repossessed wheat and corn on the phone. He had a warmth and a generosity in his spirit, and he could relate to people without losing his temper. As a result–and I observed this personally–where most people who were in trouble would turn out to hate their banker or whatever, everyone had the greatest affection and respect for my father. He managed to maintain most relationships, and it was not artificial. He was a genuine person who came across as such–he was a guy with a heart!

My mother doted on me. She was thirty-three when I was born, which was pretty late, so I guess I was special to her. Mother was bright and talented, but she was raised in a time when women's horizons were limited, and I don't think she had any education beyond high school. However, she was a secretary to the attorney general of Illinois for many years, and, make no mistake about it, she took credit for keeping him literate. [laughter] She thought that his dictation was terrible and his briefs were awful. She always claimed that she rewrote every-thing he wrote, and, knowing her, I think she did. My mother was skilled and fast with a pen or pencil or typewriter, and she liked to write poetry. She also had rudimentary drawing skill: she didn't paint, but she liked to sketch.

My mother was brilliant; there was no question about that–not bright: brilliant! She did a lot of strange things, though. She was terribly concerned, for example, that I wouldn't get a balanced diet, or that I would eat foods that would be bad for me. One of the foods that she thought would be bad for me was ham. Pork was OK (we weren't Jewish), but she thought that ham was too highly seasoned for a young boy's stomach. The same was true with mustard and catsup. When we went to picnics or things, if there were ham sandwiches, we couldn't have one; so, of course, I ate all the ham I could as soon as nobody was around! But that was eccentricity rather than stupidity on my mother's part. She just firmly believed in those things . . . but she did not believe so firmly in socializing.

We had a social life as far as family relationships were concerned, but not a social life as far as country club member-ships or entertaining or that sort of thing. My mother had nice silver and china, and we had a nice dining room, but our principal dinner guests, Dr. Howard Metcalf and his wife, came to dinner at our house probably no more than two or three times in my total recollection.

Dr. Metcalf was a typical Middle Western physician who had a mustache and drove a Buick. I liked Dr. Metcalf because he would always do tricks with me, and he was a *loving* doctor. When the Metcalfs came over we children didn't sit at the dinner table, because it was later than our hour, and my brother and I would already have been fed. We would be part of the greeting in the living room, and then the adults would sit at the dining table and John Brown and I would be off to bed. This was all when we were quite young. Once the Depression really set in, we had no guests for dinner; none whatsoever.

We had the UCDs, the Usual Childhood Diseases that were prevalent in those days. Besides the UCDs, the favorite name for many illnesses was the croup–I suspect that today it would be described as a chest cold. I had every childhood disease that you could have, and for some we were quarantined with big red signs on the outside of the house–things like smallpox or chicken pox or German measles or the mumps. For almost every illness, Dr. Metcalf would come to the house with his satchel and he would prescribe either calcidine or calomine–one was pink and the other was charcoal in color.

One of the worst things that ever happened to me–and it had a profound effect upon my life–was getting hit by an automobile while on my way to a music lesson. My mother wanted me to play musical instruments, but she had no percep-tion of the necessity of staying with one until you could conquer it. (She always was the one who would pick out the instrument.) One day I was walking over to Second Street for piano lessons in a beautiful old home, and the next thing I remember clearly was waking up in a white room in the hospital. I had been hit by an automobile as I tried to cross Second Street. That started a series of events which I am told affected my health.

My mother was an absolute nut on education, and as soon as I got out of the hospital, whether I was able to move or not, she insisted I go back to school. I developed an infection in my ears, supposedly the result of a weakened immune system, and it resulted in a period of hospitalization. They did lots of ear punctures, operations in which they just cut through my eardrum to relieve pressure, and it was always very painful. It seems to me that in my youth the majority of three winters were spent in the hospital, but that is probably an overestimation. I'd go in when there were no leaves on the trees in the terrible winter, and by the time I would emerge from the hospital, the trees would have bloomed and the leaves would be on them.

While I was in the hospital I had a lot of pain. One time my father hired so many doctors that it looked like there was a convention—just a group of men in black standing around. I had a nurse who read to me; and I had lots of books, and as I recovered I read a lot. My hospitalization periods would run from sixty to ninety days, which meant I wasn't studying in school, but I never had any trouble with my schoolwork in grade school because of being read to. For years I had severe earaches and pain in the winter, but that's just physical adversity; everybody gets used to that.

Although my mother *really* drummed into me the need for education, she and my father did not push me to adopt a particular career. Their attitude was that you must do what it is that drives you. One of her favorite sayings to me was, "If you want to be a plumber, be a plumber; but be a good plumber!" (She must have had a run-in with a plumber at some time.) [laughter] Then there was a period when she got on a kick that I should be a journalist, because I think that's what *she* had wanted to be. To her, journalism would have been the highest calling, because it would have given her freedom of expression, and she loved to express herself. Then they got on a kick that I should go to Harvard. But mainly, they would have been happy no matter what my profession, as long as I was good at it. I always felt relaxed in that respect, but on the other hand, I had no direction; I did not have a strong, defined career path, one that I dreamed about. I was interested in almost everything, and I could do almost anything, so I had a broad spectrum. Much later, as a lawyer, I could do anything that any lawyer could do–it didn't make any difference to me what the specialty was, I was ready to learn that specialty when I practiced law in order to be able to do it.

I had some pre-kindergarten training at a nearby private home, then kindergarten through the eighth grade was at Hay-Edwards School, fortuitously situated two blocks away on Lawrence Avenue, the same street we lived on. In those days we had a one-hour break for dinner at noon, and I would say that almost 100 percent of the students at Hay-Edwards went home. An occasional student might stay with a brown bag lunch, but the school served a population that was within walking distance.

There were two buildings–the old building (Hay) and the new building (Edwards)–joined by an auditorium. Our first four grades met in the new building, and the last four grades were in the old; and we were really happy to get into the old building, because that meant we had some seniority around the school! (Hay was a multi-story, old-fashioned school building, and if something was old fashioned in the 1920s, that meant *really* old.) The first four grades were non-departmental, which meant that we would go to our classroom and stay there. The last four grades were departmental, meaning we moved from classroom to classroom.

The students were primarily from lower middle-class families, but we were oblivious to ethnicity–perhaps we were too young to know about that sort of thing. One girl, Millicent Davis, was a colored girl who was accepted without any problem, and she played with all of us as though there were no racial divisions. Two girls who I thought were very attractive were Evelyn Fishman and Rose Yaffe, and one of my best friends was a kid named Eddie Baer. I did not know that there was a religious difference between us–that they were Jewish. We simply were all good friends, and we did all of the grade school activities together.

Our home on Spring and Lawrence was just two blocks west of the railroad tracks, near the coal miners' neighborhood. (Washington Park, an upper class neighborhood, was about a mile further to the west.) There were not a lot of Catholics in our part of town, and there were no Catholics in our school, because the Catholics went to parochial school. Half a block away from us lived a boy named Leo, who was Catholic. As I would walk to school by Leo's house, I would sometimes see him dressed in some kind of uniform, and he had different school holidays. He had been pointed out to me as Catholic, but I didn't really know what that meant, and every time I walked by his house I would look. Leo didn't associate with us, and he didn't come out and play football with us in the street. It was as though he were withdrawn or shy, and he would stand on his porch and look, but not come off it to play.

Going up from the first four grades into the last four I encountered shocking change. Each teacher in the upper grades was a specialist in one subject, and there seemed to be less of a close relationship between you and your teachers. We were also exposed then to teachers with different temperaments, like Miss Freund, who had a terrible disposition and liked to spank children with a ruler. She used to spank my hands every now and then. (She spanked everybody, right through the eighth grade.)

We had all the usual diversions in grade school, such as eating paste out of a paste jar with a ruler when the teacher wasn't looking–things like that. Miss Barnes taught English, and one of the favorite stunts of the boys in Miss Barnes's class was to fart loudly. That would set Miss Barnes off, and she would stop the class and clap her hands and say, "See here. No bodily noises!" Everybody in the class would laugh, and as soon as she turned her back somebody else would try it. If you couldn't create a natural fart, you could squeeze your hand under your arm and sound an artificial one. Poor Miss Barnes seemed older than time, and we kept her uncomfortable, but she never spanked anybody.

There was a huge basement underneath the school, and that's where the toilets were. We had two recesses a day, one in the morning and one in the afternoon. In the fall and spring we went outside, but in the wintertime we stayed inside and ran down in the basement. When it was nice weather we would play marbles or baseball or other games, or swing on the monkey bars and all. The school yard wouldn't pass standards today in the sense that instead of having grass, it had cinders all around the buildings. (Cinders were cheap in Illinois, because they were a by-product of coal.) If you fell or scuffled on the playground, you really got cut and scratched pretty badly.

There were inkwells in our desks, and we were taught to write the Palmer System, with pen and ink. Occasionally a devilish student–and I fell into that category–would bring some calcium carbide to school to create mischief. (The coal miners mixed carbide with water to create acetylene gas to burn in the brass lamps they wore on their hats. A lamp had a carbide chamber in its base, a water container above it, and a small valve which allowed the water to drip onto the carbide. The resulting acetylene gas came out through a jet in front of a reflector, with a little flint to light it.) If you put some carbide in an inkwell and corked it, half an hour later the cork would blow out, and, of course, ink would blow out with the cork. It was scary, but one of the fun things to do as long as you didn't get caught, and nobody would ever tell.

We had a dress code. When we started grade school we wore knickers, and it was not until we got close to the eighth grade that we could wear long pants. Every boy, obviously, wanted long pants, and the earlier you could talk your parents into allowing you to wear long pants, the better. I had a hard time convincing my parents to get me long pants. I was a little bit bashful about asking, and my mother had strong convictions about keeping me in knickers as long as she could . . . I was probably in the last third of the class to get into long pants. Then, of course, it wasn't just *any* long pants. Corduroys were the "in" pants, and you had to wear cords, if you could. Everyone wanted to be like everyone else. Grade school was a piece of cake. I had no trouble with grades, and I suspect I was close to a straight-*A* student. I might not always have gotten an *A* in conduct, which was one of the things we were graded on, but I had no serious disciplinary problems, and no reason for my parents to see the teachers or anything like that. Once I was sent to see the principal for being naughty. Raymond Fildes was the principal. He had a clock in his office that somehow was connected pneumatically to clocks throughout the Edwards building, so Mr. Fildes could control time. He would change the time on his master clock, and pull some levers, and all of the clocks in all of the classrooms would change time. He also had control of the bells for the fire system and for the breaks of the classes, and so forth.

Mr. Fildes wasn't a bad person, but he scared me to death. I walked in and stood in front of him, and he told me what I had been accused of, and how bad it was, and that he had decided that I had to be punished. His punishment would be that I would stay after school for X number of days for X number of minutes. Certainly, I wasn't the only person who had to stay after school, but with a mother as motivated as mine, and aunts as motivated as mine who wanted me to succeed and excel . . . . It was difficult for me to take the punishment, because I wanted to live up to their expectations; yet, at the same time I had all of the irrepressibility that any growing boy had.

There were no martinets in our family. We were treated as though we were intelligent, competent human beings, but if we did something wrong, we were disciplined for it. Kids didn't get away with what they get to do today. (I don't understand Dr. Spock and all the rest of that stuff.) You were made to mind; hell, you were punished in grade school if you didn't mind. The worst I ever got was a spanking with a ruler, but students who were misbehaving were often taken into the cloak room and spanked by the principal with a razor strop. If I was real bad, I got spanked at home with my dad's razor strop. I hated that. It didn't happen very often, but it was serious and it hurt. (My dad used a straight razor like everyone else did in those days, and I learned to shave with a straight razor.) The razor strop hung in the bathroom, and that was probably the visible symbol that kept us all straight. I didn't ever get a spanking that I didn't deserve!

I was by no means a star pupil and a sissy. I tried to be one of the guys and part of the group, but at the same time to get good grades. Such things as neatness and penmanship gave me the worst trouble: I detested the Palmer System, and I wasn't real good at cutting out Valentines and pasting little things together. I was much better when it came to reading and comprehensive skills and answering questions. In mathematics you were given a booklet in which you worked out all the problems for your particular class. You'd review it each day, and it was my habit to go through and do the whole damn text in maybe the first third of the school year, and have the text done for the last two-thirds of the class . . . just sit there and look at the book.

As far as reading was concerned, I read every Tom Swift book that was ever written [laughter] . . . and *G-8 and His Battle Aces*, periodicals, and all of the World War I boy's adventure junk. As I got older, I read Lincoln Steffens's muckraker stories–I was fascinated about the effect of graft and corruption in politics, and Boss Tweed and Tammany Hall and that sort of thing. I read a lot about Abraham Lincoln; I read a lot about government. There were a number of sensational writers in those days writing about the Rockefellers and the Standard Oil trusts and trust-busting and Teddy Roosevelt and the Rough Riders . . . all of that sort of thing. I also occasionally would read poetry that my mother wanted me to read.

I was born in innocent years, years of learning, years of good family experience, years of insulation from the cruelties of the world; and up through grammar school we were rich. In effect, I was pink, clean and baby-cheeked, and just happy to be alive and full of energy. Oh, the family had some eccentricities: exercise with dumbbells, taking musical lessons, and that sort of thing. But it was a full, exciting, and quite protected life. Nineteen thirty-one to 1933 were all "down" years financially, but they certainly were not down from the standpoint of family love and affection and centrality. However, by the time I got to high school, everything was breaking down in our family and in our economy, and my whole attitude towards school and life changed. Grade school was the halcyon period, and high school was a different period in my life.

Mother was one of seven sisters, all of whom were as bright as brass buttons. The whole brood of them came back home during the Depression to live in Grandmother's house next door . . . their families and children shoehorned in there. So I had the fortune (or misfortune) of having most of my aunts live immediately next door to me. They were always working on me, making me do my homework, and we used to have spelling bees and that sort of thing. We had a very lively, active, mentally alert group of people without television or those diversions. It was a different kind of situation than you have today . . . .

My aunt Pearl had lived in Baltimore. Her husband, a contractor, shot himself because of the Depression, so she came home with her two children. Aunt Daisy had lived in Los Angeles. Her husband was an importer, and he went out of business, so Daisy also came back with two of her children. So there were Pearl and Daisy and their children, all of various ages, and there were aunts Kate and Ethel and Josie . . . . With my aunts and their children, there were twelve to fifteen people living in Grandmother's house. It was kind of a swinging society. They had a little kitchen where everybody gathered to eat and talk, and it was almost like being on a movie set, because there was lots of conversation–lots of people talking. And only one bathroom in the whole damn house! Can you imagine all those people living in a house with one bathroom? Today, you wouldn't do it, but we didn't think anything about it . . . lucky it was indoors, I guess. [laughter] But that was the way people coped with the Depression–not only in our family, but others, too. You use the resources that you have.

We were nominally Presbyterians, but various aunts tried every religion there was. I think my mother also played around with religion a bit, but as a family, we only went to the Presbyterian Church. I was required to go to Sunday school and church, and that took up half a day; then in the evening, Christian Endeavor took up a lot of time. But there were no religious fanatics in our family.

My father was active politically; to some extent everybody was. Politics was important, because when the Depression hit there was no welfare, and, stated very simply, it was your political party that took care of the poor people in your precinct. If you wanted to be a party precinct committeeman, you had to go on a ballot and be elected, just as if you wanted to be the mayor of the city . . . except that your jurisdiction was only your specific precinct.

We have all heard the term "ward heelers". If you lived in Cook County in Chicago you were in wards, and if you lived in a smaller town like Springfield you were in precincts. But the principle was the same: if you knew your precinct committeeman and you had a problem, or if you knew a family in your district that was cold and hungry, the committeeman would find somebody who would make a donation. Coal was the big thing in the winter. (Springfield was a coal town.) The Democratic county chairman, a fellow named Pete Rossiter, was in the coal business. He would hit up Peabody, which had many mines around Springfield, to deliver a ton of coal to any family in need; in return, I suspect that Peabody would depend upon Rossiter for political favors. Those were the trade-offs.

My family were Roosevelt people, and I got a very early political baptism. The neighborhood in which we lived was not a very good one, and it gave me the ability to observe the political system in operation. We lived next to a barbershop, which was our polling place in the forty-first precinct, and there I learned first-hand how Democratic politics worked. One of my jobs every election year, beginning in grade school, was to go to the barbershop when the polls closed, and periodically run back to a telephone and call the *Illinois State Journal* to give them a tally of the votes as they were counted until the presses closed about midnight. I learned a lot about politics and about how the party system worked.

Although we were better off than a lot of people for a while, eventually we were overcome by the Depression. Under Illinois state law, if you were a stockholder in a bank you were liable to be assessed for the financial losses of the bank. My father was a stockholder in Ridgely Farmers State Bank. One day, I think it was in 1931, the phones stopped working, or all the phone lines were busy, and I was asked to get on my bicycle and go downtown to find out what was going on. I rode downtown, and there were great mobs around Ridgely Farmers State Bank. The bank had closed. It had gone busted. In our family's case, that meant losing not only what money we had in the bank, and losing the value of our bank stock, but it also meant that my father was assessed for the liabilities of the bank up to his percentage of stock ownership. That, in effect, wiped out most of his life savings–a rather tragic event.

During the Depression, with whatever money he had left over after paying bills, my dad bought groceries. We were not totally without resources, but we were dipping into our reserves, and by the time he died, my dad was broke. He had no money . . . none! We had enough to live on during his lifetime–less and less each year, but our house was paid for, so we didn't have anybody foreclosing on us. We had very little clothing, and my mother would dye my clothing to change its color periodically. If I had a white sweater one year, for example, she'd dye it blue, and I'd wear it the next year. You didn't change your clothes every day, either. People today say, "Well, I wore that suit yesterday. I can't wear it again today." That wasn't the way it was then, but we were just kids and didn't think that was a hardship. We just grew up, and we didn't think we were poor–we knew we couldn't spend any money, but that didn't mean anything.

Oak Knolls was where all of the fine homes were, and where all of the old money or the well-to-do people lived. People who lived in that area associated with people in that area, and those people who lived close to the railroad tracks associated with people around the railroad tracks. There was a pretty clear separation of groups, but I had genuine friends, not phony friends, in both groups.

I started as a member of the YMCA as early as I could, and I worked there on Friday nights and weekends for my membership. (Working at the YMCA was something my well-off friends did not do.)

On Friday nights I would stay over at the Y and sleep on the floor. Saturday mornings, I would go to radio station WCBS in Springfield and announce an exercise program. It would be at six o'clock in the morning, and I would say, "Good morning," as cheerfully as I could, and then, "It's time for exercise!" I would try to describe the exercise routines almost as though you were in the military–"Bend over . . . one, two, three, four"–and I was just a kid! I don't think anybody in his right mind would ever listen to the program, but I put it on. Then I would come back and work in the locker room at the Y.

The kids who came in smelled; they were dirty! When they took off their underwear, it was usually black from coal dust; their socks were black and filthy, too. After they had participated in their basketball or their swimming they would come back to my little locker room, and I would give them their basket of black clothes, and they would put on those filthy clothes with holes in their socks and go out of the YMCA with their hands and faces looking clean, but their clothes just as ragged and dirty as they had come in.

I tried to get started in the Boy Scouts Troop 11 at the Presbyterian Church. Initial dues were five cents, but the Presbyterian Church had a lousy troop, and it was a total failure. So I went to Baptist Church Troop 33, where we had a real eager bunch of Boy Scouts; I went through the Eagle Scout regime there and learned a lot. We in Troop 33 were kind of middle-of-the-road. Troop 33 was wonderfully competitive and very enthusiastic, but we had substantially less than Troop 7 in the way of equipment. Troop 7 was the "silk stocking" regiment–they had everything; they had tents and canteens and full uniforms. When we had the Jamborees and the contests, they had all of the equipment that the Boy Scout handbook called for. Troop 7 won everything. They were the New York Yankees of the Boy Scouts.

We learned a lot in Boy Scouts–knot tying, starting a fire by friction, and so forth, and we went over to the railroads where we saw how locomotives worked. Bird study was very interesting, because we had a Harvard student who taught us, and another student taught us tree study. I remember being able to identify a tremendous number of birds either by sight or sound, and a large number of trees. Today I can barely tell an oak tree from a pine, or a crow from an eagle! But in those days I was reasonably sharp, so when we spent our summers on the river, I felt perfectly at home in the botanical scene. On the river, my habit was to get up every morning at six o'clock and go out into the woods before my parents or my mother or anyone else was awake–just walk in the woods, and come back and have breakfast, and then spend the rest of the day in the willows or on the river.

We had several family vacations, but the most memorable were one to Michigan in 1926 and one to California in 1927. On the first, we drove a Dodge from Springfield to Traverse City, Michigan, over a period of several days. (The luggage was strapped on the outside on big luggage racks, and there was an external trunk on the car.) We explored various places to try to find a place to stay. One place we stopped, I never will forget–we turned on the water in the bathtub, and a fish came out of the faucet! That was quite exciting, and shows how simple water systems were in those days. Places we stayed generally had kerosene stoves and very poor beds and furniture.

Eventually we stopped on what I think was called East Bay at Traverse City, Michigan, and found a place that was satisfactory. The lake was clear–if you think Tahoe was clear, East Bay was clear! It was a very gradual slope, so that you could walk out into the water for what seemed to be miles and was maybe a couple of hundred feet . . . the water simply very gradually grew deeper, so that Mother was not afraid that we were going to drown. That is where I learned to swim–I'd walk out in that shallow water and then crawl on all fours as a dog might walk or as a kid might crawl on the floor. Eventually, I found that I could go out just a little further with my hands paddling and my feet kicking. Then I drew my head out of the water, and I no longer had to hold my hands and feet on the bottom; I'd make a little U-turn and come back. That's the way I taught myself how to swim in 1926. Over a period of years, I became an excellent swimmer. I could beat anybody in high school in any kind of swimming event.

Our other vacation was to California, where Aunt Daisy and her family lived. We spent a good part of that summer at Manhattan Beach, and we used to come in from the water covered with oil tar, which was really sticky when it got in your hair. It stuck to your feet, to your body, and nobody thought of damning the oil companies. There weren't any environmentalists; instead, it was just a fact of life that there was a lot of oil in the ocean. We had to clean it off with Energine or something like that.

During the summers when I was in grammar school, from the late 1920s up through the beginning of high school, we spent most of our time at Havana, Illinois. We had a place there on Quiver Lake, which was a little lake off the Illinois River. My father would take us up there and leave us. He would come back to town and work, and then come up on the weekends and for his vacation period. I learned everything there was to learn about nature that you can learn without instruction.

My dad had a little boat built. Today, you would laugh at it–it was a little wooden boat about twelve or fourteen feet long, small enough that a boy could row it comfortably. I would get in that boat and travel and swim and explore, so there was no part of the outdoor world that was a secret to me. I learned a lot about swimming in dirty waters. For example, I learned how to dive in the water and never penetrate more than twelve inches beneath the surface, where kids who were raised with clear swimming pools would dive into muddy water and break their necks on concealed objects. (I am exaggerating somewhat, but it's quite true that you learn to swim and dive differently when you are in mud flats and logs and trees than you do when you learn to swim in the swimming pools that people have today.)

During our summers in Havana, I planted a lot of trees. I'd go out in the woods and find a small tree that I wanted to put around our place, and I would dig it up and transplant it. I did that with various vines and herbs, and I built trellises and things for them to grow on. Bittersweet was a plant which I often planted, and I also used sassafras root to make sassafras tea.

In those days, we had a great desire to smoke. Mother would not let my younger brother or me smoke tobacco, but we could smoke other things. So it evolved into smoking corn silk in corncob pipes–it was terrible smoke; very hot! Somebody invented smoking coffee, and we smoked a lot of coffee, which didn't seem to bother us at all. If nobody was looking, you could shove some cigarette tobacco in there, and you were head and shoulders above the game . . . . Cigarette smoking was strictly for adults, and it was like long pants in grade school: what you wanted to do was graduate to cigarettes as soon as you could! (Of course, everybody who was *anybody* smoked in high school. There was always the nice, so-called John Wolaver group, the intellectual group, the goody-two-shoes group, who didn't do anything . . . but I was not one of those. I was right down and earthy in high school.)

Next door, the Chapman kids would be up for two weeks in the summer; their family ran a laundry in Springfield. They were nice, and they were roughly our age, but during these years my brother was my summer companion, mostly. John Brown Dixon is four years younger than I, and we get along today as we did then: we were partners and best friends. He grew up differently than I did in many respects, but we were and are able to communicate with each other almost without using words. We have the same sense of humor, the same perspective on things in many ways. He looks at life a little differently, in that he's more conservative and has never taken some of the gambles that I've taken, but he's a great person, and our relationship from his infancy to today has always been very close.

My brother was a little kid, but he was a tough little guy. We experimented with all kinds of things, such as taking coffee grounds and putting them out in a certain place every day to see if you could attract earthworms, because they were very important for fishing. I did a lot of fishing and cleaned a lot of fish; we ate a lot of fish. We learned how to put out what are called trotlines from stump to stump, with maybe as many as fifty baited hooks. We didn't use the cheese balls or things that people use today; we used worms, and we had great success.

My brother and I did lots of things when my dad was around. We built fish ponds and we painted the interior of the house and we worked on the exterior. We had big projects, like digging a garbage pit; I mean, it was something to dig a garbage pit! We had all kinds of activities, so it wasn't simply Huck Finn out fishing, and I learned a lot about life. One of the things we did was to mix our own lead paint. You had red lead or white lead, and it came in gallon cans. We had to mix the lead with boiled oil to get a vehicle, and then we mixed pigments in. It was very difficult to stir: it seemed to take hours to mix the lead and the oil together, to make it smooth, and then to get the pigment smooth and homogeneous in it. (If lead can get in your blood stream, I must be full of lead, because I have stirred so much lead paint.)

Our summer house wasn't much of a place, but it was better than most because it was cooler–it was plugged into the side of a hill. The upstairs floor was level with the ground as you walked in; the basement floor was level to the ground as you walked out. The summer house enabled us to escape from the city heat, which was so suffocating. In the city in the summer, everyone had difficulty sleeping, and you tried to sleep on the floor under a window. The heat and the humidity were very uncomfortable, and you slept with wet sheets . . . so our summer home was our refuge from the terror of the city heat.

Our house was reasonably primitive, but we had a pump and good well water, and we eventually put in a water system with an electric pump and a toilet instead of having to use an outhouse. We lived in the cool, concrete-block basement, mostly, which had in it a long, narrow, rectangular wood stove; you could cook on top of it. We also had a gasoline stove, which was an advance over kerosene, and when electricity came along, we put in an electric stove . . . so we had three stoves in the basement. We had an ice chest that was four feet high, perhaps, and three feet deep and eight feet long, lined with galvanized steel. When you'd go to town you'd buy a hundred pounds of ice, and put it on your bumper and bring it home. You had to break it in two—nobody could lift one hundred pounds of ice. (There were perforations on the block so it broke easily.) That was our refrigeration, and it would last about a week.

My brother and I knew every farmer within ten miles. We walked through the woods and the various farms and up the streams, and there was a lot of country there: Quiver Creek, the old levee district, the Illinois River, the paddle-wheel steamers–it was big country for a little boy. I would start out sometimes to walk someplace, following paths through the woods and through the farmers' fields. I never took a canteen of water; never took any food; would drink the river water, which you weren't supposed to do. If I got thirsty enough, I stopped at a farm house and got water out of a pump. You could just go forever, and you got to know the people. If you missed the noon meal, you missed the noon meal; that was all. Life was one big exploration.

One day when I was at Quiver Creek there was a family having a picnic beside the dam. They began screaming because one of their children, who might have been ten years old, was out there caught in the eddy, drowning. So I ran out on top of the dam and dove off, swam through, took the kid, knew how to get under the water, moved him downstream, and brought him ashore. Oh, they all jumped up and down; they thought that was wonderful! They had a lot of food there–watermelon and lemonade and sandwiches and everything else, and I was starved. But they didn't offer me so much as a peanut. I thought to myself, "You know, I really would like something to eat." But they didn't offer me anything. [laughter] So I just went on with wherever my adventure was taking me that day, hungry as could be.

During the Prohibition years, my dad used to make home brew. We had great big ceramic crocks in the basement, and made a lot of home brew. I would bottle it by the quart with a bottle machine and a capper and hose . . . you suck on the siphon to get it started out of the crock, and so forth. When repeal came you could get Al Capone's beer, Prima beer. It was only "near beer", so the people next door used to spike it, and we'd go and help them out. They would get two or three cases of Prima and take the cap off and pour a little near-beer out, and then spike it with grain alcohol, Everclear. You'd pour in about an ounce of grain alcohol, and go to the capping machine and recap it.

After the repeal of Prohibition, Illinois was pretty wide open for casino gambling. Springfield had at least three major casinos–major for us, anyway. About 1934 I became more mobile, because I had my own car. Our family had disintegrated, but I drove down to Havana and looked around. There was a street that ran along the river, and they had a real interesting horse book there, exactly like you used to see in old Reno–not like you see in Reno or Vegas today. It was a small horse book with all of the tracks and the cards and stuff, and you could walk right in. Across the street from the courthouse was a place called Shawgo and Long's, and there were two or three other places–well, hell, every drug store had a slot machine! I guess there was also some Twenty-one, but craps was the big game in Illinois. So you had slots and craps and a book, and it would be in a store front, just like in early Nevada–these were joints that were twenty-five feet wide in front. You could look in from the street through the plate glass window; it was open, and there was gambling.

I do not remember my father ever going in a joint, and my mother would not even have thought of it; but as I started working, I started putting my nickels in the slot machines. Down around the boat docks there were slot machines, Jennings Indians–you put the money in, and you thought you were going to get a jackpot, because you could see the nickels build up in the machine behind the glass. The more full it got with nickels . . . you figured, "Gee, it's got to hit anytime now." I found that you could lose all your money pretty easy. [laughter]

I started high school at Central High, a very old red brick school with turrets on it. Central was exclusively for freshmen, ninth-graders, and there must have been about a thousand of us. (The last three years of high school were at Springfield High, about a block west of Central.) I was totally unsophisticated and unprepared, and I guess I was a little bit behind the social scene. I didn't know how to adjust to high school; I didn't understand it. We had a *huge* class, and it seemed that I didn't know anybody. All I remember is the president of our freshman class was a kid named Cookie Roberts, who appeared to know everything.

In high school my mother insisted that I take band . . . not orchestra, but band! There were three electives that you could take–band, orchestra or the normal course, and by taking band or orchestra, you were out of the normal course. I went to band practice every day, and I had no athletics at all–no gymnasium; no associating in that sense with a greater group of people. I often wondered why my mother was so insistent that I learn to play an instrument. This time she insisted that I learn the C flute and the D piccolo, so I did. I had a flute made out of pot metal that she bought from some guy who used to play in the Spring-field Watch factory band. (She always tried to buy everything second-hand.)

By being in the band, I was isolated with a small group, whereas all the *real* people went to gym and other events and would do a lot of things together. The musical group was a bunch of kooks! Why would you ever want to learn how to play the flute and make it a career? I can't figure that one out, but that's what I had to do! So I was deprived of any participation in the group that made up the popular social club. We had two social clubs: one was called the Wranglers and one was called the Delphics. They were supposed to be debating societies, but that wasn't entirely the case. Everybody who was "in" made the Wranglers and everybody who was "out", who was unpopular or regarded as undesirable, made the Delphics. Naturally, I would be a Delphic.

We had a shop teacher, Anthony "Fuzzy" LaFauce, who was as mean as could be. He did a lot of things to hurt me, and I never will get over that son of a bitch. We had to make some-thing–I forget what it was–but I had to buy my materials, so I went to Woolworth's and bought some stain or varnish there. I came in to class, proud of having put my piece together, but he took my stain away from me, and berated me in front of the class for buying this cheap stuff. Hell, I didn't have much money, and I didn't need to be humiliated. I was an innocent kid trying to succeed, but I was tortured by that guy. There are only a few people whose asses I still would love to kick today, but he's definitely one.

The next year, things were different. By then I was already working as much as I could, and wherever I could, and school was secondary to me . . . I didn't know what I was doing in high school. As a freshman I had gotten straight A's in Latin, but my sophomore year my Latin teacher was Marguerite McPhillimey. For some reason, she and I could not see eye to eye: I could not do *anything* to satisfy that woman and get a good grade. So I took care of Marguerite–I put thumbtacks on her chair. She sat down and they stuck her in the derriere, and she jumped up and screamed. I also put snow in her seat, because snow would melt and turn into ice water, and then she would sit down and get wet. I took all the erasers out of the classroom and threw them in the big ventilator that went up the wall, so that when she gave a class, she could never find any erasers. In other words, we had friction. Finally, she said that she would permit me to pass if I would promise never to take another foreign language. I said, "That's all right with me," and I think I got a *C* as my final grade. I kept my word and didn't take any more foreign languages, but I'm sorry now that I didn't. On the other hand, the idea that to be a lawyer you had to know Latin was a lot of garbage, and I later knew all types of lawyers who quoted Latin but couldn't find their way in or out of a courtroom.

My mind was elsewhere during my high school years, probably because of family problems. My father was by then unemployed, and life just didn't seem to have its blossom. I didn't have goals or motivation; I didn't know what I was going to do. My friends drank straight rye and bourbon whiskey in high school, and I did that, and I learned how to drink beer pretty good . . . learned how to dance with girls. But I didn't pursue the curriculum. While I wasn't one of the bad boys, I played around with resisting conventions–not studying too hard, but trying to become a person. I admired some people who had tremendous intellect, but who were always causing trouble . . . and that doesn't help you get credits toward getting into college.

The school had its cliques. Ed Hohenstein, Don McNelley, Bob Enochs were tough, strong guys from the wrong side of the tracks who would just as soon punch you in the nose as not. They worked in service stations, and so forth, and they were good guys . . . they were like me, and they taught me how to drink whiskey. [laughter] Then there were the more intellectual types from the clean side of town: Junie Robert, whose father owned the big fish market, was one; Bill Thoma was an intellectual, and still a great friend of mine–a very creative guy; and Gersham Greening became a doctor and remains a good friend today. But I don't think those fellows bridged both sides of the tracks or both strata of society the way I did. I did not know what group I belonged to. In retrospect, I recognize that my family lived in a very closed little world, out of step and out of place with the other parts of the world . . . or so I thought. My high school experience was a growth into the bigger world.

I bought my first automobile at fourteen years of age in 1934, paying five dollars for it. But, by God, I *earned* the money. At the Springfield High School cafeteria, the basic lunch was twenty-five cents, but I always managed to get by on fourteen cents' worth of lunch, which gave me a margin of eleven cents. That margin of eleven cents was what I used for spending money. [laughter] I also earned money by car-running, or whatever else, down at Kish Motors as a night boy in the garage. I didn't know anything about automobiles, but I sure learned, and the desire to own a car is what really got me to work. I had also worked at the Y, and at a number of cloakrooms around town. We had an armory, and when they would have public events there, I would work in the checkroom just to make tokes–people would give you a dime if you hung up their coat. But from age fourteen on, I worked part-time jobs for long hours in the school year, and full-time jobs every summer.

When I graduated from high school in 1937 my grades were not distinguished, and I was not particularly proud to be on the platform in a cap and gown; I just went through the motions.

[laughter] The distinguished students got the great diplomas, and I got a piece of paper like everyone else. After I graduated I was asked to go out in the back yard and talk with my father, who was sitting in a wicker chair. It was embarrassing to me–the substance of what he said was, "Son, I always wanted to send you to college, but I can't."

My response was, "That's OK, Dad. Can I help you?" because by that time I had saved and saved, and I had almost five hundred dollars. He hadn't made me contribute my income to the family like other kids had to do, so whatever I could earn, I had saved. That was difficult for him to say; difficult for me to say.

My parents got along well, but I guess the last couple of years of my father's life, when he didn't have anything to do, were difficult. (He died in 1938 at the age of sixty-five.) There was some friction, but you can't be a person who has been successful, and then have your world wiped out, and go along and have everything be peaches and cream. There was some family concern about survival, and who's in the way, and all that sort of thing, but by and large it was as good a marriage as you could expect–in fact, better than you could expect in most instances. My mother and father were different in personality, but they were compatible.

All my well-to-do friends were going off to the University of Illinois or Yale or the University of Chicago or Northwestern, but I had no money to go anywhere, and no theory of how to get anywhere. In September the people that I had known and associated with all disappeared–all going to their schools and their careers–and I knew loneliness and a feeling of separation. It was the kind of feeling you have when you miss a train . . . and I've missed a few! So I had to make some decisions.

Beginning in 1937 I spent three years working for the Kerasoteses, a Greek family who owned a chain of theaters. I began as an usher at the Senate Theater, starting work at noon every day. (Our hours were roughly from noon until eleven o'clock at night–fifty-six hours a week for twenty-five cents an hour, and we did the fifty-six hours in six days.) In September I enrolled in Springfield Junior College, a relatively new Catholic institution. Their tuition was low, and I had the advantage of living at home. I had Fridays off at the theater, but I could take no courses that met afternoons on the other days of the week. Accounting met in the mornings, so I took it.

Accounting was taught by a professor named Doc Zimmerman, who had been on the faculty at the University of Illinois. He was distinguished by his age, his disposition, by the cigarettes that he chain-smoked in a cigarette holder, and by the fact that he had no toes, they having been frozen off sometime in his childhood. All those things contributed to his personality and strange ways . . . but he was a pretty good guy. In those days, we had school on Saturdays, and I went into an eight o'clock class one Saturday morning for accounting, and had not completed my project. Zimmerman said, "Where is your work?"

I said, "I'm sorry, Doctor. I didn't get it finished. I had to work all week."

He said, "Mr. Dixon, that is no excuse; it's unacceptable. If you want to pass this course your work will be completed every week on time, and I don't want to hear you complain."

Now, that was totally different from the experiences I had had in grade school or high school, where if I had a cold or didn't feel well, I could always raise my hand and say, "Teacher, I didn't get my work done." This was a lesson in reality. From then on, I got my accounting work done and turned in by Saturday morning at eight o'clock. Zimmerman's approach was to give loads of work; *tons* of work: ledgers and balance sheets and income statements and so forth, and you had to do it all by pen and ink. There were no calculators, so you did everything in your head, and the sheer volume and tediousness of it was overwhelming. The bottom line was that usually I would spend all afternoon and all night on most Fridays doing the week's accounting work in order to be able to hand it in. It was very tiring, very debilitating, but I did it and got my work in instead of quitting the course. In retrospect, I think I probably should have quit the course.

One of my very best friends, Bill Cullen, was the doorman at the Orpheum Theater. He had a much better job than I, and less hours, and I think he had the vision not to take accounting. [laughter] Cullen was a handsome, strong, intelligent man whose father worked for the state of Illinois, and he was very aware of politics. One day in 1938 outside Springfield Junior College, Bill came over to my car and said, "Dixon what are you going to do with yourself?"

I said, "I don't know what I am going to do."

He said, "Why don't you come with me? I am going to the University of Missouri to prepare for law school. If you come with me, you can be a lawyer." To make a long story short, that's what I did. I entered the Business and Public Administration school at the University of Missouri.

When we arrived at the university, Cullen got work in a clothing store. We rented an apartment in the fall of 1939, and we took in five other students, whom we charged eleven dollars a week to live there. We tried hiring a cook part-time, but it didn't work out–it cost too much money, so I did the cooking. That was pretty tough on the boarders, but they had room *and* board for eleven dollars a week. I went to Ward's and bought a .22 single-shot rifle, because there were squirrels in the trees outside the apartment, and they were easy to shoot. We cooked a lot of squirrels, and vegetables were cheap. [laughter] And hog jowl was cheap: ten cents a pound, as I recall. Hell, I don't think the guys who lived with us had ever heard of hog jowl, but I knew how to cook it.

I did not get a degree before starting law school in 1940, and that tracked me all through the service in World War II. It was a big mistake. A number of law schools had special programs (remember, this is the Depression) in which you could, after your junior year, enroll in law school as the fourth year of your bachelor's program. If you did that you could get a bachelor's degree at the end of the fourth year by following the right curriculum, if that was what you wanted to do. That was not what I wanted to do. I wanted to get a law degree as quickly as possible, and I didn't bother with the bachelor's degree. I saw no reason for it. I recognize that that particular path to a law degree was a poor man's key to the courthouse, but it was there, and a number of us took advantage of it.

I started in Missouri's school of law in 1940, and did very well. I was admitted to law review, and was slated for Order of Coif, which is the highest honor you can get in a law school. I was even admitted to Phi Delta Phi, which, although they drank too much, was the "exclusive" legal fraternity. [laughter] In short, law school was my meat, and I did very well.

Now, you could see World War II coming. I registered for the draft on October 16, 1940, and my draft number was something like 8673. I decided that I would go all out to try to finish law school before any war came, so I talked with my mother. We had a little money left from my father's life insurance, and I talked with my mother and said, "I've got to get through school more quickly, but I can't keep on working and still get through before war breaks out." She was kind enough to help me with what cash resources she had, so along with a group of three or four of my friends from the University of Missouri School of Law I enrolled in the University of Colorado's 1941 summer law session. Byron "Whizzer" White (who later became a supreme court justice) was there in my class, and we became friends, drank a little beer together. I won't tell about the girls. [laughter]

I got back to Springfield at the end of August, 1941, and found my mother in very ill health; I put her in the hospital. I delayed going back to the University of Missouri until mid-September, when I took my mother out of the hospital. My standing in law school was good, even though I was two weeks late returning, but I was only there for maybe ten days when Aunt Pearl called and said, "Your mother is sick again; you had better come home!" So I started out, but I only got about three blocks from my apartment when my car caught fire, and it burned to ashes. I was stranded in Columbia, Missouri, with all of my clothes burned up in my car. Al Hoffman gave me enough money to take a bus to Springfield. I got home, and sure enough, the old lady was really sick, so I put her in the hospital again. She had cirrhosis of the liver. I sat with her while she died.

I had to do something to pay doctor bills, hospital bills, and whatnot, so I dropped out of law school and started working for Allis-Chalmers on one of those goofy shifts that started at five o'clock and ran until four-thirty in the morning–an eleven-and-a-half-hour shift, which meant that it was really twelve hours by the time I punched in and out. It was always the wrong time, because when you got home at six in the morning, what in the hell were you going to do? Sleep? I had my little brother at home, too, because I was his legal guardian. To keep things going, I got a contractor and made a duplex out of our house and rented out half of it.

How much fun it would have been to have gone through college with time to study, talk, and read–and to learn not only the subjects, but how to be a person! Instead, I went to school with the idea that it was something you have to get through–you have to be able to pass, but you don't have enough time to study; you don't have enough time to participate in activities. It was only a fragment of trying to survive. When I talk to people now, and they tell me about their college days, I think, "Wouldn't college have been wonderful, had it been like that?" I missed that wholeness of the college experience.

[2]

From Army Private To Nevada Attorney

THE AUTOMOBILE DEALERS IN SPRINGFIELD had a program—anybody who had any kind of education or skill could sign up with one of them and go into a special army ordnance company that was being formed with local recruits. If you did that, you had a little breather before you had to report. I signed up right after Pearl Harbor, and that gave me a couple of months to get the duplex put together and to figure out how I was going to take care of my brother and so forth, before leaving. I left and went to Chicago, took off all of my clothes, and stood in that huge armory while they gave the physical exam . . . and then got on a train and went to Camp Davis, North Carolina, for training.

In transit I contracted pneumonia, and while in the Camp Davis hospital I heard artillery firing and decided that was the branch I wanted into. When I rejoined my battalion, they had no uniforms, and I had to do all of my work and drills in wing tip shoes . . . and no meat can to eat out of. (At meals, you'd stand in line and get one that someone else had already eaten from.) My first assignment was to dig latrines in the clay. I had thought I was going to get some training; I had thought I was going to be a contributor to our war effort, but it didn't turn out that way. So I went on watching the military, trying to learn (as I've always tried) to fit into society and not make waves. I just did my job every day, and tried not to volunteer . . . watched Sergeant Radowich. Radowich was a big, mean bastard who would assign you to the worst duties that he could if you said anything wrong. I always steered clear of him.

Our officers must have been totally P.I. officers–Political Influence officers, guys who . . . hell, they couldn't tell their left foot from their right! The captain of our company was an oil millionaire from Texas, and we used to march to his tune of "Gush, Gush, Gush." He was such an ass. I had read about Officer Candidate School, and how to get accepted, but nobody in the command was allowed to apply for OCS because the Texan did not want to strip his unit of valuable people. So there was no OCS for me; I could see that.

It was kind of a miserable period, and the whole unit suffered from terrible morale. I had a cousin, Sherwood Dixon, who was a colonel who became a general during World War II. I wrote him a letter and said that this life is pretty tough, and he wrote back and said, "The most important thing you can do is wash your socks every night." That's what I did. [laughter]

It was so bad that the Inspector General (I.G.) was called in by some people who were complaining to their families about their terrible situation in this unit. A special tent was set up, and everybody had to go see the I.G. They would go in and moan about how terrible things were, and the I.G.'s aide would write it all down. When it was my turn, I found myself before the Inspector General (a major from Washington), with Captain Cocanaur sitting next to him at a desk. I saluted and did all the proper things, and the major said, "Private, what's your feeling about this unit and its readiness to go to war?"

I said, "I think it is splendid, really great; and I am anxious to be of service to the country. I am competent and skilled, but I have a problem. I have four and a half years of college behind me, and I believe I could contribute a lot to the war effort if I were allowed to expand upon my abilities instead of washing dishes and digging latrines."

He said, "Why haven't you applied for Officer Candidate School?"

I said, "Captain Cocanaur will not permit it."

So he turns to the captain and says, "Is that right?"

The captain, of course, had apoplexy, and said, "Well, that's my rule!"

So the major turned to me and said, "I want you to fill out an application for Officer Candidate School."

I saluted and said, "Thank you, sir."

You *know* what happened to me when I got back to the company . . . I got shit detail. I could not even get an application form! I knew that if I wanted to succeed I would have to help myself. My struggle, which had started in high school with trying to find my identity, turned into a drive to survive and a drive to try to accomplish my goals. So I went down in the middle of the night to a quartermaster's outfit, and got an application form, and went into a warehouse and typed up the form for Officer Candidate School. I took it to the company executive officer the next day, saluted, and handed him my application.

I made my application to OCS while we were at Camp Davis, and then our ordnance battalion got on a train and went to Savanna, Illinois, to the Savanna Ordnance Depot, and froze to death . . . it was a very miserable place on the river. All I did was load ordnance–work civilians were supposed to do–till I got my orders to report for officer's training in anti-aircraft artillery, which was delightful to me. I went through OCS, and became commissioned as a second lieutenant assigned to the 496th AAA (anti-aircraft artillery) Battalion.

After maneuvers in Tennessee, we came West to Camp Pendleton for amphibious training, and we did a lot of desert training in the Mojave Desert. Then we were to go overseas. By this time I was a first lieutenant and the BSO–battalion supply officer. I went to San Francisco and spent a month getting everything organized for the unit to go overseas–all of the supplies, uniforms, shipping data, where the staging area would be . . . in other words, all of the logistics for going overseas. (While organizing this, I shared a room for a month in the Senator Hotel with my supply sergeant, which officers were not supposed to do . . . but he was a real good guy.) Before going overseas I went down to Fort Mason and had one of those examinations with the doctor in his office. You just open the door, and he says, "You pass." We sailed in January of 1944.

We went to Milne Bay in New Guinea, and we hopscotched our way as far as Cape Sansapor. There, I learned how things work. I gave an Air Force sergeant an electric generating unit (which we had enough of), so they could play poker in the middle of the night. After that there was nothing I couldn't get out of the troop carrier command, the TCC. Anyplace I wanted to go, anytime, all I had to know was Sergeant so-and-so at such-and-such a place, and the doors opened. Since I knew these guys, when we needed to re-supply I'd go out to the air strips and just get on an airplane. I'd go to Hollandia, which was MacArthur's headquarters, and I'd say, "Sergeant so-and-so sent me."

And the guy says, "OK. You're on; get on," and throws some bird colonel off, puts me on the airplane, and I got priority. All the priority I have is that I know Sergeant so-and-so.

Another class of people who would help you were second lieutenants. When we were still having supply problems, because we were at the furthermost penetration of American forces and were being bombed by the Japanese quite a bit, I'd go to Biak, where they had a lot of supplies. Wandering around there, I found where the supplies were, and I found a whole lot of things that we needed. But now how am I going to get them to where we're going? I wandered around the airport, went into a hangar, and there was a second lieutenant sitting there, real happy. [laughter] I said, "Hey, I got a problem."

He said, "What's your problem?

I explained the problem and said, "I got to get these supplies over to our base on Middleberg Island."

"Well," he says, "maybe I can help. We are sending out a C-47 training mission." [laughter] So we loaded up the supplies and took them to Middleburg Island. Eventually, we ran a lot of flights like that. I would get on the radio and send out a priority message with Rhubarb tail number so-and-so (we called those airplanes Rhubarbs), ETA whatever the code for Middleburg was, and our fellows would be there to meet me and help unload it. We got a whole bunch of stuff (on one flight we even flew in a jeep), and Brigade wanted to court-martial "the captain who is sending all the priority radio messages." [laughter] I managed to slip by that rap, and we were re-supplied.

On Morotai, they began to convert our unit from anti-aircraft to infantry. We landed at Leyte in the Philippines, and then were ordered to the island of Mindanao. At Mindanao we were completely equipped as infantry, and a gook regiment was attached to us. (Filipino Constabulary was what MacArthur called them; we called them gooks.) I went out in advance of the unit with my little crew, and we located where we wanted to put headquarters and our various batteries, and set up command posts. Our job was to clear the Japanese out of the mountains, but we were *alone* out there. (I was awarded the Bronze Star "for meritorious achievement between 5 June 1945 and 8 August 1945." Primarily this was for finding and supporting a lost detachment. It was a lot of work and took some guts and brains, but I always called it rescuing a cook stove.)

We managed on one patrol to capture twenty-four Japanese, and under orders from 24th Division I took the prisoners to a Moro group. On this twelve-hour trip Filipinos kept coming and bravely "attacking" our convoy to kill the Japs, though by God they hadn't been so brave before! In fact, most of the gooks in our regiment would run the minute they heard rifle fire. When I surrendered the troops to Datu (Sultan) Delangauwan of the Moros, who was a major in the Constabulary, he invited me in for coffee, and he asked for U.S. equipment, clearly for his black market. While I sat there, his troops walked by with the heads of the Jap prisoners we had guarded so carefully. These Moro bastards had beheaded our prisoners while I was drinking coffee with their crooked major!

Even though I was only a captain, I was the senior officer in my battalion from September through December, 1945. My C.O. had been reassigned after V-J Day, and I became *de facto* battalion commander. It was our job to try to pacify Mindanao; there were nine provinces, and I had patrols in each. As the Marines left, they had sold or abandoned their weapons to the Moros, and the Moros were trying to chase us off the island. There were also Japs who had not surrendered, so in fact V-J Day didn't change things much for us, except that we were left on our own without any real support.

When we finally got orders that we could leave and report to Leyte for transport back to the states, I had people everywhere. I said, "Get to Leyte the best way you can!" [laughter] And that's what they did. I mean, they took small boats and various things, but we all managed to re-assemble in Leyte. That was the end of the war for me. I left Leyte in January, 1946, and was discharged at Jefferson Barracks, St. Louis, after being promoted to terminal-leave major in the Army reserve.

My approach to getting through my service years had been somewhat unconventional, and not always in conformance with regulations, but as far as taking things into my own hands, I didn't do that whimsically; I didn't rebel against every cause. There are simply turning points when you are either going to succeed or not succeed, and I never tried to substitute chicanery or trickery for merit. I always felt that whatever I was doing, if it was meritorious and right and strong, I could still continue to go ahead even if I encountered some obstacle. I had to believe that. You can't see all your friends go away to school without you; you can't see them all getting an education; you can't see events passing you by without digging in and getting some traction and grabbing hold of life.

The war also taught me that you can't go home again. Everyone envisioned that as soon as the war was over, we'd go home; but you go home, and it ain't there. Where you lived, your high school friends . . . all that's gone; all the girls you know are married and gone away. Your possessions are gone. I went back to my house–things I had put away in the attic had disappeared. I guess the tenants stole them while I was gone–who knows? You don't have the same circle of friends–they're gone, and the whole social scene has changed. War teaches you that you can't go home again.

After the war I found myself looking at the practice of law and feeling more and more that that was what I wanted to do. I couldn't be fired if I was a lawyer, and to me that was important–I wouldn't have to depend upon someone else for a career, and I wouldn't have to be part of a system. (I don't think I could ever have been house counsel–not that it's a bad job, but it isn't me.) Whatever I did, I wanted to do it well, so I could feel good about it. I *always* wanted to be proud of my work and the results that I was able to accomplish.

When I returned home after being discharged, I attended Springfield's Lincoln College of Law night school for a while. That held a special meaning, because the classes were in my father's old building, and Lincoln was a school that he and my mother had been fond of. Many of the lawyers in Springfield had gone to Lincoln, which was fundamentally a night school taught by local lawyers, but I came to the conclusion that it was really not the challenge that I wanted. In the summer of 1946, I decided to enroll at Northwestern School of Law in Chicago.

In the fall I entered Northwestern on the G.I. Bill to finish law school, but my health was not good. I guess the war had been hard on me: I weighed very little and had blue fingernails at the time . . . they were like a dead man's fingernails! I had a class in administrative law with a professor who was a real jackass. (We used to call him The Brain.) One day The Brain was talking about administrative law, and my heart began to beat heavily. I smoked in those days, and a pack of Camels was in the pocket of my shirt, and the pack began to move in and out, and jump around. I thought, "Jesus Christ, what's going on now?" My heart beat faster and faster, and then all of a sudden I keeled over and fell to the floor and lay there–I couldn't move. The Brain didn't even stop talking. A fellow from clear across the room came over and put his hand on me and said, "Are you all right?" I couldn't answer him. He called some medics and they hauled me off.

Continuing like that was not for me, and in my condition I wanted a better climate than Chicago's in the winter, so I dropped out of Northwestern and drove out West. I stayed briefly in Tucson before moving up to Boulder City, Nevada, where I worked in the government service that ran Boulder Dam and Boulder City. I knew something about surveying–chain work, and that sort of thing–and that's all I did, until I decided that I had to get involved in something pertaining to law. In Nevada, if you had training and experience equivalent to a law school education, you could pass the bar, and I figured I ought to be able to do that. I went in to Las Vegas and met Frank McNamee, who was a district court judge. Frank became my sponsor; he liked me. Through Frank, I got a job as bailiff in 1947 in the Eighth Judicial District Court for the county of Clark. I did legal research for Frank, and I got to go into chambers with him and hear him tell me how dumb the local lawyers were. [laughter]

While I was working in Frank's court I decided that if I wanted to take the bar, I'd better get law office experience. So I became, in effect, a law clerk with the Ralli and Rudiak firm, which gave me an opportunity for the first time to see how you actually did this work hands-on. And I thought, "Well, hell, life is great; life is rosy, and I'll be able to take the bar examination like Abraham Lincoln did or like all the . . . . " When I was young we had lots of prominent lawyers in Springfield who had never gotten through school. So I was just still living in a pioneer era–skinny, dumb and happy.

I'd known Jane Diller since high school in Springfield. We had known each other pretty well, but I wouldn't say we were high school sweethearts, because I wasn't that kind of a guy. [laughter] But after I got the job at the courthouse in Las Vegas she moved out, and we were married in July of 1947. (Our daughter Ann was born in 1949 at the University of California Hospital. My oldest boy, Sherwood–a vascular surgeon of some stature in the Reno medical community–and my third child, Drake, were born in Reno.)

So I was working, and I had a wife and a home, and before we had children I began thinking about taking the Nevada bar exam. Bernard E. Witkin, author of *Summary of California Law*, ran a refresher course in law, and he had the finest reputation for this sort of thing. I was still thinking I might be permitted to take the Nevada bar without a degree (I was a young man in a hurry) so in July of 1948 I went to San Francisco to take Witkin's cram course in preparation for taking the Nevada bar. After I finished the Witkin course I had a conversation with Bert

Goldwater, a prominent Reno attorney who was secretary of the state bar. Goldwater said, "Yes, it is true: Nevada will permit you to take the bar examination without a law degree, but if you do, I want a commitment from you that you won't practice in Reno; that you'll practice law in Elko." Bert said that to me; I swear that on a stack of Bibles! (There was an extreme amount of politics in the bar association and in becoming a lawyer in Nevada.) I concluded then I had to finish law school . . . but ultimately I *did* take the bar before I finished.

I still had the G.I. Bill, and I wanted to complete my education in the Bay Area, so I interviewed at Hastings College of Law, at Stanford, and at the University of San Francisco. I could have been admitted to any of them, but both Stanford and Hastings required two residence years of matriculation at the school for a degree. Dean Hogan at USF said, "I understand your problem. At USF you can finish your course work as rapidly as possible, and get on with your life. I will withhold your degree until the two years have elapsed, but you can be on your way." My goal was to finish two years' required work in one year, and at the same time I asked the bar association in Nevada to allow me to take the bar examination before completing college.

Jane and I rented a little place over in Marin County, and I commuted to San Francisco every day. It was real easy in those days. You had no traffic; nobody lived there–just cows! [laughter] Zip right in to the USF campus; zip on back. Jane's sister lived in Sausalito, and that's how we heard of Marin County. We drove around and found this one-bedroom apartment in Corte Madera–it was only about as big as this office, and Jane was pregnant, and then my brother came out. I was on the G.I. Bill, and I used what little savings I had left over from various sources . . . some small amount of stock called dividend shares, and I can't remember what else. We lived *just* within our means. I had a house with a down payment on it in Las Vegas that we rented out, and that took care of that obligation.

I had applied to take the Nevada bar exam while still in school, and in September of 1949 I got a phone call from Paul

Ralli in Las Vegas. He says,"They're going to let you take the bar, and the examination is next week."

I said, "I can't believe it!"

I'd done no bar review or anything else. What was I going to do? I said, "I'm going to take it," but it worried the hell out of me, because the failure rate was very high in those days in Nevada. (Law students who had been Nevada residents before World War II were admitted to the bar after the war without being required to take the bar exam, but I had not been a pre-war citizen . . . droves of people had been admitted to the bar without exam, and those who were taking the exam were having tough luck.)

I got to Vegas, worried like hell, and started the examination, which lasted three days and required essay answers. The night after the first day of the exam I was very nervous and couldn't sleep, so I drank a few beers, which always puts me to sleep, but that didn't work. After the second day of the exam I was desperate. I called Karl Krause, a doctor, and said, "I'm taking the bar, and I can't sleep. I'm just wearing myself out!"

He said, "Been on the Bennies, eh?"[1]

I said, "No, I just can't sleep."

He said, "Oh, I'll give you a prescription for Seconal." First sleeping pill I ever took in my life. I took one, but it didn't do anything. So I gave him another call, but I got somebody else. I said, "Hey, I took one, but it didn't do anything. Can I take another?"

He said, "Sure."

I took another "red bird"–that's what they used to be called. I slept! When I woke up the next morning, I whistled and sang and danced all the way to city hall. The third day went well for me; I never had a more beautiful day in my life, and I wrote the examination and worked hard.

About twenty people were taking the exam, and during the three days of its duration, some of the guys would ask each other questions when the monitor was out of the room. I had been

---

[1] From Benzedrine, a trademarked amphetamine.

raised on the honor system, and that bothered me. The third day, some fellows who are prominent Nevada lawyers today started checking with each other on the answers to questions after the exam was supposed to be over. So Dixon appointed himself: I just went around and picked up the papers from everybody, and turned them in. I had had enough of this nonsense!

When the initial grading came through, the board of bar examiners had passed three. The supreme court raised that number to eleven, and it turned out that I was number one on the bar examination. This was plain luck, because I hadn't finished law school and hadn't done my preparation . . . but I was admitted to the bar. When the results of the bar exam were posted in October or November, I remember coming to Reno by plane, and riding in a taxicab to Carson City to get sworn in by the supreme court all by myself. The taxicab barely got up Washoe Hill, and I thought, "Jesus, this is a horrible experience." [laughter] But I got the piece of paper in my hand with "Esquire" after my name, which made me feel pretty good. It didn't put any bread on the table, but it was my first degree; it was my key to the kingdom.

[3]

Early Law Practice in Reno

GOING BACK AND FORTH between San Francisco and Las Vegas, Reno became so attractive to me, with the mountains and the trees, that I decided it was the place to live. I moved to Reno in January of 1950, and I've been here ever since. (I didn't get my degree from USF until May of 1950.) There are lots of lawyers who start out practicing in Reno and end up moving to Vegas, because that's where the money is; that's where the jobs are; that's where the action is. Reno was a tough place to earn a living–it was a town that was dominated in those days by Norman Biltz and John Mueller. "Keep the town small; discourage growth"–that was their credo. Nothing's wrong with that, but most lawyers who wanted to succeed moved out of town. The Foleys, Howard Babcock . . . oh, I could probably name twenty or thirty lawyers who started their practice in Reno and gave up and moved to Vegas because of the lack of economic opportunity in Reno.

Reno was a very close-knit society in those days, and Norman Biltz and John V. Mueller were the political heavyweights. If you wanted to run for office you went to see Norman, because he was a source of money. John Mueller was his point man, and they were Pat McCarran supporters and got their power from Pat. Norman and his group, and lots of the people who lived here, wanted to keep Reno the way it was.

The houses on Court Street, that are today doctors' and lawyers' offices and wedding chapels, were respectable homes back then, and Court Street had a kind of Reno history and community feel to it. Unlike Las Vegas, Reno was an established society to which you either belonged or you didn't. It was not easy to break into, but Reno did not seem to be aggressive, and its law firms were relatively stagnant. The so-called powerhouse firm of William Woodburn, Sr. (it became Woodburn, Thatcher, and Forman), was the only group that you could even call a law firm in Reno, and I think they had four lawyers in it. The Thatchers and the Formans and the Woodburns were pillars of the legal society and of Reno society in general.

There were people who said that Norman Biltz's no-growth policy was why Reno was not Las Vegas, but I don't believe that a political establishment or a social establishment alone could keep Reno small. (Norman Biltz and Johnny Mueller would be turning over in their graves today if they could see how much Reno has grown.) Las Vegas was Las Vegas because of its proximity to Los Angeles, and a year-round automobile route to Los Angeles. What built Las Vegas gambling was Los Angeles; San Francisco did *not* build Reno gambling. In the winter you often couldn't get over the Sierra on the two-lane highway (Route 40) between San Francisco and Reno, and when you could, it was an eight-hour drive. Southern California also had a much bigger population base to draw upon. The combination of climate and geographical location tied Las Vegas to the Los Angeles market and the great population explosion in southern California.

In the late 1940s and early 1950s, the city of Reno restricted gambling to the east side of Virginia Street, and you couldn't gamble outside the so-called red-lined district downtown. As a matter of local policy, gambling was restricted fundamentally to the block that Harolds Club sat in. (Of course, the Riverside and the Mapes were exceptions, and the Cal-Neva was kind of grandfathered in to the downtown zone that was set aside for gaming.) On the other hand, the politicians who ran Las Vegas *encouraged* the growth of gaming. The Reno mindset of the 1950s through the 1960s was that they were not going to let gambling expand and turn Reno into a gambling town.

After I passed the bar and got my degree, I went around and knocked on every door in Reno trying to find out what law firms existed and how I could get involved. (In those days the bar restricted its members–you couldn't get your name or picture in the paper; if you did, somebody would call up and raise hell with you.) I could not find a position. I finally got started when Stanley Brown, who was a year behind me at USF, said his father-in-law, John Belford, would help me, and he introduced me to him. Belford said, "Mead, you can use my law library; there's a desk in there. Anything that you can get in the way of practice is yours, and in return for your help, I will charge you no rent."

I sat in that law library, but I didn't have any clients. One day I saw some guy stalk out of John's office, and I asked Lynn Quill, his secretary, what had happened.

She said, "Mr. Belford just sent that client away."

I said, "John–what happened?"

He said, "The man wanted a divorce, but he wouldn't pay my minimum fee, which is two hundred and fifty dollars. He only wanted to pay a hundred and fifty."

I said, "John, I need the money. Send him across to me."

He said, "Mead, you wouldn't want a practice like that." (John had no feeling or sensitivity for my needs.) [laughter]

John had a good law library, and E. Frandsen "Bud" Loomis, a prominent attorney, used to come down and use it. Bud knew my problems, but he had the same concept that Belford had, which was that he had certain minimum fee standards. However, he knew I needed the bread, and so when he would reject a client, he would send that client to me. I got the castoffs: I got the blacks; I got people in domestic disputes; I got everything. Then Stanley Brown graduated from law school and joined the Belford firm, and he had to have a place, so I had to go.

I found three adjacent office rooms for rent as a package, but I couldn't handle that alone. About this time, Grant Bowen was leaving the district attorney's office, so we talked, and I told him, "Grant, I've got three offices put together, so why don't the two of us go in together and share the reception area?" It would cost us seventy-five dollars a month apiece, and he thought that would be a good idea; but he backed out when he found a cheaper place. So Grant went his way, and I went mine.

I ended up in two rooms next to Oliver Custer in the Stack building, trying to survive. Oliver was fairly well connected, and he was the same kind of friend to me that Bud Loomis was: he sent me all his trash. [laughter] As I recall, Oliver got throw-aways from the Woodburn firm, among others; and then what he would throw away, he'd throw to me. So here I had a law office, trying to scrape together a practice, but I had no furniture or stationery. Del Machabee of Morrill and Machabee said, "I trust you, and I'll give you credit. I'll put in a desk for you, and you're going to need a lamp; you're going to need a chair. You pay me when you can." He did that, and I have never forgotten it.

Another lawyer who had a little office over in the Arcade was selling his furniture, and for seventy-five dollars I bought all of it. Now I had two offices full of furniture, but no books, so I subscribed to *American Jurisprudence*. And then Jim Boyd died and Oliver Custer took me on as an assistant while he was handling the estate. We went out to O'Connell's warehouse, took apart the whole library and whatnot, and Oliver either gave me or sold me at a bargain price the fundamental law books that had belonged to Jim. (Those law books are still down in the Vargas library as a foundation for their reports. I built a better law library than George Vargas and John Bartlett had ever heard of, and it started right there.) So it was through the help and friendship of Bud Loomis, Oliver Custer and Del Machabee that I got my law practice started.

I was still starving for work when I got a phone call from Sam Platt, an extremely reputable lawyer, but also a somewhat pompous guy. He says, "Mr. Dixon, my associate, Bruce Lehman, has died." Bruce was an up-and-coming young lawyer who worked for Sam. (Bruce had been a bird colonel in the Air Force. At his funeral his widow played the song, "Cool, Cool Water", and it was so tragic I couldn't stand it. Even today, it gives me creeps when I hear that song.) Sam said, "I'm looking for a new assis-tant, and John Belford has given me your name."

I said, "Fine, what are you going to pay?"

He said, "I've been paying Bruce two hundred dollars a month."

"I can't do that," I said, but I talked with Sam, and we struck a deal for three hundred dollars a month . . . and anything that I could make independently from his assignments would be mine.

Sam would introduce me to his clients as his assistant. I tried a case or two for him, took some very difficult cases for him, and did good work–pulled some of his chestnuts out of the fire, to be candid. After being there for eight or nine months, I felt it was time for me to find out about my future, so I had a talk with him. Sam said, "You're my assistant. You will never be my associate; I will not have an associate. You will never be my partner." I thought about that a little bit, and it didn't sit well with me.

By December I had concluded that I had to leave. Sam decided to take his usual three-week Christmas vacation, and I said to myself,"Good-bye, Mr. Platt! While you're on vacation, I will clean up the files that I have." [laughter] I wanted to make his vacation a happy one, him knowing that there would be nobody else to worry about in the office when he returned. I stayed in the office through December thirty-first with Cecilia Priest, a great girl, a great secretary. Then I left Mr. Platt and the three hundred dollars a month behind, and started out as an independent on my career in practicing law.

I found that local clients were really not worth very much, in the sense that they couldn't afford to have a lawyer do careful work for them. Quite often someone would call me and say, "I need a lease." Well, they think a lease is a commodity that you just take off a shelf. But there's a lot more involved. You couldn't afford to do thoughtful work, because in those days if you spent seventy-five dollars' worth of time . . . . In the first place, a client called you. Then you had to get a lot of people to work together and understand what he was trying to do. Then you had to get it typed, and with those old typewriters you had to get it typed about three times. Then you sat down and met with your client, and maybe met with other guys, and then maybe you found that the lease wasn't quite right. But, hell . . . you charge seventy-five dollars, and everybody has a fit: "We can't afford a lawyer!" So of course you can't do all that.

The ordinary small Reno business could not afford competent legal help, or didn't believe it could, so I asked myself where the legal business was in the community. For instance, how about the tax situation? CPA firms were just beginning in Reno after the war–Semenza and Kottinger had been the only CPA firm until then–and the PAs (and later the CPAs) guided their business clients in tax matters. If a tax problem was too big for the accountant, the client was sent to San Francisco, and the accountant was the interface with the San Francisco lawyer. So at that time it was almost impossible to hold yourself out as a tax lawyer and earn a living in Reno. CPAs were the secret; basically you couldn't be a successful local tax attorney unless a CPA sent a client to you. They were the source of legal business, estate planning, and income tax litigation. I am sure that has changed, but back then it was a chicken-and-egg situation.

There was a very hard-working guy by the name of Emerson Wilson, who was successful because he started his own title company, the Nevada Title Guarantee. Before that, there had been only one–Pioneer Title Insurance Company, which had Sidney Robinson as their counsel. (They ran all of their real estate transactions through Sidney, who had a deed mill. He had secretaries who just sat there all day long typing deeds and deeds of trust and promissory notes, from which they generated some real estate practice.) Well, Emerson Wilson sat over here in a basement on First Street, and he finally built his book–which was hard to do in the early days–so he could become a title company. (There are differences between the way the county recorder records data and the way the title companies record data. Once you build your book, then you have quick access to data and you can become a title insurance company. If you had to go through the county recorder's system, you'd be as old as Methuselah before you could check all the records in order to be able to insure title.)

Emerson became not only an owner of a successful title insurance company; he also developed a strong rapport with contractors and developers, and he became preeminent as a real estate lawyer. He was able to put together complex transactions–they wouldn't be complex today, but they were complex then–and he was a pioneer in land development and the documentation that went with it. He could help put together a subdivision quickly, efficiently, and effectively, and be able to make it work for the developer and the land owner. Emerson did a lot of that work, and he did a lot in pioneering legal documentation in Nevada. I admired him and his long hours, which would run until midnight every night–he even had a dictating machine in his automobile, and one at home.

In 1951 I got involved with Howard Hughes in the Husite development in Vegas–zoning, and taxation politics, and county commissioners and Bob Cahill–and the case opened an envelope of law to me. Hughes owned about 25,000 acres of land west of the Strip, out to Red Rock, and when the county commission put together a road and development plan for this area, Hughes's property taxes went up. He felt that the increase was too much, but he failed to appeal to the county board of equalization until it was too late. After that deadline had passed, he hired me to get his taxes reduced . . . which I did, but in the process I had to identify Hughes as my client, and this meant that his situation became publicly known. When word got to him that I had used his name, he said that too much attention had been brought to him, and he fired me.

The Husite case gave me a foundation when ten years later I took on the case of Jack Schumacher, the Ormsby County assessor. I had to quickly become acquainted with how land is assessed in Nevada, and the law governing assessment. Basically, an assessor is to appraise the value of a house and lot, and then assign it an assessed value for purposes of determining the property tax. The tax rate derives from the assessed value, not the purchase price or market value. Household goods were figured at 10 percent of the assessed value of the property, because the assessor is not going to go in a home and count furniture, books, radios, and TVs, and appraise them. (The law said they were supposed to do that, but they never did . . .

impossible!) That was the way things were until they decided to summarily remove Jack Schumacher from office.

Without question, Jack's removal was strictly a political play. Jack had followed all the rules, but he got unfairly caught up in politics with Judges Frank Gregory and Dick Waters of Carson City, and Frank McNamee, my dear old friend on the supreme court. (Frank was as political a judge as there ever was–he was very bright and competent, but he knew how he wanted his cases to come out. He could design the result, and he did, but not malevolently.) Jack Schumacher was assessing property at 35 percent of its fair market value. To this he would add 10 percent as the estimated assessed value of the household goods on the property–the rule of thumb. (Both of those rules had been honored for years.) But when he assessed some *undeveloped* property that Judge Jack Ross and his son, Tom, had, the Rosses decided to get rid of him.

I agreed to defend Jack, who had been given ten day's notice of removal, but I knew I would have trouble before Frank Gregory, who was a tough and arbitrary judge. I drove to Carson City with a petition for an extension of time, and Gregory said, "I am not going to allow you an extension of time."

I said, "Well, Judge, I've got news for you: I'm going to disqualify you. Here's my twenty-five dollars." (In those days, we had a statute where lawyers could pay twenty-five dollars and disqualify a judge.)

He said, "Very well, I am disqualified. I assign the case to Judge Waters."

So, I walked into Judge Waters's chambers, and I said, "Judge, this case has just been assigned to you. Here's my petition for extension of time."

He said, "We've been waiting to get Schumacher. Petition denied!"

I knew I was trapped, but I got a short extension from the supreme court and full cooperation from the Nevada Tax Commission people, who testified, "Yes, we instructed Schumacher; we worked with him; he is following procedures that are universally followed throughout the state of Nevada." But the court found cause for removal on seven counts. As I recall,

I won appeals on six of the seven, but lost on the last one, and Schumacher was impeached and removed from office. As a consequence of that, the legislature over a period of time amended the statutes relating to assessments so that now they are substantially similar to the way the Tax Commission and Jack Schumacher were doing things when he was removed from office.

Some of my earliest cases were Public Service Commission work–I represented a good portion of the major trucking carriers before the Public Service Commission of Nevada. One of the interesting cases was when Senator Johnson[1] sold Nevada Truck Lines to Dale McLeod. (I was still working for John Belford at that time.) The highlight of that case was a two-week hearing before the commission, and the court reporter left town because he had a nervous breakdown. He was unable to copy the proceedings down, and he went to Florida; and if he didn't commit suicide, he should have, because all the records were lost.

(In the early 1970s I got involved with trucking again when *every* two-bit carrier in Nevada objected to United Parcel Service [UPS] doing business in the state. Every technicality that you can imagine was raised by their lawyers, who were usually tedious people, buried in regulations, buried in tariffs: how many pounds of nails fit into a box, and is a nail a commodity, or is it steel that is a commodity; or is it hardware or construction materials . . . ? They were worried over all kinds of minute detail that would drive you absolutely crazy. Generally, the lawyers who argued these cases were so deeply into technicalities that they missed the high points. I was a better trial lawyer than any of them, and I had a relatively successful part-time career with Public Service Commission cases because I didn't get bogged down in the garbage. I also knew how to take the wind out of windbags–and most people who testified in those cases were

---

[1] Kenneth F. Johnson was a state senator from Ormsby County from 1943 to 1957.

windbags! We were eventually successful in bringing UPS into Nevada, and that was probably the last significant common carrier case I ever got involved in, because I had other fish to fry by that time.)

John Drendel and I had a little law partnership for a while in 1952 and 1953. Gardnerville was Drendel's hometown, and we had an office above the Adaven Cafe there. We would take turns going down to Gardnerville one day a week, seeing farmers or whoever else might become our clients. Although it didn't turn out to be a very productive relationship, I was introduced to a great many fine people–the locals in the Minden and Gardnerville area were living thirty years behind the times, but they were honest, hardworking farmers.

We represented the Minden Cooperative Creamery Company (or certainly, I did), and its Windmill-brand products. But I learned that you can't very well manage a cooperative when the board of directors has more experience with a milking machine than they do with running a business! [laughter] They had all the prejudices that come from being hard-working, fundamental German farmers who don't recognize the passage of time, and don't understand the modern, competitive, corporate world. These poor guys were in over their heads. They did *excellent* jobs with respect to the product that they raised on the ranch, but they did a terrible job with marketing and sales and management. They didn't even know how to keep books . . . but they tried.

The Minden Cooperative Creamery and the Windmill products brand got into trouble with the entire Nevada dairy system, which itself was in trouble nationally. The problem that dairy farmers always had in Nevada was that when their milk was collected they would take whatever price and rating was given it by the dairy that collected it. One reason Minden wanted to be a co-op was because they thought they'd get an honest count, and they did. But milk in those days had two pricing standards: grade A and grade B. All pricing was measured on butterfat–not on volume, not on the skim, not on the whole milk, but only on the butterfat content and grade. Originally, grade B milk had been milk where a farmer just put it in the cans, which were collected once a week or so, and it was sour milk that turned into butter. (I've watched that, and it stinks!)

The rule of thumb was that all milk ought to be at least 3.5 percent butterfat. Milk from Guernsey cows would be 4.2, and Holstein might be a little bit lower. But 3.5 percent was the rule of thumb, and you either got a grade A or grade B price. Grade A might be $1.12 per pound of butterfat; grade B might be thirty-five cents per pound of butterfat. In reality, how your milk got *used* determined the price you got; it had nothing to do with the quality. Milk that was cooled and shipped daily was still paid for on the grade-A or grade-B basis, and it was easy for a guy in the dairy business to pay the farmer grade B prices for milk that was really used for grade A purposes, in order to make his bottom line work out.

By meeting all the ranchers, I was introduced to the county commissioners. Eventually, I became engaged to help establish a dairy control law for Nevada after a fellow named Bill Tyson came out from Washington, D.C., and started a dairy farm in Jack's Valley; he also started a price war. It was in large part because of Tyson (and Perle Mesta, who provided the money for the price war) that the Minden Cooperative Creamery and its Windmill Brand failed to survive. (Part of the failure to survive, however, was absolute inadequacy of management, period.) The Tyson situation attracted the attention of the state dairy commission, and may even have motivated its foundation . . . I can't recall the genesis of it now.

About 1957 I was hired as counsel for the Nevada State Dairy Commission, and later I became special deputy attorney general under Harvey Dickerson, assigned to the dairy commission. Trying to regulate the dairy business was a much bigger and more political exercise than might seem likely, but consider that it involved every retail outlet in the state of Nevada–every grocery, every restaurant . . . . Combine this with efforts on behalf of *all* of these people to change a fixed, inflexible pricing system to some system that would favor them, and you can see that it was not only a political and business ferment, it was an exercise in ingenuity. Some of the significant players were

Raley's stores, Eagle-Thrifty Drugs, the major supermarkets in Las Vegas . . . and Kenny Cyril, who was very strong in a Mormon group, as well as in the business world of Las Vegas. Dairy price controls and that sort of thing can lead you into meetings with Tom and Jimmy Bahan of Model Dairy in Reno; with old Sam Murray of Old Home Dairy; with Barry Brooks; Norman Snow, when he had Velvet. Even Perle Mesta in Washington, D.C., was involved. Everyone was paying lip service to the law; everyone was saying, "Yes, we want a dairy commission; yes, we want fair trade . . . but I want a way around it for myself." Had I been politically motivated or a crusader–which I was not–I suspect that I could have caused a lot of trouble for a lot of very prominent people. But my goal was to try to keep the industry stabilized, and to keep compliance organized.

Once we established the dairy commission, we were trying to swim upstream against the law of economics. If you take the principle that all milk (as a commodity) has to be sold to all persons at the same price for every transaction, you are flying in the face of human nature. You are really flying in the face of the law of economics, but that's what we did in the state of Nevada. During years of trying to get the dairy commission established, and years of dealing with prominent people who you would expect to say, "Certainly, I will obey the law," I found that everybody felt that his own case was exceptional–everybody tried to figure out a way to avoid the application of the rules and regulations. But I tried to keep the dairy commission from flexing too much arbitrary muscle.

I finally severed my relationship with the dairy commission because it had become a burden, in the sense that to do the job right took too much time to be simply a lawyer to the commission, and not a voting member. Secondly, it took a lot of political work with the members to try to keep the commission going the way you felt it should. Thirdly, it required a lot of personal time and intervention with the businessmen involved. In the long run, I decided to go to greener pastures. I have never regretted the experience I had on the dairy commission, but I have never regretted my departure, either. And the money I made from the commission was nothing–seven hundred and fifty dollars a month.

I handled divorce cases during the whole time I practiced law, but I did a very substantial divorce business from 1963 to 1967 . . . and I don't know why. I eventually developed some excellent connections with major law firms in the East because I responded promptly; I responded intelligently; I handled their clients well. There wasn't a single client that they sent out to me as a VIP divorce who didn't come away with a good feeling.

The way they used to do it in Las Vegas (I've watched this) is the client would come for a divorce, go in to see the Las Vegas lawyer and give him a couple of pieces of information. The lawyer would say, "I will see you in six weeks." The client would come in in six weeks, and the lawyer would say, "Sign here!" They would go to court while the poor client was sitting there wondering what the hell was happening, going crazy. I never worked a VIP divorce client or any other divorce client that way. I took the time and the patience to counsel and talk with them about their divorce, and I didn't pry into their marital secrets. I tried to acquaint them with the concept of divorce, with the Nevada law, and with the law of the state they'd come from, giving them background on why they had to be in Nevada, what the philosophy was, and why they had to put in a residence.

I would reinforce the relationship with my client periodically during the six-week period to make sure that the client didn't feel abandoned. They would come into the office, or we would have a telephone conversation at the very least. With every significant divorce client that I had–and even some pretty damn poor ones–I built a good relationship. That takes a lot of time and effort, and you don't get home on time when you do that. The consequence of this was that over a period of time I think I built up as good a divorce practice of important clientele and impor- tant law offices as one could get–New York City, Boston, Philadel- phia. The premier firms would send me their premier clients, because they always came back with good results and good feelings.

In a nutshell, that's the way I practiced law, and the way I did everything I did. I am not going to say I succeeded in everything that I did–far from it. But I always tried to make the best effort I could; always tried to treat each client and each case as though it was important, and I really worked hard so that every piece of paper that went out of my office was a good piece of paper instead of a casual one. I didn't make as much money as some successful lawyers, but I had success in working with clients, and reasonably good success in keeping clients.

When the war was over, and I was still debating what I was going to do, I almost bought some surplus airplanes, because I thought that air transportation and air freight would be a growing business. I traveled around to see if various companies would be interested in a service like the Flying Tigers (air cargo line), and how much they'd be willing to pay. But I concluded there was no sense in buying any surplus C-47s and trying to start in the aviation business, because it wasn't going to pay.

After I had been a lawyer for some years, I deliberately set out to get involved in aviation defense work. I thought it would pay a lot more than who-hit-who cases, and it would give me insight into a field that I liked. There was a period from about 1965 to 1975 when General Dynamics F-111s were tearing their wings off, and there were also crashes in southern and eastern Nevada because of flaws in their terrain-following radar systems. I got involved in the analysis of this for the Associated Aviation Underwriters, and with John Brennan, the president of the United States Aviation Insurance Group. It was very interesting work, but eventually I grew disenchanted with the compensation system. I was being paid well–by their standards, at least–but I didn't get paid for good results; I just got paid every day for the work that I put in. If I did an exceptional job, I still only got paid per hour, whether my hour was a good hour or not a very good hour. That's not the color of my jib, but insurance carriers love to see how you spend your day, and how many hours you charge, and how much you charge an hour. I could be a genius, and you could have the IQ of a light bulb, but everybody gets paid the same. I don't like that.

Not only did I represent aviation clients, I also flew my own airplanes. One day I looked up at the blue sky in Nevada and thought, "My God. Here is my escape; here is my boat. I don't have an ocean, and I don't have a Mississippi River, but I have the sky." And that's how I got involved in aviation. I got my pilot's license in 1964, and I have pursued it ever since in a very serious and adult way–not as a Sunday flier who goes up and says, "Oh, gee, here I am."

Aviation has been a great escape for me, a great outlet for my energies. Although it's fun, sometimes it's really hard work if you're doing it right. *Can* you do it right? I recently got typed in the Citation, which was flying to ATP standards–I don't have an ATP rating because I'm over age and my eyesight is too poor to qualify, but I got the type rating. Flying my own planes has been a great experience, but I would have been many dollars ahead if I had never gotten involved in aviation, and just went everywhere on commercial flights or by car or Greyhound bus.

I've always been relatively quiet and withdrawn, and my social life in Reno was limited. My wife and I became involved in St. John's Presbyterian Church when it was meeting at the Reno Little Theater with a pastor named Rafe Martin. (Rafe was a Scotchman–a fun guy, a ball of fire, an organizer.) William Kottinger, an important accountant in Reno, gave St. John's Church a five-acre parcel over on Plumb Lane, and I went through a long period when I attended meetings, helped with the financing drive and worked on the construction of the church building on that property. When Herb Hallman, the Chevrolet king, came to town he became a very significant force in that church. He brought all the drive and strength that he must have exhibited in becoming an important Chevrolet dealer. A lot of us would devote an hour a day to going over and working on the building, and we built St. John's Church.

Some of us in that church in the early days would occasion-ally meet at someone's home. Unfortunately, if you went to a church gathering at somebody's house, it was one of the dullest gatherings you could imagine. It was cookies and tea, and nobody could use any four-letter words, and nobody could have a drink;

nobody could tell a story. You were always on your goody-goody behavior–I don't mean that in a negative way; that was just the way it was in Protestantism in the 1950s and 1960s, because religion was so perfect. Presbyterians always went out of their way to not really be themselves, and to be on their good behavior. From a childhood of Christian Endeavor to being an adult in Reno, I found that lots of so-called "good, Christian people" were totally different when they got together in a barroom somewhere!

I worked hard all day, and before I went to any meeting of the elders or deacons or church committees in the evening, I'd always take a big slug of bourbon, and I would smell like I was full of whiskey. In effect, that was a challenge. I'd walk into this nice room, and . . . "Here comes Dixon, all tooted up, smelling of whiskey." I kept waiting for somebody to say, "Dixon, are you drinking? Because people in our church don't drink!" Nobody ever raised that issue. [laughter]

They made me a deacon of the church, probably because I wore a clean shirt now and then. [laughter] Then eventually they made me an elder. I was a little bit over my head trying to understand Christianity and the church and where it was going, but there were a lot of positive things about it, a lot of good feelings–it was nice to build something, and it was nice to *belong* to something. I even taught Sunday School for a while. With the limited tools that were available to me, I was trying to teach young people about the book of Genesis, which really doesn't mean what it says, and about Matthew, Mark, Luke and John. The best-selling book in the world is the Bible, and it's probably the least-read. I've tried to read it many times, and I can't get past who begat whom. The miracles befuddled me, because to prove that he was the son of God, Jesus had to perform miracles, and yet you still see people lying in the gutter, in pain and suffering. There's such an incongruity . . . . The Bible doesn't stand up to analytical scrutiny, in my opinion, so I've had some problems with that.

Lots of good and decent people attended St. John's, but there were also some prudes . . . and there were some who were just absolute business sharks, but who went to the church, anyhow. They think they can do anything they want to in the business world, but on Sundays they go to church. I had all the doubts about organized religion that I suspect anybody has.

Eventually Jane, who had been devoted to the church and who had pulled me into it, had a complete personality revolution, and decided that she would have no more to do with the church or with Christianity or with any religion. It was a very difficult period, and it led to a break with the preacher and a lot of our friends in the congregation. A strong emotional wall went up, and it was a very strained period in my life. It pretty much ended my relationship with St. John's Church, and I have had very limited church affiliation of any kind since those days.

Attorneys used to have to take on a certain amount of criminal defense work for the federal government at our own expense–it was called *pro bono* work. We were required to do it, and I had a number of cases. The federal system would go through the roster of attorneys who were admitted to practice before the district court here, and they'd summon them to do the *pro bono* defense work on some equitable basis . . . but it seemed that it was usually the younger attorneys who got all the cases. [laughter] I got more than my share, and it seemed that I spent months in Carson City at my own expense. Fortunately, my practice was so meager that it didn't mean a great loss of other clientele that I could have been serving. [laughter] I tried a number of cases, and consulted on others, and in the process I became acquainted with Bruce Thompson, who was then Assistant United States Attorney under Jack Pike. Bruce was tough! I was highly successful in my defense work, and the only lawyer who caused me serious trouble was Bruce Thompson.

I lost a case to Bruce that, in my opinion, I should not have lost. [laughter] The case involved stolen travelers checks, and I thought I had the government where it would hurt, because they had to *prove* that these checks were stolen. I didn't see how they were going to do that. But Bruce produced a letter–this was in the days of trial by surprise–in which the owner of the travelers checks had written his bank and said, "Gentlemen, this is to report that my travelers checks have been stolen," or words to that effect. Bruce attempted to introduce the letter into evidence, but to me the letter was clearly hearsay. There was no way to examine the guy, but they were introducing it to prove that the checks had been stolen, so I objected to the admission of the letter in evidence.

Judge Foley really embarrassed me in front of the jury, and I think he probably meant to. (He was a dominant kind of judge.) He said, "Young man, I want you to approach the bench." Judge Foley was sitting in this great, high federal bench in the old court house, and he had the *United States Code, Annotated* out–a big red book. He said, "I want you to read this statute." Hell, I knew the statute; I knew it better than the judge did. It was a business record statute. (If you don't know the big business record statute or the business records law, you shouldn't be practicing law.) Fundamentally, it says that records that are kept in the ordinary course of business are admissible in evidence. That meant that certain kinds of business records which are kept are inherently so trustworthy that, at least in the first instance, they are allowed to be admitted as evidence. Then you are allowed maybe to cross examine to show that there is something wrong with the record. But in my view a letter from someone outside the bank *to* the bank was not a business record that the bank kept. I am satisfied that "business record" means a record the bank was keeping of its own business.

Foley admitted the letter, and the way he had me come up and read that statute book made me look like a dumbbell in front of the jury. Bruce won that case, and I told him, "Thompson, the only way you won that case was through Foley. You got that letter, and it shouldn't have been admitted as evidence, and you are the only guy who could have whipped me!" We had fun with it, and that was the way I met Bruce Thompson. We were part of the reasonably small Nevada State Bar, and we also went to Democratic party meetings together, so I knew Bruce almost from my arrival in Reno in 1950.

When I was on my own I did not get involved in who-hit-who cases, although I could have gone into the plaintiff side and made some money. But I guess that relates to how you get started, and how many people have lectured you about what you should and shouldn't do–all that business about ethics and whether or not you should be an ambulance chaser; whether you hire a so-called private investigator who goes to the hospital and signs up clients . . . . That's the way Gordon Rice got started. He invented the personal injury law business in Nevada by garnering all the claims out of the hospital. To me that violated the ethics of the legal profession as they were laid down, so I didn't ambulance chase.

The money is all on the plaintiff side of who-hit-who. You could settle a case for a million dollars, and get $350,000 or $400,000 for a fee. On the other hand, the guy who is defending the insurance carrier or the defendant on the other side earns two or three thousand dollars for defending the case. That is the economics of it. Fortunately, my practice didn't come even remotely close to insurance defense work until I joined up with George Vargas and John Bartlett. Vargas used to say, "Insurance defense work is the bread and butter of this office." Well, there was bread, but there wasn't any butter on it, so I declined that aspect of the practice.

By 1957 I had become unhappy with my legal career. I hadn't been able to get it going the way I wanted it to go, but I didn't want to get involved in personal injury claimants practice. One day–this was a spur-of-the-moment decision–I was on the courthouse steps, and I saw George Springmeyer, who was a feisty, thin little man . . . one of the few people, I guess, who are smaller than I am. George was walking up the courthouse steps, and I had an idea–it just struck me like lightning. On the fourth floor of the First National Bank building, where George and Bruce Thompson had the offices of their firm, was a door with the name Sally Springmeyer on it. Sally was George's wife, and I knew Sally did not practice law. I thought, "Here is a chance for me to rent an office in the bank building where I can get more prestige from location." I said, "George, could I rent that office from you?"

"Well," he said, "maybe. I'll think about that."

Maybe two or three days later, I got a call from Bruce Thompson, who said, "Come on over. I want to talk with you." So

I met Bruce in the coffee shop of the Mapes Hotel, and in effect he said, "How would you like to come to work for us?"

I said, "That's not a bad idea."

Then Bruce said, "How old are you?"

I think I said, "I'm forty years old." (I might have said, "I'm thirty-five;" I don't know.) [laughter]

Whatever I said, he says, "You're too old to work for us. You've got to come in as a partner."

I said, "Well, that's fine with me."

So we sat down, and we discussed it a bit, and we created the firm of Springmeyer, Thompson, and Dixon. I took over the office that said Sally Springmeyer on the door, and it worked out very well. It was the opening of a whole new experience in the field of law for me, because Springmeyer and Thompson were well established . . . particularly Bruce. Oh, I was probably a pretty good lawyer too. My reputation was good enough for them to want me in their firm.

When I started practicing law, at the end of each month I would add up all of my bills, and if I had enough money, I paid them. I kept books in a rather formal way, and I had a practice of taking money from clients, but not spending it for my personal use until I performed the service. For example, if I received a retainer of five hundred dollars to take a case, that was really my money, but I would put it in a special trust account and *not* take the money down until I performed services. The reason I did that was I didn't want to be lazy; I didn't want to do what so many lawyers do: take in money and spend it, and then not perform the work. You should never co-mingle retainer money with your own funds. When I paid the bills at the end of the month, that made me hustle and work; it motivated me.

When I joined the Springmeyer and Thompson firm, I had a culture shock. I had a good law library, which I had entered as an asset on my books. I had office furniture and typewriters and so forth, and also had those written up as assets. I had a depreciation schedule, and I had maintained my trust accounts practice. But I noticed that when a bill came into the office, Mary

McKinnon, our secretary, would write a check for it, and pay it the day it arrived. I said to Bruce, "How can we do that?"

He said, "Well, we always pay our bills the day they arrive."

I said, "I have always waited until the end of the month to see if I have enough money to pay the bills."

He said, "We don't have that problem in this firm." That was lesson number one.

Later we bought a new typewriter or Xerox machine or something, and wrote a check for it, and just charged it to expenses. I said, "Bruce, that's not an expense; that's a capital item."

He said, "Hell, we don't have any capital. I've been in this business for years. If we buy books, we pay for them; if we buy typewriters, we pay for them; if we buy desks, we pay for them, and we just charge it all to expenses. It all works out the same in the long run, and the Internal Revenue Service has never bothered us." And here I was being careful with the depreciation schedules!

As I recall, George Springmeyer–dear George–never kept a time record. I don't think Bruce did either. When George got through with a case, he would send the client a bill for what he thought was a reasonable fee for the services rendered. George often took cases for friends or clients, and didn't charge any retainer. When a case was done, he would just send out an estimated bill. I used to say, "George, you've got to think small. I mean, you're doing all kinds of work around here that you never bill for, because you don't write it down. Start thinking small."

He used to laugh and say, "Boy, I can't think small. All I do is I send out a bill when I think I've earned some money."

Bruce was a supporter of John Kennedy for the presidency, and there were many telephone calls from Teddy Kennedy to our office, calling Bruce to ask about the campaign and how it was going in Nevada. I don't know what Bruce did for the Kennedys, but it seemed that every time the phone rang, Mary McKinnon would buzz Bruce, and it would be Teddy Kennedy on the line.

In 1963 Bruce was offered a judgeship, and we talked about it. He said, "You know, I hate to leave the partnership, but I've always wanted to be a federal judge. The opportunity is just too good for me to pass up."

I said, "Fine. I'm pleased that you have the opportunity."

When Bruce took the appointment to the federal bench, we were still then Springmeyer, Thompson, and Dixon. George Springmeyer was not well, and we had a fellow working for us named Bob Groves, a lawyer. I figured I would continue the practice of law, keep Bob on, and work out my relationship with George, which I did.

One day I ran into Ken Dillon in the shower room at the YMCA, and we got to talking. Ken was my idea of a really competent lawyer. He was an excellent business lawyer; he understood finance; he understood corporations–he had a broad perspective on the practice of law. Ken was not a country lawyer; he was a New York lawyer with experience in a big-city law firm, who had initially come to Nevada for a divorce–*Dillon v. Dillon*, which had gone to the Nevada Supreme Court. Although he was in the Vargas firm, Dillon was not a Vargas-type lawyer, and he filled a niche in the Vargas firm that really had been missing. He was not a trial lawyer, and he was not interested in insurance defense work: he was interested in a different kind of law–maybe more the kind of law that I was working in. I thought we had a commonality of view in many ways.

Ken said, "What are you doing now that Bruce is gone? How do you get along with George Vargas?"

(In my first years in Reno I would see George around town, but I hadn't had much to do with him. His firm then was Griswold and Vargas; Morley Griswold was his partner in Elko. One of my early contacts with George occurred when Bill Griswold, who I believe was Morley's son, wanted to get a divorce, and his wife, Marilyn, came to see me. I called George, and we settled the case reasonably quickly and amicably; and, as I recall, I didn't charge any money because of the Griswold and Vargas connection. My second contact with George was when Johnny Bartlett was over in the district attorney's office. George needed somebody to do the defense work in the who-hit-who cases [he really believed that these were the bread and butter cases], so he proposed to Bartlett, who had developed a good reputation as a trial lawyer, that he come over to Vargas's firm. John Bartlett called me up and said, "I'm going to go with George Vargas. Why don't you come over here and take my job in the district attorney's office?"

I thought about that . . . the politics, and so forth. I thought, "Do I want to go over to the district attorney's office? Do I want to run for the assembly?" [laughter] I decided I didn't want to, and that I should try to devote my time to practicing law on my own. That was probably the wrong thing for me to have done career-wise, but I didn't want to go over and work for a district attorney; I didn't want to be part of the government system, period. So I did not take the offer.)

Ken Dillon suggested that we talk about the possibility of a partnership between our firms. So we did. We looked at their practice, and they looked at mine, and we decided that there would be room to bring the two together. (We were even in the same building at that time–the Union Federal Savings and Loan building along Court and Sierra, as I recall.)

We created the firm known as Vargas, Dillon, Bartlett and Dixon, and we went through the usual problems that any merger of law firms and law practices brings: How do you set up accounts? What is your capital account? What sort of cases do you bring in? What do you do with your excess law library? What kind of a law library do you have? And desks and furniture and chattel and that sort of thing.

With the Vargas, Dillon, Bartlett and Dixon law firm, there was meticulous, hourly accounting for every hour of the day that you were in the office, for everything you did. [laughter] Ken Dillon was very much involved in maintaining accurate produc-

tivity records on each lawyer, monitoring the amount of work
that each put forth, and managing a law office on that basis, even
though it was a relatively small law office. Everything was run on
a *totally* businesslike basis, which was a night-and-day switch
from Springmeyer, Thompson and Dixon. I soon learned how
things were done, and I grew with the firm and became a
significant producer.

Sadly, Ken Dillon died in my first or second year with that
firm. I had asked Ken to help me on a couple of significant
Harrah's matters that involved finance and New York. I could go
to him and say, "Ken, would you do this?" and he not only would
do it, but he'd do it well. There were not many lawyers who
could do the kinds of things that he could do. But I'm not going
to say that that's the reason I miss him . . . he was a loss to me
as a good lawyer, but I miss him as a friend. (His wife, Barbara,
is now Barbara Vucanovich, our congresswoman.) Ken was
probably the reason that our firm created its particular practices
and methods of doing business, and his death was a real loss to
the law firm. I wish he could have stayed with us for years and
years because I think we would have had a stronger and better
law firm with his talents.

Bruce Thompson and George Vargas were two totally
different people. Each respected the other, and yet their personalities were almost as different as night and day. Bruce Thompson was a lawyer who practiced law by putting the seat of his
pants to the seat of a chair. Beside his desk he had a typewriter,
and he could turn from facing his desk to his right side and sit
down and type his letters or documents. It helped him think.
(I've often found in my own life that typing or writing helps you
think. I would use pen or pencil and yellow, lined manuscript to
write out my thoughts.)

Bruce had a peculiar habit: every year at Paterson's fall sale
he bought a brown suit and a blue suit. That was as far as his
interest in clothing went. [laughter] We used to laugh about it,
because one day he'd wear the brown suit, and the next day he'd
wear the blue. He'd alternate brown and blue, and brown and

blue, and brown and blue, and he'd wear the hell out of those suits.

Bruce was a member of a Reno horseman's group, the White Hats, and he used to ride in all their parades. I once saw him wrestle a steer to the ground at the rodeo, and I couldn't believe it. Bruce was aggressive that way. He would never hunt ducks with me because, he said, "I can't sit still. I don't like the idea of sitting there waiting for a duck to fly by." Yet Bruce and I would often hunt upland game, and we'd walk for hours. He wouldn't play golf, "because I can't stand the slowness of the game or spending half a day at it. I want to play tennis so I can get it over in an hour at the most." And that's what he did.

George Vargas was just the opposite in so many respects. He was not a golfer, but he was flamboyant: he loved bright blue suits, bright clothing . . . totally white suits and white shoes. Everything George had was tailored, and he was dressed almost outrageously, so you might have thought he was an entertainer. He was almost as flamboyant in his practice of law as in his clothing. George loved to dictate, and he would dictate a document or a letter and never read it back, because he knew that whatever he dictated was right. He didn't have to correct it or go back and edit it, and George was a genius in that regard. But when he was through with a case, he was through. He was not a seat-of-the-pants-to-the-seat-of-the-chair guy. You could never imagine him sitting down as Bruce did and spending long hours, and the result was that they had a totally different clientele and different results.

George liked representing insurance companies; Bruce didn't. George felt insurance defense work was the bread and butter of the firm, whereas Bruce couldn't accept those cases because he couldn't have agreed to the regimentation that the insurance adjusters or the insurance carriers imposed upon defense lawyers. George was at his high point emotionally when he was trying a case in a courtroom, and he was a great Nevada trial lawyer. Bruce was a good trial lawyer, but he was probably better at research and legal education. George liked to work very hard and play very hard, and he didn't have the same consistency as Bruce.

George Vargas was one of the first guys I knew who had a four-wheel drive Jeep utility wagon that wasn't painted all brown and yellow to sort of imitate wood like the first ones were. George's Jeep had everything on it: he had it completely equipped with a winch, shovel, a handyman jack–all of the equipment–and this famous lawyer would drive to work in that car. (George had a pretty good reputation for being a good hunter as well as a good lawyer.)

Different as they were, George and Bruce liked and respected one another. They kidded each other, and they got along well. I knew them both intimately, and I never knew either of them to have a thought of dishonesty, a thought of misrepresentation, a thought of chicanery. They didn't believe in cutting corners–they just were not that kind of people. Each always told the truth, and they would tell you where they stood, and their word could never be questioned. Whatever they said they would do, they did. They were God's people; they were the right kind of people. They were both giants in their field, and although they will be forgotten in a few years, the people who knew them will long remember them.

Between the Vargas and Thompson approaches to law, I was probably closer to the Thompson side of the thing. George Vargas was almost a one-shot lawyer–that is, he didn't build a clientele with repeated, long, repetitive relationships. You'd go to George Vargas if you had serious trouble, and he'd do a good job, but then he might go hunting. On the other hand, he was extremely successful as a lobbyist, when Bruce probably would not have succeeded. Every legislative session George gave a red velvet party in Carson City, at which there was lots of red wine drunk, and George would perform and sing. (George loved to play the drums. If he had his way, he might have been an entertainer.) [laughter] Bruce, of course, was more private than that, and I fell somewhere between the two. I'm sure Bruce used to think I was frivolous at times, and George used to think I was too serious. One of my problems was that I always thought I could do

everything or anything . . . or at least I always *tried* to do
everything or anything. [laughter]

[4]

Party Politician

THE VERY FIRST DEMOCRATIC MEETING I went to in Nevada was in the Odd Fellows Building in Reno, and it was an eye opener. I was taken there by Bill Kane, who was the deputy U.S. attorney under Jack Pike (Miles N. Pike). Les Leggett was the chairman at the time, and I think Virgil Wedge was also involved. It was one of the most amazing political meetings I had ever seen. Leggett sat up there as chairman and rapped the gavel, and if there was somebody that he didn't want to speak, they didn't get a chance to speak. It was really bang, bang, bang, like something out of Tammany Hall.

When I was involved in party politics in the county, it seemed like all of us were active . . . like Bill Berry, who must be in his mid-eighties by now. Bill was a stringer, I think, for New York newspapers, like the *New York Daily News*. There were also Bryn Armstrong and Ed Olsen–Ed was with the Associated Press, and I guess Bryn was with one of the local Reno newspapers. Frank McCullough was with the *Nevada Labor News*, as I recall; Frank later became an editor and vice president of *Time* magazine.

John Squire Drendel and Tom Cooke and I were kind of firebrands or young Turks in the Democratic Party in the early

1950s, and we had our concerns about Pat McCarran.[1] None of us had been to Georgetown University Law School, or had been fortunate enough to have the patronage of Pat. Grant Sawyer, of course, was one of Pat's boys. Jack Pike was United States attorney, and John T. McLaughlin was in his office. Leslie Leggett was also a McCarran devotee. Then there were Bill Kane, and Bob McDonald, who was with Alan Bible. All these people were prominent in the Democratic Party in Nevada, and they were all part of the McCarran group.

A bunch of us rebels with a cause decided to go against McCarran's wishes and support Tom Mechling in his 1952 campaign for a U.S. Senate seat. Mechling had married a girl from Wells, Nevada, Margaret DiGrazia, and he came here from Washington, D.C., and astounded us all when he announced that he was going to run for the Democratic nomination for the United States Senate against Alan Bible. Mechling had no residence in Nevada–he was totally an outsider–but he came on with a tremendously good line and great effort to run against Bible, who had been Nevada's attorney general.

Alan Bible's greatest campaign slogan–I never will forget it–was "Native Nevadan". He had signs all over the state,"Alan Bible, Native Nevadan". I guess Alan thought that in those days that was enough. Among ourselves, we sort of thought we needed new blood. We didn't need more of the McCarran machine; we didn't need Alan; and we decided to support Mechling, because we were enthusiastic about what he was saying. So we worked at night, and we solicited our friends. We had campaign literature printed and we distributed it . . . probably annoyed everybody by putting it under their windshield wipers. [laughter]

Mechling defeated Bible in the primary. Then, in October–following some harsh accusations Mechling had made about an arrangement between his Republican opponent, George "Molly" Malone and Pat McCarran–McCarran publicly repudiated

[1] Patrick McCarran (Dem.) served as a United States senator from Nevada from 1933 until his death in 1954.

Mechling and urged all of his friends to vote in the general election for Malone! Shortly thereafter, if my memory is correct, Norman Biltz went public with tapes that he had secretly recorded at a meeting that he and Mueller had had with Tom Mechling the month before. Unbeknownst to our naive little group, Mechling had gone to Biltz, who was an ardent McCarran supporter, I think to solicit funds and McCarran's endorsement in exchange for favors if he was elected. This shocked us–we had supported him because he was pure and clean and new and honest, just like we were. Norm had a tape of their conversation, and, as I recall, he released its substance to the newspapers. He also rushed over to radio station KOH, but a lot of the guys who were working there were Mechling supporters, so they in turn put together a doctored tape, which had Pat McCarran supporting Tom Mechling, as I recall. [laughter] The idea was that the Mechling campaign would play the doctored tape to show that the Norman Biltz tape must have been doctored also!

Mechling told us that the tape was a phony; that anybody could make a tape say anything. But we all felt disillusioned, because whether or not Mechling was actually lying to us, we concluded that there was something wrong with his representation–so all of the enthusiasm that we had for him failed. Of course, the result was that Mechling did not make it to the United States Senate, and Malone was reelected.

This was kind of an initiation for me into Nevada politics. I became as active in the Democratic Party as anyone could become, and eventually, I became chairman of the Washoe County Democratic Central Committee.

Pat McCarran died in office in 1954. Pat, the silver-haired gentleman, had been a skilled politician, a mover and shaker. He had built up a coterie of young lawyers whom he had befriended, and who were good McCarran Democrats because of what Pat had done for them and for the state. I didn't have the indebtedness to him that many Nevada lawyers had–lawyers who had gotten their law degrees from Georgetown (Grant Sawyer being one)–and since I was not a McCarran insider, I don't know how influential he was, except by hearsay. He was significant in the completion of the Flamingo Hotel in Vegas because of his political clout–at least I was told that when I was there–and he was instrumental in getting the Mapes built in Reno. (Again, that's hearsay.) I met with him, and I've had coffee with him. He had his little table at the Riverside Hotel, and when he was in town he put his body in that chair at his table, and that's where he held court. [laughter] Norman Biltz also had a table in the Riverside; Norm was there every day with Johnny Mueller, and they were staunch McCarran people.

Pat was not only a competent politician, but an erudite lawyer. If you go back and read the opinions of the Nevada Supreme Court that Pat McCarran wrote, his opinions were lucid and clear. Perhaps to some people the language would seem simple, but his opinions weren't filled with a lot of the garbage that judges of the time usually wrote, so I was impressed with the guy. A lot of my friends would say, "McCarran is terrible; he wields too much power," but I don't recall anybody saying he was corrupt, even though he was criticized heavily by lots of liberal Democrats. I thought the guy was highly competent and intelligent. Maybe some of the things that he had done I wouldn't have voted for, but . . . .

Pat had the knack of knowing everybody in the state of Nevada, and when Nevada was a rural state, rural power was important to him. I rode around with Walter Baring when he was eating peanuts and trying to copy Pat's style. McCarran could drive through the Nevada countryside, and he would know the name of every ranch and every rancher. If he drove into the town of Austin, he knew the name of the guys who ran the grocery store, the service station, the bar, the saloon, the hotel. He was at home with his Nevada people, and he did not ignore his homework. His passing was an event of national significance. No Nevadan that I know of ever achieved the stature and the power that McCarran had, and we certainly don't have anybody like him today.

When I was chairman of the central committee in Washoe County, Floyd Lamb was the Clark County leader, and he was very powerful in those days. At a Democratic Central Committee meeting following McCarran's death (Bruce Thompson was with me), we agreed to support Alan Bible for United States Senate, a complete turnaround from the position we had had earlier. I was enough of a friend of Alan's and active enough by that time that I had the privilege of driving him to Carson City to the secretary of state's office, where we filed his petition for his candidacy.[1] After that, Alan and I were always, I thought, good friends. Sometimes his political views were more conservative than mine, but I grew to like and to respect him. Sure, I laughed at some of the things he said, and I am sure he laughed at some of the things I did, but he was successful in his campaign.

After I had served my term as chairman of the Washoe County Central Committee, I just fell away from politics pretty much. The position of county chairman is not a very high position, but the demands of a practice of law and other interests intervened, and politics did not offer a career path for me. I had no interest in becoming an assemblyman, nor had I any interest in working for the district attorney's office. (I had job offers there, but I had no interest in becoming a political employee or a politician.) And I had a problem with the caucus system.

Politics was totally different in Illinois in the 1930s than it was in Nevada in the early 1950s. In Illinois, both the Democratic and Republican party systems were based upon election rather than the caucus principle that Nevada uses. I think it is unfortunate that Nevada has relied upon the caucus to select representatives for state and county committees, and for the national conventions, because caucuses . . . well, I know how we used to run our Democratic caucuses when Pat McCarran was still alive. The abuse of the caucus system was amusing, but it was probably one way that democracy is taken from the people.

My disenchantment with the party and its caucus system made me think, "What the hell am I doing with a bunch of people like this?" The people who controlled the Democratic Party

[1] Bible defeated Cliff Young for United States senator in 1956 by a plurality of 4,965 votes.

through its caucus system were really not representative of the population. I don't want to say it was a professional group, but it was a very limited group of people that would go to the caucus meetings. As a matter of fact, Joe Cleary (there's a name from the past) used to say, "Let me help you pick the houses where we're going to have the caucus meetings, and we will pick houses that nobody can find so nobody will show up." They'd even announce that a meeting would start at eight o'clock; then they would start the heart of the meeting before eight, and by the time everybody arrived, they'd say, "Well, we're sorry, but the meeting is over." That was the way the caucus system was running the state of Nevada.

In the 1950s, casino gambling was becoming successful in Nevada, and Las Vegas was growing by leaps and bounds, but gambling's future in the state was certainly not politically assured. When I became involved in representing Harrah's in 1957, I was concerned (as were Bill Harrah and other people I associated with) that we had two threats to the future of gambling in Nevada: one was federal intervention; the other was–let me be sacrilegious–the threat of Christianity . . . the churches. A number of tracts were published by various religious groups, largely Protestant, condemning gambling as being immoral or wrong. At that time I belonged to St. John's Presbyterian Church. Some people who belonged to that church, and who worked at Harolds Club, had *terrible* internal torture, because they were going to a church where, in effect, the congregation was saying, "Gambling is wrong," and these people were earning a living from gambling. They had to ask themselves, "How can I be a Presbyterian (or how can I be a Protestant or a Christian) and still work for Harolds Club?"

The movement to reform Nevada didn't get very far, but it was a threat. One consequence was that many legal documents of that era contained clauses that allowed termination of contracts in the event that gambling should be outlawed or suppressed by reason of excessive taxation, federal intervention, or by Nevada legislation. (That was before the rise of corporate gaming.) There was a period of several years in which that was a concern, and I think that our governors (certainly Governor Grant Sawyer) were cognizant of the possibility of federal intervention to suppress or interfere with Nevada gaming.

I knew Grant Sawyer when he was prosecuting attorney in Elko, and his father was a doctor in Fallon. Grant was a dynamic governor, who had some principles, and he stood up for his principles. One of them was the protection of the Nevada gaming industry. In later years the federal threat became more apparent than the threat of reforming Nevada from inside, and the so-called Christian threat gradually subsided because it hadn't enough political clout. Today we have the economic threat. Our country has gone through a tremendous change, so that every-body in the United States is now legalizing gambling . . . or it seems that way.

After Bible was elected, my only active party participation was trying to support Grant Sawyer when he ran for governor. (I was able to persuade Jimmy Contratto to make a contribution to Grant's campaign, even though Contratto said that he wanted to give the money to Governor Russell, because he thought that a Republican ought to be in office.) [laughter] Grant was success-ful, and that was about the end of my political involvement. I always knew the people who were in office, but I had no other activity in politics.

I was impressed with Grant. He was a McCarran man, but there was nothing intrinsically wrong with that. I had first met him when the party had a convention at Boulder City, I think. We talked, and Grant impressed me as being sincere, competent, and eager. As governor, I thought he was far preferable to Charlie Russell, whom he was running against. Since my background had been Democratic politics, and Grant was the Democratic nominee, naturally I supported him.

Grant was a good leader and a good governor. He had poise, presence, a good speaking voice, and I thought he was good for our state. I had some problems when he came out in support of the right of eighteen-year-olds to vote, but that became a national trend, and I suspect that I was a little behind the times in thinking that they should at least wait until age twenty-one to vote. (As it's turned out, I don't think many eighteen-year-olds vote.) I could envision a whole panoply of related changes that could arise if you could vote at eighteen: Are you old enough to sign a contract? Have you reached the age of maturity? Are you legally responsible? Can you drink beer or whiskey? Can you gamble? My recollection is that in most states, if you were eighteen years old you could vote, sign a binding contract, sue and be sued, but you couldn't drink or go into casinos. That's a strange distinction–you are an adult for some purposes, but not for others. Had I been governor in Grant Sawyer's time I would have opposed the eighteen-year-old situation . . . but Grant was on the cutting edge.

Grant was good for gaming, and he made good appointments at a time when gaming was evolving in the state. What had been good for gaming in 1950 might not have been good in 1960, and some of the things that Grant stood for would not necessarily be good for gaming today, but at the time and the place he brought respectability to the governorship, and he was good for gaming and good for the state of Nevada. The public thought so, and he is still very highly regarded in this state.

Paul Laxalt, of course, was a conservative, but he brought a certain stature to the governor's office because he carried himself very well. It was under Paul's administration that Howard Hughes became licensed. People have criticized Paul for licensing Hughes, but that was pivotal in the development of gaming in Nevada. All the credibility and prestige of Howard Hughes came to Las Vegas, and by virtue of his acquiring ownership of a large number of hotels, it is said that he cleaned up the state by buying out a lot of unsavory people. That's an exaggeration, but there is a certain degree of truth to it.

Paul Laxalt was wise enough to say, "It's important enough to the state of Nevada that we are going to license Howard Hughes, whether Hughes goes through all of the required procedures or not." Had Paul been rigid and unwilling to use some common sense and discretion, Hughes would never have been licensed, because Hughes would never appear in public and bare his soul. I am glad that Paul had the wisdom to recognize that Hughes was unique; Paul was criticized for this, but he had the courage to be flexible when the situation required it.

While I was chairman of the Washoe County Democratic Central Committee, Mike O'Callaghan[1] occupied the same role for Clark County. I met with him in Las Vegas on a number of occasions, as well as at the party conventions. O'Callaghan very much admired policemen, and one of his litmus tests was that a person was a good guy if he'd ridden around in the back seat of a cop's or trooper's car for a while, and seen that side of life. He had a firm belief that people who had had that exposure made more of their lives, were better citizens, and had better understanding than people who hadn't. I sometimes wondered if he was shooting barbs at me, because I hadn't done that . . . . I had done a lot of things in life, but I hadn't ridden around in the back seat of a sheriff's car! [laughter] And I always wondered why that was such an important thing to Mike.

After he became governor, I had my disagreements with Mike . . . he tended to allow personality to affect him perhaps more than some others. And he had the misfortune of being governor just when the state was beginning to burst at her seams–Atlantic City was coming along, and there was tremendous pressure put on O'Callaghan to allow operators to go out of the state for gaming ventures. He had a foot in both camps: he was part of the past, and yet the future was upon him. Mike O'Callaghan would very much have liked to stay in the past without accepting change, and he would have loved to see Nevada have a monopoly on casino gaming, so he had a hard time adjusting to Atlantic City. One of his statements about New Jersey was, "Where are they going to get their gamblers?" It was clear to me that the state might be able to lock a Nevada casino company in to the state of Nevada, but they couldn't lock people in here. I told Mike there was no reason why a New Jersey company couldn't call up and employ anybody from any Nevada

---

[1] Donal N. "Mike" O'Callaghan (Dem.) was governor of Nevada from 1971 to 1979.

casino. Therefore, we as casino operators ought to be able to go out of state also. My arguments didn't carry very well, but I know that Mike had the best interests of Nevada at heart. Those were wrenching times for all of us. It took months and months, and a lot of effort was put into establishing the policy that eventually allowed Nevada gaming operators to go into New Jersey.

[5]

Lady Luck and Hacienda

THE DEVELOPMENT OF THE LADY LUCK, which eventually became the Las Vegas Hacienda, began around 1954. At the time that I started to work on the Lady Luck, Nevada did not have a gaming control board.[1] Bud Loomis was a private attorney representing the tax commission, as I recall, and he was instrumental in the formation of the first GCB . . . but Bud didn't like to do much grunt work. Bud got Howard "Harry" McKissick–the lawyer whose dad was United States marshal here–involved in drafting the Gaming Control Act, an act that I always thought was poorly drafted . . . but that's simply a personal opinion. Like everything else, it had to be legislatively expedient to pass, but it worked, and it didn't affect my practice in any way. Obviously, a lawyer in my situation had to keep up with what was going on, but any change in the Nevada statutes relating to gaming control would only affect my clients, not me.

About the time the Gaming Control Board was being established, we were trying to get the Lady Luck casino together in Vegas. I was introduced to Carlton Adair, who liked me. He took me into this project, because he thought that I understood Nevada gaming laws, and how to get along with politicians and

---

[1] The three-member Gaming Control Board (GCB) was created in 1955, during the administration of Governor Charles Russell, to act as the investigative and enforcement arm of state gaming regulation.

deal with political and regulatory problems. For instance, Jack Stratton–who eventually became a member of the Gaming Control Board–was a clerk at the GCB offices who sat in a little desk out in the hallway; but I had a good relationship with him, because I knew if you wanted to get through the door, you had to get through Jack Stratton.

We were in a race to open and get operating before the Tropicana. Carlton Adair was the promoter for the Lady Luck, and he got Stanley Burke, the hamburger king from Sacramento who owned the site, to commit the land. Then he got Frank Hoefus from the Del Mar Club involved. (Frank had a secret interest in the Golden in Reno, but he was really *persona non grata* with gaming authorities. Consequently, they had to evaporate a little bit because of Frank's lack of acceptability.) Adair also got Warren "Doc" Bayley, who had the Fresno Hacienda and the Bakersfield Hacienda, which were tremendous motel chain successes in California, to come in for the hotel side.

The package that Adair was promoting was that he and his group would, as he said, keep the goose that laid the golden egg: they'd keep the casino operation. Stanley Burke would have the land and the buildings, and Doc Bayley and his group would have the hotel operation–this was the consortium that would go together. You could not sell public stock; you could not sell participating interests; and you were limited to *fifty* ownerships. That was kind of a vague number, and not well defined. It derived from the tax commission rule of thumb, inspired by Senator Ken Johnson from Carson City: when, in 1955, they decided to impose a 3 percent gross revenue tax on casinos, they also determined that there were too many assignees in Nevada; and in fact assignees *were* an accepted way of doing business. Somebody who was licensable and had a participating interest in a casino would assign all or part of that interest to an assignee, who thus acquired a hidden interest in the casino. The flow of money to assignees was common.

Robbins Cahill and Bud Loomis decided that they would limit the number of licensees to fifty in any joint, but they didn't know how they were going to define eligibility. Loomis wanted to say that nobody could own less than 2 percent of a casino, thereby limiting the maximum number of owners to fifty. (Everybody called percentages "points", and points were common. Cliff Jones had five points in the Pioneer, for example, and other guys had points here and there.) So in effect, you had to have two points in a joint or you couldn't participate in its license. The other side of *that* coin was that there would be no more assignees, because they had to be licensed and counted in the fifty. This was going on with the tax commission about the time that the Gaming Control Board was being created.

We had to comply with all sorts of securities rules and regulations. As our corporate counsel, we employed Gibson, Dunn and Crutcher of Los Angeles, instead of some other significant law firm in Beverly Hills or Los Angeles that had Las Vegas ties. Gibson, Dunn had none; it was old establishment. The Hacienda[1] couldn't have come in without some heavyweight lawyers, and Gibson, Dunn tried to keep noses clean with respect to California laws, securities, all interstate regulations, and so forth.

We worked on the financing of the project for a couple of years, it seems to me, and I spent days and days in Las Vegas meeting with investors. About that time, the Riviera and the Royal Nevada were going up. Morry Mason built the Riviera; he also built the Fontainebleu in Miami–that was his claim to fame. One of our guys in the Hacienda group knew Mason, so I got to stay free in the Riviera before it was open to the public, and could thus afford to spend more time in Las Vegas. I also knew a security guard at the Royal Nevada, so I used to stay there free of charge, too. (I'd walk right across the parking lot to the Silver Slipper and get my breakfast for almost nothing.) It really made it more economical for me as a Reno lawyer to help handle this Las Vegas project, which otherwise would have been a big problem.

---

[1] Begun as Lady Luck, this hotel-casino project was renamed Hacienda before completion. The two names are used interchangeably in this chapter.

I had no trouble being accepted in the Las Vegas community. I knew people there, and I fit into the community well, but there was still always a line of demarcation between Vegas and Reno. You had to be on-site pretty much if you were going to succeed. On the other hand, you also had to know Carson City if you were going to succeed. In fact, the reason the Hacienda group chose me was because I was a pretty good lawyer, and I knew the tax commission people, knew Carson City, and had considerable experience in other aspects of government. People would go to regulators and say, "Gee, we don't have counsel in Nevada. Who should we see?"

And the regulator would say, "I've had experience with Dixon. Why don't you go talk with him?" I always have had the ability of coming across to government regulators as a straight shooter–a no-BS guy. I could talk to them; they could talk to me. So I always had good relationships with almost any office in the state.

From the beginning, we struggled with the Hacienda, trying to get people to invest money. Carlton Adair would give away pieces of anything, as long as he could hold his hands together and say, "I'm going to control the goose that laid the golden egg," meaning the casino. We could get money for a hotel; we could get money for land; we could get money for operations; but we couldn't get money into Carlton's casino in any significant amount to balance the three-legged stool that we were standing on. It became apparent that at some point we were going to have to take the strong players (and the only *really* strong player was Bayley) and make them the pivotal interest in the project, instead of the Adair group . . . and we had to get rid of Frank Hoefus.

We had formed two limited partnerships: South Nevada Investors, Ltd., and South Virginia Investors, Ltd., because at the same time that we were considering trying to build a casino in Las Vegas, we had property out by Brown School on South Virginia Street in Reno. The decision was whether to build a casino on South Virginia Street on the Avansino property, or go ahead in Vegas. I created limited partnerships for both the Reno and Las Vegas projects. We finally went with South Nevada. (If I had wanted *you* to sign up for a limited partnership, would you have signed up on Virginia Street in Reno or on the Las Vegas Strip?) Actually, we had a poor location on the Strip for the Hacienda, because we were so far out. Not only were we past the Flamingo, we were past the Tropicana! And we didn't have a clear property definition for building to begin with . . . but everything evolved toward Las Vegas because we had to get investors.

In those days, for the most part investors were not only people who liked Las Vegas, but they liked bourbon whiskey and fast women. You didn't have a whole lot of dentists and doctors–you had fast-track people who could afford to spend the money, lose the money, and who liked the fast life and believed in Vegas. You have to remember there was a strong concern in this period that either the people of Nevada or the people in the federal government were going to stop gaming, so it was a risky venture. But the point is this: I had meetings with many potential investors, and they usually involved drinking whiskey and smoking cigars. I will tell you that I have signed a lot of participating contracts as late as four o'clock in the morning in the DI (Desert Inn) or some other place, and Bayley used to charter DC-3s to come up out of Fresno, and we'd sit in Reno in the Riverside, working things out. What I wanted was signatures and commitments to flesh out our financial package so we could get the Lady Luck going.

Investors came from many backgrounds. We had car dealers . . . we had Orville Chedister, who was a Bakersfield cotton farmer, and a rather significant investor in our project. We had a lot of documents to sign, and Orville would always sign anything you put in front of him. I once said, "Orville, it's kind of interesting–you never ask any questions; you just sign the papers."

He says, "Yes, but let me tell you: I went into the bank one time down in Bakersfield . . . . " Now, you got to remember this is one of the largest cotton growers in the valley. He told me he went in the bank to borrow some money, and the banker brought out some contracts. Orville started to read them, and the banker asked him, "What are you doing?"

Orville said, "Well, I'm trying to read this contract. My daddy told me not to sign any contract until I've read it."

The banker said, "Orville, it doesn't make any difference whether you read it or not. If you don't sign the contract, you don't get the money." [laughter]

Then Orville said, "In that case, I'm going to sign the contract."

It was fun putting this transaction together with guys like Orville, who would sign as long as you said, "It's OK. Sign this document."

Adair tried to beat the bushes for money everywhere. One of the last meetings we had with Carlton Adair was on Las Vegas Boulevard, South, just a block north of Charleston Avenue. I can see the building, but I can't remember its name or address. How I got there at two o'clock in the morning, I'll never know, but we all came into a darkened room . . . only a dim light over a conference table. This meeting was going to make or break the Lady Luck casino, and Carlton was desperate to hold us all together and to hold his position in Lady Luck. There were several people there: Carlton, Bayley, myself . . . maybe Chuck DiSantis of Gibson, Dunn. It was fish or cut bait, and Carlton was at the head of the table. He said, "Gentlemen, I have all our problems solved. I have a commitment for all of the necessary money for the casino."

Somebody said, "Well, Carlton, you've got to do more than talk. You've got to show us."

He said, "I will show you." He put his hand on the table and turned his hand up, opened it, and there was a bunch of diamonds in his hand. [laughter] I looked at those diamonds; I didn't know if they were real diamonds or zircons, and neither did anybody else.

Somebody said, "Carlton, what are those?"

Carlton lowered his voice, and in a confidential tone said, "The Waterman diamonds!"

At one point in time, the Waterman Fountain Pen Company was a very prominent company. As his story went, Carlton had gotten a commitment from a widow or some woman in the Waterman family to finance his end of the joint. He needed evidence that she had the ability, and she had given him a handful of diamonds. That was his story. But the bottom line was that you couldn't write a check against them, so we made no deal that night, and concluded that the house of cards was going to tumble. At this point, bills were coming due, and the project had to get some direction. So Bayley took over, cut out Carlton Adair (who later became employed at the Dunes), and changed the name to the Las Vegas Hacienda, because he had run the Hacienda chain of hotels in California. From there the project went forward, was built and was completed.

Construction of the Hacienda began in 1956. Homer Rissman was the architect; he is still an architect in Vegas. He had a neat concept–the Hacienda would have the same design that early Las Vegas casinos had: there would be a central casino building, housing all of the restaurants and so forth, and then there would be various motel units or bedroom units–dormitories, if you will. It was to be built like the Sands, but with a very significant difference: Rissman was the first to connect all of the sleeping rooms to the main casino with enclosed corridors. There would be half a dozen different rooming units in a big semicircle around the rear of the Hacienda, all connected to the casino with slate-floored, glass-walled walkways, with air conditioning in the summer and heat in the winter. In effect, no one would have to go outside. Rissman believed–and I think he was right–that glassing-in the corridors would add to the attraction of the Las Vegas Hacienda. The hotel opened in the summer of 1956, and the casino early in 1957.

Gaming licensing was in its nascent period, and we had to find a competent casino operator for our place, because as Bob Cahill[1] used to say, "I'm not going to license a bunch of lawyers

---

[1] Robbins E. Cahill was perhaps the most powerful figure in the early regulation of casino gaming in Nevada. He served on the Nevada State Tax Commission (the first state gaming regulatory agency) from 1945 to 1963, and was chairman of the Gaming Control Board from 1955 to 1958.

and dentists and doctors, period." He said, "I realize that you've got to get knowledgeable operators from somewhere, and that gamblers from outside the state always paid off the sheriff–they always lived outside the law. But the only way we're going to get gambling going in Nevada is to use people who have gambled illegally, and we're going to license them if we think they're clean," or words to that effect. They weren't going to hold against them the fact that they had operated illegally in another state.

We tried to get Jake Kozloff licensed to run the Hacienda. Jake had been at the Frontier, and his was a big name in Las Vegas. Doc Bayley and Jake hit it off well, so Kozloff was going to run the Hacienda; but he had to get past the Gaming Control Board of Cahill, Bill Sinnott, and Newell Hancock, and for some reason Bob Cahill had it in for him.

Jake owned three mid-1950s Cadillacs, all pink; and he smoked big cigars, probably twelve inches long, and handmade. Jake was an extrovert, and he had the old Nevada way of impressing the straights. (I was a straight; Bayley was a straight.) [laughter] When you'd go to dinner, wherever you went, Jake always gave what he called "complimentary play" . . . . If you were really an old-time gambler, you never walked into some-body else's store without you gave them some complimentary play–that is, you'd gamble a hundred or two hundred dollars on a crap table *just as a courtesy*. A hundred dollars is about the minimum; that's the standard unit for complimentary play.

(I was with Bill Harrah when Jessie Beck took over the Riverside Hotel. When she opened, Bill gave Jessie some compli-mentary play, and Bill very seldom played. The way I understand it, if I had gone in and done it, it would not have been compli-mentary play, because I wasn't an owner, a proprietor or an old-timer. That was kind of the courtesy that one showed the other, and it was expected. I've been with Jimmy Contratto up at the lake, and he would go over to a table to give some complimen-tary play–just walk right up to the craps table and lay down a hundred or two hundred bucks, and roll those dice. And as soon as he lost . . . . Of course, you could win and pick it up and walk; I've seen that happen. But you didn't stay there all day shooting craps like a flat crap player would. And everybody in this business knows you win or you lose, and nobody cries over winning or losing, either way: "Smile! Them dice can't hear!")

Jake would start with hundred-dollar bills, and shoot craps. He would also call his friends in advance, so that if we happened to go by the Sahara and Louis Prima was there with his orchestra, Louis'd stop and say, "Here's Jake Kozloff! Welcome, Jake!" Wherever we went, they always greeted Jake, but that didn't happen because he walked in and somebody recognized him; it happened because Jake was connected. Oh, that impressed the investors in the Hacienda! We'd take a couple of investors out, and we'd walk into some important place, and they'd say, "Here comes Mr. Kozloff." That impressed them, and Jake would go through his complimentary play, and then they'd have dinner.

We wanted Kozloff licensed to operate the Hacienda, but how were we going to do it with Cahill so opposed? We had to hire somebody who had some juice, and I think we got Clark Guild, Governor Russell's brother-in-law, to represent Jake. But you've got to say this about Cahill: even Governor Russell, "Alligator Charlie," could not get Kozloff a license over Cahill's opposition . . . and he tried.

We'd go to hearings on the application for a license, and the three members of the control board would sit there and say, "Proceed." We'd wonder, what in the hell are we going to do next? Cahill would say something like, "The burden of proof is upon you to show that you are qualified for a gaming license. So go ahead and prove it."

Kozloff would say, "What did I do? I ain't done nothing!"

And Cahill says, "You have the burden of proof."

We had hearing after hearing, which never got beyond that point. And when we had staff consultations with these guys, they'd say, "We don't think Kozloff is entitled to a license. It's up to you to prove that he's entitled."

"Tell me what's wrong."

They'd say, "We don't have to tell you what's wrong. You prove that he is qualified."

This went on for month after month after month, until finally Kozloff quit. He was dead in Nevada. I remember seeing his pink Cadillacs on a used car lot; it was sad. I used to go to his house, and we'd sit and talk. Jake was a nice guy, a knowledge-able guy. I don't know where he got in trouble with Cahill, but Bob Cahill was just *not* going to license Jake Kozloff.

(Eventually, Kozloff and Cliff Jones got together, and Cliff sold all of his Nevada holdings and went to Aruba with Jake to start casinos. You could not have foreign interests if you were a licensee in Nevada–Nevada would not permit you to gamble outside the state–but Cliff thought this was an opportunity. Cliff was confident of his ability to make money in the new venture. He did not.)

In those days, the control board and the tax commission had the kind of dynamite power where you were not entitled to due process; you were not entitled to a hearing in the ordinary sense. And people believed that was the way it should be: they believed that it was proper that gamblers could be turned down for a gaming license for any reason, arbitrary or not. When in 1955 Judge Merwyn Brown decided not to let the tax commission's earlier revocation of the license of Marion Hicks in the Thunderbird stand, but to give Hicks a hearing, that shocked the Nevada gaming community. All of a sudden, here's a guy who's got a chance for a hearing!

How Bayley kept the Hacienda alive as long as he did is a story in itself, because the property was not successful. Finally, he started to promote business at the Hacienda by flying customers in, and then the question became whether or not the Las Vegas Hacienda was engaged as an air carrier. The *United States v. the Las Vegas Hacienda* became a key case in FAA secondary air transportation regulation, and it is always studied by lawyers who get into air transportation. In any event, the Hacienda got built, but once it was up and running, I had no further contacts (other than socially) with the group. My job was done.

[6]

Jimmy Contratto and the Cal-Neva

RIGHT AFTER THE WAR there were only three joints on the Las Vegas Strip: the El Rancho, built by Tommy Hull just before the war, was the most beautiful, with lawns, bungalows, tile roofs, pretty girls, a nice casino, and a swimming pool. Then down the road toward Los Angeles was the Last Frontier . . . Bill Moore. That was another story. (Bill Moore was on the Nevada Tax Commission, and he was theoretically the owner-operator of the Last Frontier.) Then there was Bugsy Siegel's joint, the Flamingo, which was not really a part of Las Vegas–it was six miles out from Charleston Avenue, and it was the beginning of a changing Las Vegas.

When they started the Flamingo in 1946, Senator Pat McCarran was very influential. Right after World War II, there were many shortages in construction materials, and a government agency passed a rule on non-essential projects. Casinos were obviously in that category. The fundamental rule was that you could continue any project that was underway on a building, but you could not add new buildings. So Bugsy Siegel and his group modified their plans for the Flamingo with the blessing of Pat and the power of his juice in Washington. The Flamingo had a semicircular design. (It had started out as a series of individual buildings, but if you look at what's left of the old Flamingo, you will find that every building is attached, one to the other.) The individual motel rooms, scattered around the back of the Flamingo casino, were in effect all tied together only by lattice work–two-by-fours between one building and the other, and a little overhanging roof. But by the interpretation that prevailed, aided by McCarran, these were *not* separate buildings which could not be started under regs–they were all one building. (I was court bailiff in Las Vegas when a lot of this litigation came up. By listening to the lawyers and the witnesses, I learned something about how the Flamingo got built during the moratorium when you weren't supposed to have new buildings; how the suppliers cheated one another and nobody got paid; how the liens got filed, and so forth and so on.)

Sanford "Sandy" Adler was extremely prominent in Nevada gaming after the war: to the public he *was* the El Rancho Vegas. When Sandy was told to get out of the El Rancho Vegas, he took issue (this is documented in Las Vegas newspaper accounts), so somebody broke a beer bottle over his head while he was in the men's room at the El Rancho, and left him unconscious in the toilet. Sandy decided to leave town in a hurry. He came north and bought the Cal-Neva at the lake and the Cal-Neva in Reno . . . and Christ, he couldn't handle them! He couldn't make any money. He ended up selling the Reno Cal-Neva to a group led by Jimmy Contratto, who was really an old-time gambler.

Contratto had run an illegal book down in Gardena for years, and he had so many telephones that it almost gave him the Alexander Graham Bell award. He knew how to get along in the Los Angeles community, but he finally came to Nevada when they closed down gambling in California during World War II. The first thing Jimmy did was go to the Flamingo. In those days, it seemed anybody who had a connection could buy points in the Flamingo, and I think Jimmy took three or four. He was sophisticated–he understood gambling; he understood people. Jimmy said, "I was there a certain period of time, and pretty soon I understood what was going on." Jimmy told them, "Fellows, let's make this a three-ring circus," but they wouldn't cut him in, so he moved out and came to the Colony Club in Reno.

(There are other stories about the Flamingo that are roughly the same. I mean, you could have points in the Flamingo, but if you weren't part of the inside group, you weren't getting any of the so-called "inside benefits." There were two kinds of investors in the Flamingo: people who were getting their money after it had been counted, and the people who were getting their share before it had been counted. If you were not part of the inside group, you were just SOL–shit out of luck. Jimmy was not that kind of operator, and he tried to run the Cal-Neva as a straight joint, and as a straight, honest man.)

Jimmy Contratto was famous for his part in the Kefauver Committee hearings.[1] When Estes came through the state (I guess Jimmy might have been at the Flamingo at the time) there was a piece of paper under question that was initialed "J. C.", and Kefauver asked Mr. Contratto, "Could J. C. mean James Contratto?"

Jimmy's answer was, "Senator, J. C. could not *possibly* mean James Contratto!" That didn't make any sense, but it was typical Contratto. [laughter]

When a group decided to buy the Cal-Neva (which was in trouble) from Sandy Adler, they needed a guy to run it, a guy to put up some cash money, and that was James Contratto. Contratto's group included Leon Nightingale; Cap VanCitter; Dr. Franks, a weirdo dentist from Beverly Hills (I say he was a weirdo because he believed in hypnosis and tried to hypnotize me by looking at me); Al Rogal, whose brother was a movie producer, and a couple of others. I knew Jimmy from the Colony Club, and I became the lawyer to put the deal together, just at the time Internal Revenue was going to seize all the money off the tables–something you can't have happen in a joint and keep it open.

I was concerned about how we could put this deal together and keep the property open, but luckily we got consulting help

---

[1] In November 1950 Tennessee Senator Estes Kefauver's Select Committee on Organized Crime came to Las Vegas, investigating Nevada casinos. Hearings were held, and a number of casino gambling figures were questioned. The committee concluded that major crime syndicates were indeed operating in Las Vegas, but Kefauver's subsequent proposal to regulate casino gambling at the federal level was killed in committee.

from a prominent Los Angeles attorney whom Dr. Franks and Al Rogal knew. Joe Ross, from the Beverly Hills firm of Ross, Warn, Pacht, and Bernhard, came to Reno to help me. He said, "Mead, I know how we can handle this in a way that will pass Gaming Control Board scrutiny. I've done it in Vegas a number of times." This was part of an eyeopening experience for me, because as a Nevada lawyer I thought that you were either *on* the license or not on the license . . . but this was an arrangement something like the Del Webb lease.[1] (Actually, the Del Webb lease hadn't been invented yet, or I would have been a whole lot smarter, instead of being an innocent Nevada lawyer who believed that everything that came out of Carson City was not only gospel but principle; and I sure believed in principle.) Joe showed me how to draw up a contract that would have our group in control of the Cal-Neva during the several months that it took us to get gaming licenses, and also give us profits for our endeavors. It was a scheme that I had not the genius or the ability to come up with, and it worked very well. "What we do," said Joe, "is we enter into a management contract, but we have no participation in the finances. We will have your (Contratto's) group sign a contract to manage the Cal-Neva without participating in the earnings or profits, *and* they will have an option to buy. When you have completed your licensing requirements and exercise your option to buy, we are going to adjust the purchase price based upon how much money you made while you were operating the place. So you get your earnings that way."

I said, "Joe, that's a hell of a good idea!" And fundamentally that's what we did. We threw our money in after the IRS took the money off the tables.

Jimmy always paid his bills, and he always told me, "Cash talks, kid! Cash talks!" When we got him licensed, and got the group licensed, I went to Eddie Questa, who was chairman of First National Bank, to borrow some money. I said, "I've got to

---

[1] For an explanation of the Del Webb lease, see page 226.

have seventy-five thou for the Cal-Neva." (Nobody else would lend the Cal-Neva any money.)

Eddie said, "OK, you've got it!" He made a phone call downstairs, I went down and got seventy-five thousand dollars in cash. That's the way Contratto liked to take money: in cash. When he had to pay for our city gaming license (we had to be licensed by the city before we went to the state) we had to have the money for the slot machine taxes and so forth, and we were in a hell of a hurry. I went to the city clerk's office and counted out cash, and the sum might have been fifty thousand . . . I can't remember. I was in too big a hurry to even wait for the clerk to make up a proper receipt. I looked him in the eye and said, "I will come back for my receipt. You had better be here!" and we went on to Carson. It all worked out.

Becoming counsel for the Cal-Neva, spending time with my clients (and not charging for spending time with them), and getting to know them and their business was an invaluable experience for me. I got to know the Cal-Neva inside out–the kitchens, the philosophy, counting money . . . . I got paid for what I did, but I wasn't the kind of lawyer who wouldn't talk to you if you didn't have a case for me. I spent a lot of time at the Cal-Neva, and learned a lot about people and about gaming. It was partly social, partly educational, and by getting to know the operation and all the people involved, I could anticipate and understand their problems, instead of being the abstract lawyer who waits for the client to come to his office and bring him a problem. I became, in effect, part of the group.

Most of the people who have casino ownerships or participations like to take advantage of perks, naturally. That's how some of the guys in the Cal-Neva were: they would say, "Well, let's take a few steaks home or a beef roast."

Contratto would say, "No. You can't take even a stick of butter out of the joint. If the help sees the boss taking a stick of butter out, they say, 'Hey, that's a successful guy. Look how he lives. I could be a success too. I'll take a stick of butter out.'" Well, that was a bone of contention between some of the owners of the Cal-Neva and Contratto, but that was Contratto's policy. The world did not look upon Jimmy Contratto as Mr. Clean, but I tell you he had his philosophy on how to run a joint, and that's the way he ran it.

A fellow came into the joint one day, and a problem developed, and it ended up in Jimmy's lap. The guy said, "I want to play Twenty-one as long as I can play head-to-head, and I don't want a lot of people around bugging me."

Jimmy said, "Well, fine, let's go! We'll deal to you single deck; we'll deal to you head on." The guy was there for forty-eight hours, and he almost took all the money in the house. Nobody could figure out how he kept winning or how he knew when to bet. They changed decks; they thought he had coolers,[1] but there wasn't anything wrong–the guy was just counting. Back then nobody understood that you could change the odds in Twenty-one by counting cards. (In hindsight, that was what I concluded was going on.) This was many, many years before anybody heard of counting. We finally had to cut him off before the joint ran out of money. *You* would have thought (*I* would have thought; *Jimmy* thought) that the odds in Twenty-one favored the house, and the longer you played, the greater the certainty that the odds were going to turn in the house's favor. But the odds never turned with that guy, from the moment he sat down to the moment he quit playing. That guy had to be a skilled card counter, and he knew how to play the game.

Jimmy Contratto was a gambler from the old school, and he was on the premises all day long. He loved to go to Harrah's barbershop and be shaved and have his shoes shined and get a manicure. (I think Jimmy would have had a manicure every day of his life if he could have.) He loved to smoke cigars and run every bit of the show as an individual who had grown up in illegal gambling, and the culture of the Cal-Neva in Reno on Second and

---

[1] Coolers are decks of cards that have been introduced into the game from the outside, with card sequences prearranged to produce the desired results.

Center Streets was entirely the individual culture of Jimmy Contratto.

Jimmy and his two or three key pit bosses were the people who ran the Cal-Neva, along with Everett Adams, the so-called auditor. Auditor was a term that was universally used in the old days in gaming casinos–you didn't have a bookkeeper; you didn't have an accountant; you had an auditor who kept all the records. It must have been a high-sounding name, because it was in common use in gaming casinos in the early fifties.

There was constant friction between Jimmy and the Cal-Neva investors, perhaps because the property didn't produce as much income as the California people thought it should. There were too many bosses, and Jimmy didn't think much of Al Rogal, who was a windbag, and Dr. Franks, the hypnotist–they were on the phone all the time. After numerous meetings of the board, which I attended, and constant criticism and argument, we decided to divide the house. (This must have been sometime in 1953.) We made a financial arrangement whereby Jimmy took over the operation of the casino and ran it, and Dr. Franks's group took ownership of the physical property. There was a lease arrangement, and at the expiration of the lease, Contratto would be gone, and Dr. Franks's group would own the property and could choose their own operator. The numbers worked out to the satisfaction of everyone.

The biggest investment that anybody had in the Cal-Neva was twenty-five thousand dollars, and the arrangement would pay them back substantially more than that, as well as insure them future ownership of the property . . . but there were still hard feelings. Contratto was a typical Italian [laughter]–he wanted to get even a little bit, because he was hurt by the arrangement. (Leon Nightingale was a gentleman throughout all this. He went with Dr. Franks's group because he was an investor, not an operator, and he made the right decision by staying with the investment group. The problem with the investment group was primarily Franks and Rogal from Beverly Hills, who were really difficult to live with.)

When Jimmy's lease on the Cal-Neva was about to expire, about 1958, he decided that he had a way to get even: he would close the Cal-Neva, and under Reno city ordinances if the Cal-Neva was closed for six months it would lose its grandfather status, and would not be eligible for license renewal outside the red-lined area to which casino gaming was confined in downtown Reno. In effect, he said, "They tried to screw me. I'll show them; I'll screw *them*." So he shut the Cal-Neva for six months. He was willing to forego six months' worth of revenue or earnings in the firm belief that the law was the law; and that at the end of six months the Franks group would have a building, but they would not have a gaming license. It would be an understatement to say he was disappointed: the city council licensed Cal-Neva anyhow, without regard to the red line or the ordinance, period! [laughter] I had nothing to do with it, but as far as I know, there was no problem with the Franks group getting a license for that location, which meant that the red line did not really mean anything.

Later Art Smith, chairman of First National Bank, was influential in trying to evolve a political solution to the red line restriction. The red line was more than a city council problem, more than a gamblers' problem–the red line was a whole citywide problem. It was the same sort of situation you have today when some people say, "Turn your water faucet on and let it run, because if we can keep the city out of water, we'll have no growth." You've heard people say that; people believe in that in this town. Back then there were people who were disproportionately vocal and loud, who wanted to keep Reno small and restrict the spread of casinos. There was tremendous controversy over whether keeping the red line was to the benefit of the gamblers who were within it, or to the benefit of the city. In the early 1950s gambling was finally permitted on the west side of Virginia Street, and by the late 1960s the city council had done away with the downtown red line.

The issue of constraining the expansion of gambling in general has never been focused upon logically or unemotionally in the city of Reno. There has never been any dispassionate, impartial thinking on where we want gambling to grow, or even if we do want it to grow. It's always been an emotional issue, fraught with politics and schisms.

Mead Dixon's parents. *Above:* Louis Mead Dixon, ca. early 1930s. *Below:* Emma Pickrell Brown Dixon, ca. late 1920s.

"Mother was one of seven sisters, all of whom were as bright as brass buttons. The whole brood of them came back home during the Depression to live in Grandmother's house next door." (p. 14) Seated (*left to right*): Willie Mae, Mary Katheryn, Grandmother Brown, Emma (Mead's mother), and Elsie Pearl. Standing (*left to right*): Ethel Marie, Daisy, and Josephine, ca. 1910.

John Brown, known affectionately as "Bud," and older brother Mead in 1932.

John Brown and Mead on Christmas Day, 1926.

When Mead Dixon enlisted in the Army in 1942, military issue clothing was in short supply–note the oxford shoes.

This Dixon family portrait was taken in 1954. From left to right: Sherwood, Jane, Drake, Ann, and Mead.

Bruce Thompson, at right, practiced law with George Springmeyer and Mead Dixo
from 1957 until his appointment to the United States District Court in 1963. Also
pictured *(left to right)* are federal court judges Gordon Thompson and Roger Fole

e Showboat Hotel & Casino in Las Vegas, ca. late 1960s. Mead Dixon served on
Showboat's board of directors from 1968 to 1978 and again from 1987 to the
sent time.

Reno's downtown block of casinos in the 1940s, with Harrah's Bingo pictured at
Bill Harrah opened his first bingo parlor in Reno in 1937. The site was later occ
by the Colony Club, operated by James "Jimmy" Contratto.

Harrah's 325-room, 24-story tower in Reno opened in 1969.

Rome Andreotti, Harrah's executive vice
president of operations, ca. 1978.

Bill Harrah *(left)* with Maurice Sheppard, president of
Harrah's from 1969 to 1975.

Harrah, Robert Ring, and an unidentified employee at the Harrah's Tahoe Sports ok in 1959.

Lloyd Dyer, president of Harrah's from 1975 to 1980.

Ed Berg, master mechanic for the Harrah Automobile Collection, poses with Mead Dixon by a 1927 Stutz Blackhawk four-passenger speedster while on a trip to Sydney, Australia.

J. K. Houssels junior and senior, owners of the Showboat in Las Vegas, ca. 1975. The elder Houssels is said to have operated by the motto, "If it ain't broke, don't fix it."

Barron Hilton of the Hilton Hotels Corporation and his Staggerwing Beech, ca. 19

From 1966 to 1970, Robert Maheu was Howard
Hughes's principal assistant.

n 1947, Howard Hughes testified at senate hearings to defend his wartime
efense contracts.

Mead with his second wife, Gwendolyn, and Representative James Santini, ca. early 1980s.

Richard Goeglein, Mead Dixon, and Mike Rose sign the paperwork making the Holiday Inn/Harrah's merger official in March, 1980.

Above: "Phil Satre has the organized mind to be able to handle his obligations and his opportunities...and an analytical mind to see how he wants Harrah's positioned." (p. 203) *Below:* "John Sande was my stalwart, my principal strength in working with the Harrah estate." (p. 178)

[7]

Harrah's Club

I WAS STILL REPRESENTING THE CAL-NEVA on a retainer arrangement when I formed a law partnership with Bruce Thompson and George Springmeyer in 1957. Bruce was really the lead lawyer in our firm. He was a good lawyer–he was tough and vigorous, and he had a tremendous legal mind. Harlan Heward, Bill Harrah's lawyer, got throat cancer, and one day he walked down the hall to Bruce and said, "I can't handle this. Will you help me out?" Bruce said sure, so Bruce became, in effect, the delegate of Harlan Heward as counsel to Bill Harrah. Our firm had a problem, however, in that I was with the Cal-Neva, theoretically a competitor of Harrah's. Bruce talked to Bill about the conflict, and said that the Cal-Neva account was eventually going to close, because Dixon wasn't going to represent the Franks group, the landlord group. As soon as Contratto's lease ran out, we'd get rid of the Cal-Neva as a client. That was OK with Bill.

Harrah's guys would occasionally come over and see Bruce about a question, but he was a very busy lawyer, and he would sometimes ask me to take care of this or that matter for Harrah's. (Starting in 1955, I had already done some legal work for Bill Harrah up at Lake Tahoe, so we weren't strangers.) All of a sudden, most of the firm's work for Harrah's began to be put on my shoulders . . . maybe it was because I was around. [laughter]

When somebody from Harrah's would call, I would say, "You sit still. I am going to come over and see you." I wanted the people who worked for Bill Harrah to know that they had a lawyer, and I wanted to get ahead of their problems so I could have some anticipatory input into what was going on. If you have lunch with a guy, if you talk with him, he may be the greatest accountant or casino operator in the world, but you sometimes discover that he doesn't know politics like you know it; he doesn't know the judicial system like you know it; he doesn't know the state; he doesn't know what other casinos are doing. You can see that he is heading toward the waterfall, or that he is on the right track, and you can help your client a lot more. That was my approach to Harrah's–to try to foresee problems. Instead of simply asking, "What does Bill want?" I wanted to be of service, and, quite frankly, being visible was also a way I could sell myself. (That's where Bruce Thompson and I were totally different. Bruce would sit in his office, and if someone didn't call him and come in to see him, he was very happy, because he had plenty of legal work to do. When you did come to see him, Bruce would solve your problem, and solve it quickly and efficiently, but he never became part of your company.)

The Harrah's of 1955 or 1957 was not the Harrah's of 1977-1978. Not only did my relationship with the company grow and change, the company itself grew and changed. My earliest legal engagement with Harrah's was in 1955, and the retainer arrangement began about 1957. When I was still doing legal work for Bill on a single-case basis, the phone would ring and it would be Bill Harrah, and he would say, "I'd like to talk with you." That was something that Bill Harrah would not have done in the 1970s, but this was the 1950s.

My earliest meetings with Bill in his office were after the expansion of his Virginia Street property to fifty front feet when he got the Frontier from Pick Hobson in 1956. To get to Bill's office you would walk into the club at about the mid-section on the south side off Virginia Street, walk up a very narrow flight of stairs, and at the top of the stairs there were a couple of doors. To the left was Bill Harrah's office. If I said his office was ten by ten, I would be exaggerating–it was one of the smallest offices I have ever seen. Bill ran the club from behind a desk in that office, and he was very much hands-on in running Harrah's at that point. (This was when he was expanding into Lake Tahoe, starting his bus programs. He had acquired–and the word "acquired" is loosely used–George Cannon's Gateway Club, which was nothing. The club was at Stateline, and Bill was leasing it from George with an option to buy. All he did was buy George's lease from Ken Johnson, a senator in Carson City, who was the ultimate fee owner.)

In any event, in the beginning of my relationship with Harrah's, Bill Harrah was hands on. He not only made all the decisions, but he personally did such things as call in little people like me to deal with legal problems. Gradually, the intermediary role between Harrah's and me (or Harrah's and Bruce Thompson) began to be filled by Maurice Sheppard, then Bob Hudgens, and Lloyd Dyer after him. The legal questions gradually shifted from Bill Harrah to these gentlemen, and that's the way things evolved in my relationship with the company.

For Harrah's, I dealt with a variety of problems: zoning; expansion; building contracts; construction contracts . . . . Harrah's had labor relations counsel–Nate Burke from San Francisco–but we had some participation with the Reno business community in general labor relations after the decertification of the culinary union, which was a Bill Harrah accomplishment. Sometime in the early 1960s Bill was able to convince the employees to take a vote that complied with NLRB rules, and to decertify the union as their representative. That's an accomplishment that Bill Harrah deserves *all* the credit for. Bill decided he wanted more freedom in operation, and just as he didn't want partners (he got rid of all his partners one at a time), he decided he wanted to be free of the union. Not because he was anti-labor, though he may have been, but because he wanted freedom to make decisions, and one of the union's problems, obviously, was rigidity. (I could give you a lot of other problems. The culinary union was not easy to work with.)

The important point about the decertification is that Bill Harrah got an opportunity to speak to his employees, and that's very difficult to do under the National Labor Relations Act. (In this, he was properly guided and coached by Nate Burke.) Bill spoke to the employees, and in effect he said that Harrah's was a great club, and that he was a great boss, and that they would be happy with him. And by God they held the election and the union was decertified! It was historic. Except for what happened very recently in Vegas, it was the only time it ever happened that I know of in Nevada. Everybody else–the Mapes and all the rest of them–were always Culinary.

Harrah's remained non-union, with some maneuvering in this respect: to remain non-union and to avoid strike, you had to play a few games. One of the games was to hire a contractor instead of hiring your own maintenance man. Your contractor might hire union people, but you hired the contractor, so your *organization* didn't have union people in it. That happens also with musicians; that's pretty much the standard with the AFM (American Federation of Musicians). The so-called band leader is an independent contractor, and the musicians work for him. You pay him, and so you've got your union group, without having in-house union representation. You'd go absolutely crazy trying to understand the contracts of the various bands that were engaged by Harrah's. I reviewed many of those contracts, which were of interest to me not only from the standpoint of their binding nature and cost and duration, but also for their potential effect upon other labor relations with Harrah's.

At Bill's insistence, almost every document or contract of any consequence was reviewed by a lawyer. He said, "That's what you hire them for; it's like going to the doctor," and as he grew to know me better over time, my role increased. So I got broad exposure in the early years to the details of the growth of Harrah's and Bill's role as the decision maker; and in the beginning (until we developed the Reno hotel, at least), Harrah's Club pretty much *was* Bill Harrah and the team that worked directly under him–Bob Ring, Rome Andreotti, Maurice Sheppard, and Red Farnsworth.

(In 1937, Bob Ring had come to Reno with Bill Harrah from Venice, California, to open Harrah's first bingo parlor. He was Bill's trusted friend, and he was made president and eventually vice chairman of Harrah's. Rome Andreotti started on Harrah's floor in 1948; he had an innate understanding of the games and how they should be run, and he rose to become executive vice president of operations for Harrah's. Maurice Sheppard's expertise was in accounting and bookkeeping. He became a vice president, and then, in the 1970s, president of Harrah's. I was never really sure of the role that Red Farnsworth played, but was told that he was in charge of communications. Red drove a Dodge with the biggest engine that money could buy . . . and it was one of the ugliest cars I'd ever seen. Red liked it because it was a hot car, and you had to have a hot car to please Bill Harrah.)

The company established a policy manual, which turned out to be a very thick document. Harrah's had a policy on almost everything. For example, one policy was that all concrete should be painted. That may or may not be significant, but it gives a clue as to Bill's personality. (Actually, the policy was a little longer than that: it went on to say how it should be painted; the color that should be used for painting concrete when there was no other color coordination involved; and the requirement that it be inspected and kept painted and in good condition.) Every policy that the company adopted in this very thick book–as thick as the Manhattan telephone directory–had to be submitted to Mead Dixon for approval. In most cases there wasn't a significant legal issue, unless a policy might have a fallout effect upon some other aspect of the company, or wasn't worded in a way that was clear and consistent with what I understood Bill wanted it to be.

By following the development of Harrah's policy manual over a period of years from its inception to its conclusion, I got insight into the way Bill thought the company should be run. As I recall, there was a policy that plants and flowers be genuine and not artificial; there was a policy that real leather should be used, and not vinyl. There were many other policies which related to employees, construction, contracts, advertising, expense accounts, automobiles, and so forth and so on. The policy manual covered almost all of the operations of Harrah's, and management was supposed to be familiar with it so that their conduct was consistent with Harrah's policy in any specific case. If anything, there was overkill, and I found the book cumbersome to use. You could almost have said, "It is Harrah's policy that management should use good judgment," and that might cover it all! But that wasn't Bill's technique–he had to have it down in detail.

Bill had high standards of cleanliness and orderliness: Bob Ring was always walking through the property and seeing if there were light bulbs that were burned out. (Rome Andreotti would do the same: he would walk the Reno property every day with an eagle eye for cleanliness and for burned-out light bulbs.) Ring was president of the company, and he was concerned about a light bulb being out! Why wasn't somebody on a lesser level responsible for burned-out bulbs? Well, the truth of the matter is they were working for Bill Harrah, and Bill never wanted to walk in and see a burned-out bulb, and they knew damn well that if they didn't catch it and get it fixed before Bill walked in, Bill would be unhappy. Lots of people laughed about this . . . I shouldn't say we all did, but lots of people on the inside laughed about Bob and Rome worrying about light bulbs being burned out. But that was part of the excruciating attention to detail that Bill Harrah demanded.

Scotch tape was never allowed, so you never had a Harrah's sign put up with Scotch tape, and no hand-printed signs of any kind were allowed. You didn't have someone writing "out of order" on a piece of cardboard, and taping it to a toilet. Every sign that was put up at Harrah's was put up in a professional manner, and the sign was professionally done. It was even company policy that pictures have two hooks, so they would always be straight. (A picture that hangs on one hook isn't always straight.) This was part of Bill's personality and part of his insistence on getting as close to his idea of perfection as possible. He wanted to make a visual impact upon the customer. Carpets . . . he loved carpeting; he did not like hard floors. He loved real leather; he did not like vinyl. He wanted things to have an impact on the customer from the standpoint of physical and visual comfort, so that was the way he directed his policies.

Bill reviewed every policy himself, but the creation of the policy manual was delegated, at least in its later development, to Rome Andreotti. This was right up Rome's alley, because Rome loved to have detailed policies for every occasion. It was a combination of Bill's desire to have general policies for how the company was run, and Rome's eye for detail that was responsible for what I think was an over-proliferation of policies.

One of the things that Bill did early on–and I recall the cost was seventy-five thousand dollars, an unheard-of sum–was to hire the George S. May Company to do an engineering study on how to keep Harrah's properties clean. The product of that study was a schedule that showed which rooms had to be vacuumed, and at what time; when the walls had to be washed–the whole detail. They created, in effect, a maintenance schedule, so that if you followed the schedule, you knew the property was going to be maintained.

In those days, Harrah's was almost constantly in an expansion mode, and a lot of my legal work was to review documents that related to the expansions. Somewhere early on in my relationship with Harrah's, the Golden Hotel burned, and after it burned, it was torn down. I thought this presented an opportunity to acquire the property, and I did my best to persuade Bill to pursue it. My recollection is that Maurice Sheppard opposed me in that. Shep was a vice president at that time . . . vice president of what, I don't know. [laughter] (He was not executive vice president, not senior vice president, just plain vice president.) But Shep opposed me because of the financial condition of Harrah's and the ability of the company to take on the debt that would be required.

It was impossible to sell Bill on acquiring the Golden Hotel property, and the big hole in the ground stayed there for a long period of time after the Golden burned down. Eventually, the Tomerlin brothers (Jim and Bill) from Bakersfield, California, came to Reno and purchased the property, hired Martin Stern, and started to build a hotel. They got as far as the first floor casino and the basement, and above the first floor they put in steel for an automobile parking structure. Their concept was to build a garage over the casino, and a hotel above the garage. Unfortunately, the Tomerlins could not make it financially, so the property again became available. I really had some heart-to-heart talks with Bill about this; and although I wasn't the sole influence, I did my very best to get him to agree to the acquisition of the Golden property, and he finally did.

In 1966 we negotiated the purchase of the property with Bert Goldwater, an attorney for the Tomerlin brothers, and we bought the Tomerlins out. We made a *reasonably* intelligent negotiation, which allowed us to acquire this property under terms that were favorable to Harrah's. The Tomerlins got out with their skin, too, but it took a lot of creativity on both sides. (From the Harrah's point of view, we had to be creative to negotiate a purchase contract when we didn't have any money.) Working with Bert Goldwater, you had to be creative, because Bert was a very tough legal opponent who represented his clients very well. But fortunately, he had the ability to understand that all problems have to be solved.

One of my early jobs for Harrah's was to contract with Everett Brunzell for the construction of our Second and Center Street casino. The casino was built in 1962 on the site of the Grand Hotel, which had been owned, I think, by a Mrs. Jacobs and Sidney Robinson, a very prominent Reno lawyer, and it initially had no name except the "Jacobs building," which is what we called it for years. John Petrinovich had the Grand Cafe there, which had been a Reno landmark for years. We were able, over a period of time, to acquire legal title to those properties. We began leasing them in 1959, and one of my goals was to protect the names of the Grand Hotel and Grand Cafe, which we did by creating a corporation using those names.

We moved John Petrinovich and his Grand Cafe into properties we leased from the Robinson Group on Center Street, between the Professional Building and the One-Sixteen Club. We wanted to save the Grand Cafe because Harrah's had no food outlet of its own. Eventually, we moved the cafe into Harrah's casino property, and we used those Center Street properties for personnel offices for a number of years.

The Jacobs building had extraordinarily deep foundations and sub-basements, and it was designed to be able to support a seventeen-story building, which was then an unheard-of height for Reno. Initially, we only had enough money to build the first-

floor casino and the second-floor restaurant, and the under-
ground portion contained the building's utilities, money count
rooms, and the like.

The second floor of the Jacobs building housed Harrah's
coffee shop, which was called the Terrace Room. It was a very
popular place in Reno, and we used to eat there often. Bill ate
there every day for lunch, as near as I can recall, and he enjoyed
the fashion shows that were held there several times a week.
These girls would walk around from the various stores in Reno,
showing off the new fashions. [laughter] They would come up
and speak to Bill, and one of them *always* used to come to our
table–her name was Roxanne; Bill later married her.

When the Reno hotel was built in 1968-69, Bill wanted to
make sure that it was managed properly, so he went outside
Harrah's and hired Bill Callahan, who had been the manager of
the Regency in New York City. He was the second hotel manager
that we hired. We had hired the first manager and had him on
board for several months before we built the hotel, but he moved
on for reasons that are not known to me. Then Callahan came
from New York, so when we opened Harrah's Hotel we had a
professional manager in charge. That was the way Bill Harrah did
things.

By this time, Bill had hired Joe Fanelli out of the Kahler
system, and he put him in charge of food and beverage for all
properties. Bill had met Joe in Rochester, Minnesota, when he
was at the Mayo Clinic, and he was impressed with the food
operation at the Kahler Hotel. If I'd been Joe, I would have run
all the way to Reno to get out of Rochester, but apparently it was
hard to sell him on coming to Reno to be in charge of food and
beverage. [laughter] The point is that as we got into expansion,
Bill began to go outside Harrah's to bring in people with expertise. Of course, we were always involved with outside people who
had expertise in the *entertainment* side of this thing, and we
went through more stage managers and entertainment directors
than I care to count. [laughter] As the company grew, Fanelli
and Callahan were the two people who were really engaged as

outside experts, but the only one who remained with the company for a long period was Joe Fanelli.

In October of 1978 I decided to expand the hotel in Reno, because we were *very* weak there with respect to rooms. We only had 324 rooms, and you can't run a hotel with 324 rooms! On the old Grand Hotel site, the Jacobs building, we already had a foundation that would support seventeen floors, so I instructed Bob Martin to arrange for the San Francisco firm of Skidmore, Owings & Merrill to design a hotel tower with the maximum number of rooms possible on that site. They came up with a 220-room hotel addition, construction of which was begun in 1979 and completed in 1980.

We'd been through architectural design with many different people, but Harrah's strength was interior design, and that was strictly the responsibility of Henry Conversano, who was a *very* significant player at Harrah's. He was responsible for all the interiors of Harrah's Reno (until the merger with Holiday), and for Harrah's Tahoe–the beautiful rooms, the decor, and so forth. He knew not only what Bill Harrah wanted, he was able to give Bill Harrah good taste. (Bill Harrah wanted good taste, but Bill, just as you or I, couldn't create things that an artist could create.) Henry made Bill very happy, and made Harrah's very successful, and you could not even make a modest change in the interior without consulting him, just as you could not do anything that had to do with law or contracts or documents or property acquisition or financing without talking to Mead Dixon. Bill believed in using experts.

Steve Wynn[1] came to Reno with Bob Maxey, and looked at Harrah's; and Wynn makes no secret that he concluded that the

---

[1] Stephen Wynn is chairman of the board and chief executive officer of Mirage Resorts, Inc. Wynn started in casino gaming as a slot department manager in 1967. Profits from entrepreneurial enterprises enabled him to make a major investment in Las Vegas's Golden Nugget, Inc., in 1972, and he became chairman of the board in 1973. He oversaw the building and development of the Atlantic City Golden Nugget (1980; sold to Bally in 1987) and the Mirage in Las Vegas (1989).

way Bill Harrah did things with class was the way he wanted to
do it. Steve concluded that the interior design by Henry Conversano was a significant part of Harrah's success, and he said that
if he ever had the chance, he would employ Conversano and try
to imitate Bill Harrah in every way. Of course, that's exactly
what Steve did. If you look at his Golden Nugget in Atlantic City,
that was a Conversano project; his Golden Nugget in Las Vegas
is *all* Henry Conversano; and the Mirage in Las Vegas is Henry
Conversano. Steve Wynn was able to take lessons from Bill
Harrah, and to hire Henry to do for him what he had done for
Bill.

Although Bill used outside experts whenever necessary, his
approach to management was different. There was no management development program that I am aware of at Harrah's, no
career planning program, except the assistance that Maurice
Sheppard gave in trying to bring Lloyd Dyer along and to
advance his career. There was no lateral entry into Harrah's, and
no formal program of any kind, even though I talked with Bill
about it. I say, "even though . . . . " Hell, my opinions didn't
count for much, but I talked with Bill and Shep about the
concept of trying to get people to come into Harrah's from
universities or colleges and put them on a career development
path. That didn't fit Bill's style. Harrah's prided itself on promotion from within, except for highly specialized jobs. (Both Bob
Vice and Bob Martin were inside people in charge of purchasing
for a number of years. Later on, Bill went outside to bring
someone into purchasing, but purchasing was all inside to begin
with, until it really became a job that required some expertise
that had not "grown up" from the Harrah's floor.)

It's difficult to describe the evolution of Harrah's management, other than that Bill was the boss, and as Bob Ring used to
say, "This isn't Harrah's Club; it is *Bill* Harrah's Club." There
wasn't a person that I can recall in senior management who was
either promoted or hired without Bill being personally involved
in it. We had this strange style of a sole proprietorship, with the
entire company centered around Bill. There was not even a
succession plan in the event of Bill's death; by the same token,

there were no succession plans in the event of Rome's death or anyone else's.

Despite organization charts that made everyone say, "Harrah's is the General Motors of the gaming industry," all of the decisions were made in the corner office that Bill occupied. That was different from other gaming companies that I was associated with, because they were not really sole ownerships. But Bill did not want any partners–Virgil Smith had earlier been a partner, and Warren Nelson at one time had been a partner, but Bill was later so relieved to have no partners that he made no secret of it. He wanted to be able to make all of the decisions himself, and that was the way the company was formed.

The centralization of Harrah's management and the decision-making functions were such that even though you were general manager of a Harrah's property, you really were just a casino manager–you didn't have exposure to (or authority over), the whole property. "General manager" implies that you're the general manager, but we didn't have any real general managers. A great weakness in trying to make Harrah's grow was that we didn't have people in the organization with those talents and experience. (We *did* have Rome Andreotti, who was a great gamer. All the old-timers in the business ask about Rome–they respected his knowledge of games.)

Bill's philosophy on slot machines had always been, "Let's get all of them in that we can," but denominations and combinations of slot machines were Rome's personal bailiwick, not the property manager's. Rome controlled all gaming. He did not set the rules for Twenty-one or craps–those are basic rules–but Rome was very particular on the hand movement of dealers. Harrah's dealers were taught how to deal! Single deck was the preferred game in Twenty-one, and they were taught how to hold the cards, how to deal, and how to have their hand motions work. In fact, Harrah's preferred to hire people with no gaming experience so that they could be trained to conduct themselves in Harrah's style–they wouldn't have developed bad habits from prior casino experience. I don't mean that prior casino experience was disqualifying; I'm simply saying that Harrah's had no problem in training dealers, and they insisted that all dealers follow the Harrah's method of dealing, holding cards, and handling dice.

Rome would demonstrate to me exactly what hand motions he wanted in the various games. Ah, the comfort that gave him! If, as he walked through the casino, he saw dealers not following his prescribed methods, he became concerned that somebody wasn't managing properly, or that somebody might be trying to do something to the company. It was his way of keeping alert and trying to keep the company straight, but it didn't always work: there was the very embarrassing Joe Curry case at Lake Tahoe.

Joe Curry was the Harrah's Tahoe casino manager. (This was two or three years before Bill Harrah's death.) Harrah's was getting its brains beat in at the Twenty-one table on one specific shift, and nobody could figure out why or how. Harrah's would routinely go through all the used decks with a fine-toothed comb, and they couldn't find anything wrong with any of the decks . . . but they were still getting clipped. The way the scam worked was that Joe Curry would come in and say, "Hey, there's something wrong with this game—put in a new deck." So they'd put in a new deck and give Curry the old one. And Curry would pocket the old deck, but nobody knew he was pocketing it. (Maybe he'd leave it right there and take it out later, but nobody paid any attention to that; none of the Harrah's regulars noticed anything.)

Lynn Simons was a pit boss who had come up from Las Vegas, and normally Bill didn't hire anybody from Vegas. (He figured, "Anybody from Vegas, I don't want working for me. I'd rather train my own people." And that was one of Rome's philosophies: "We'll train our own people; therefore they won't know anything and won't have any bad habits.") [laughter] Simons sees Curry giving some orders in the pit, and he says, "There's something wrong with this." Everybody else at Harrah's was fat, dumb, and happy, but Simons was smart enough to figure that there was something wrong, and the table was losing, and Curry was going into the pit . . . into the game. So Simons watched, and he concluded that Curry was in on the action, and he got ahold of Joe Francis, who was running Harrah's Tahoe, and he blew the whistle. Sure enough, it was discovered that Curry was switching decks, and then getting the marked deck out.

So then the thing to do was to sue Joe Curry to get the money back. Which is what I did. That was kind of touchy, but as far as I know, we got all the money Joe Curry had, and all the property that he had, and we settled the case against him. Tom Yturbide and Joe Francis were involved in the trial. I had Tom Yturbide sit with me in the trial because I thought Tom made a better courtroom appearance–a little milder, a little more polite appearance than Joe Francis. (You know, Tom's running Harvey's now.) Joe was usually pretty much the big cowboy–big and strong and tough–but he was extremely anxious to settle this case. When we got an offer that was halfway decent, Joe just stood in the hallway and said, "You've got to take the offer."

I never knew why Joe settled at the point that we settled. Sure, there may have been more to the whole gambling scheme in Nevada then I ever knew about, but the Curry case was . . . not only was it heavy bucks, but there were people who threatened to kill everybody. Those were tough people who were caught cheating, and there were lots of threats of murder and people were scared of their lives. But its significance to Harrah's was that a guy from Las Vegas figured it out. All of Harrah's people were home grown, but they never discovered it; this young Simons discovered it. Curry was the casino manager, and therefore very high in the pecking order, and therefore beyond suspicion.

In this kind of business, there's always more to it than meets the eye, and there was much in this case that never met my eye, but I can't tell you what it was. Tough guys . . . they were tough guys. Everybody thinks about organized crime, and I'm sure there is organized crime, but there are also just plain tough guys. And that's what these guys were.

As far as I know, Bill was out ahead of his competition in making head counts and so forth. Long before I became connected with Harrah's, when I was over at the Cal-Neva, the so-called

Harrah's spies would come in and give Jimmy Contratto fits. But the Harrah's spies were simply looking around and seeing what the club Cal-Neva was doing, and how many people were there at various times during the day. All that intelligence came back to Bill Harrah. Bill was very much on top of his daily reports–the head counts in all the casinos, and the show counts.

Entertainment was one of the most important things in Bill's mind. He thought that without entertainment, you were lost in this business. He believed not only that entertainers were good people–he liked entertainers as people–but that entertainment was *essential* to the success of his casinos. Therefore, Harrah's went farther than anyone in catering to the comfort and the dignity of entertainers, so that every headliner that appeared at Lake Tahoe, (and sometimes Reno), had dinner at least once with Bill and Sherry . . . or with Bill and one of his other wives in later years. Bill always treated entertainers not as they were treated in Las Vegas–as hired help–but as valued friends and guests. Their every wish was catered to. The result was that Harrah's was able to get significant entertainers at prices that were less than were being paid in Las Vegas, because the entertainers loved to work at Harrah's. They loved the comforts, the so-called fringe benefits . . . that is, at Lake Tahoe they could use a boat, and they had Conversano-designed first-class accommodations–they weren't shoved into dirty, dingy dressing rooms. Entertainers got to know the boss first-hand, and Bill went out of his way to make sure that they were treated as *guests* rather than as simple employees of the company. In later years when Holmes Hendricksen was in charge of entertainment, he was responsible for continuing that tradition.

Perhaps because of the way we treated entertainers, we were able to get them for 50 percent of what you had to pay in Las Vegas. Some of the big-name entertainers were Bill Cosby, Sammy Davis, Judy Garland, Liza Minelli. You could ask them, and they'd tell you Harrah's was *the* place to come, the place where they loved to work.

Many times we tried to figure out how much money the entertainment cost, and what its earning capacity was . . . but I was never able to quantify that. If you paid X dollars a week for entertainment, how much did you make on the casino floor as a result? We tried various ways, but we could never come up with a formula that would tie entertainment cost to revenues. It was a gut instinct that Bill had that you can't go dark–that you have to have entertainers; and if you have entertainers, you have the big names in the entertainment field; and then you make money. The proof of the pudding was in the eating, because he made money.

Bill was interested in Harrah's daily financial reports, and when he was out of town, he wanted to know what they were. He was interested in the showroom head counts, and he always read the lists of everyone who was comped into the showroom. If there were ten or twenty or thirty people comped into Harrah's South Shore Room, the comp list would show their names, their affiliation, and who comped them. The comp list also had a diagram of the room, and it would show the tables at which these comped guests were seated. (I suspect that the primary reason for the diagram was so that someone could walk over to table number twenty-seven and say, "Hello, Mr. Jones. We're so glad to see that you are here.") Those reports and diagrams came to Bill Harrah on a daily basis, and he always looked to see who the comp guests were, tried to identify them in his mind, and to identify who comped them.

One of Bill's philosophies was that food doesn't cost anything–I remember him saying that. If you were born in the Midwest and were thrifty, and he said, "Come on in and sit down and have a free steak dinner," you'd say, "My God, has the man gone crazy?" Bill didn't give free steak dinners to everybody, but his basic concept was that food doesn't cost anything, and he felt that food comps were an important part of the business. But comping can get carried away in the casino industry, and the prospect scares the hell out of everybody. You can give too many people the power of the pen (authority to authorize complimentary meals, shows or rooms), and they'll comp right and left, and all over the place. That may be another reason the Harrah's comp lists all went to Bill.

When Bill reviewed the daily statements, he did not look at a lot of detail; instead, he looked at the bigger picture–he was looking at casino revenues and "hold" percentages. Those are the two keys–your revenues and your percentages–and I never heard him complain about wins and losses, as I've heard in other casinos: "Gee, we only held 16 percent today on craps." In all the time I knew Bill, I never heard him talk about the PCs (percentages) as such. (As a matter of fact, he didn't talk much about anything to anybody.) Rome would worry about the detailed PCs, but Bill looked at the big picture, the revenues. He looked at operating income on a daily basis, so that he felt comfortable with the company and its direction, and I think that was important: it was a clear message to management that Bill was interested in the numbers; that it wasn't something that people could slough off.

Bill had a principle that was interesting to me, and sort of went against my training and my concept of how you ought to run a business–that was nepotism. Bill did not have a problem with both husband and wife working for him. (I had been taught that in the casino industry you don't want family members working in the same casino.) Bill had another policy: he was happy to have his employees stay after work and drink, so employees were given drink tokes, and there was no problem with them walking up to the bar when they were off duty. This practice had some advantages: it kept the place looking busy; it made the employees happy; and it sometimes led to employees gambling.

Bill had no problem with employees gambling in their own casino. Of course, we didn't have the same problem that exists in Atlantic City: in Atlantic City there are capacity problems on weekends and during special events, when there are not enough slot machines or enough tables to meet all the guest requirements. Nevada never had that problem . . . at least, to my knowledge, it didn't have that problem. [laughter] (In Atlantic City it was illegal for any casino employee to gamble *anywhere*. Just now, in the summer of 1992, Atlantic City has begun permitting casino employees to gamble . . . in other casinos.)

Bill didn't really know the employees when we walked on the floor. They knew him when he had the twenty-five foot store, but when he got to the fifty-foot store,[1] he became more and more distant . . . at least that was my observation. I walked through all of the casinos with Bill, and every once in a while someone would say, "Hello, Bill." And he'd say, "Hi Ed." They were people who had been with the company since it was a small store on Virginia Street, when Bill was actually hands-on running it. Sometimes he would say to me, "Gee, I can't remember that guy's name, but I've known him for twenty years." By the time we had two hotels, with four thousand employees, and were running seventeen thousand covers a day in the food outlets, the magnitude of the operation was so great, and Bill's natural shyness was so great, that he obviously couldn't know all the employees.

Harrah's count rooms were reasonably controlled and sanitary, with the right numbers of people (and the right people) in them to avoid skimming. Bill Harrah himself did not go into a count room, but he wanted to insure an honest count . . . so there were plenty of tools for observation of the count—windows and cameras and other means. That is not to say that there weren't some problems with people in the count rooms trying to steal money, but everything that could be done physically was generally pretty-well done.

We once had one significant problem in the hard count, when the coin count room was manned by people who had Arabic backgrounds and worked together. They stole thousands of dollars worth of quarters out of the count room before they were caught, probably because the fellow in charge was really not on the job . . . coupled with the skill of these people in getting into the toilet with quarters in their shoes. They were able to get only a few quarters at a time, but it doesn't take long before a

---

[1] Twenty-five feet was the modular building width on downtown Virginia Street. Buildings were twenty-five, fifty, seventy-five, or one hundred feet wide.

few quarters add up to several thousand dollars. That leak was eventually plugged.

Harrah's was well-advanced in its controls to insure that all money was counted and accounted for, and Rome Andreotti was largely responsible. There was no great mystery about the principle of control. A fellow could think through the fundamentals that almost every industry has: you don't let the person responsible for the money (or for the account) get in on both ends of it–he can't count it in and count it out–and you always need to have some independent measure or method of control. If you start from that basis, it's not too hard to figure who can sign a fill slip; how money is transferred from the cage to a gaming table; how to count money into the cage; who's responsible for it; how many signatures are needed; how to leave an audit trail; how to avoid collusion. You don't need to have a rocket scientist to figure these fundamentals out–in casino gaming money is your inventory.

The big fear in the gaming industry was that everybody would get in the count room and steal money. In count rooms, when you are counting soft money, you have to be observed–that's the fundamental rule. Harrah's did that and established some pretty good procedures. But with the advent of gambling in New Jersey, with extremely strict rules, Harrah's procedures were not acceptable in that state. Nevada began to tighten up on all procedures and regulations as a result, and there's a great body of controls now that are more stringent than the ones that Harrah's had when Harrah's was the leader of the pack.

No question, Bill ran the company. In the late 1950s, Maurice Sheppard had become kind of a primary interface between Harrah's and myself and Bruce Thompson, as we were counsel for Harrah's. Then as Harrah's began to acquire parcels of property, Bob Hudgens was assigned that function; that's how I first met him. Within a few months, Maurice Sheppard brought Lloyd Dyer down to Reno from Lake Tahoe to help advance Lloyd's career. Lloyd was put in charge of property acquisition–and, in effect, in charge of property at Harrah's–and Bob

Hudgens was assigned the position of assistant to Mr. Harrah. As assistant to Mr. Harrah, Bob Hudgens became an integral part of the communications system. It wasn't long before instead of Bill calling up and saying, "Mead, I want to see you", Bob Hudgens would make the call. Sheppard, Dyer or Rome would talk to me personally about matters in their particular area . . . or Andy Iratcabal, who was secretary-treasurer, might call me for some reason. But when it was a call that Bill Harrah wanted made, Bob Hudgens would make it.

As time passed, Bob Hudgens became more and more Bill Harrah's right arm, but not his leader or creative manager or that sort of thing–he was Bill's "gopher". What Bob did was anticipate Bill's needs and carry out Bill's instructions. For example, Bob might call the garage and say, "Mr. Harrah is going to leave at nine-thirty for Lake Tahoe. Have his car ready." The car would be ready. Or if Bill wanted to drive a specific car out of the number that were available, Bob might call the garage and say, "Bill wants to drive the Ferrari today," or, "he wants to take the Wagoneer," or whatever. Bob Hudgens was the interface, generally speaking, between Bill and the world.

Bill made notes on everything, and he would say to Bob, "I noticed this. Would you speak to so-and-so about it?" And Bob would get on the phone. That relieved Bill of a whole lot of responsibility for making calls to people, and it helped him withdraw from immediate contact with many things that bothered him. In my view, Bob Hudgens did an admirable job of carrying out Bill's wishes and making things comfortable for him–whether it was making sure that Bill's clothes were cleaned, or making sure that Bill had a reservation if he went to New York . . . or if Bill complained that there was a tear in the carpet in one of the casinos, or if one of his friends had been in town and hadn't been able to see him, the interface was done by Bob Hudgens.

Bob was really loyal to Bill–he worked his tail off for him–but he had a personality problem: he did not know how to handle authority or how to treat people. Many of the people who worked at Harrah's began to resent Bob, partially because they did not regard him as their equal, but as somebody who was just kind of a flunky for Bill. Perhaps they also didn't like the way that Bob spoke to them or followed up on efforts to make sure that everything was done just the way Bill Harrah wanted it.

After Bill's death I attempted to keep a place for Bob Hudgens in the company. Although I did my very best, I could not find any place where I could keep him meaningfully employed. Initially I used him in Atlantic City to help with real estate transactions, because Bob was very skillful in those areas. When it came to placing him in Reno or Lake Tahoe, I tried without being a dictator to find him a place. I kept asking various people in the company, "Can you find a place for Bob Hudgens?" I got a unanimous "No!" Lloyd Dyer explained the reason to me. The people here simply were tired of Bob Hudgens. They didn't like him, and they didn't want him, and they wouldn't find any place for him because he had been so demanding in carrying out Bill's wishes. [laughter] They wanted to kill the messenger rather than Bill Harrah.

I couldn't find anybody who would accept Bob, and although I kept him on for a couple of years after Bill's death, I finally had to let him go. It was very unhappy for me, because I knew how loyal Bob had been to Bill–he lived and died and grieved for Bill Harrah and Harrah's. Bob, unfortunately, began to view me with animosity, and when I sent him a Christmas card he wrote on the face, "Return to Sender". He would not even accept my Christmas card after his termination; nor would he speak to me. It was regrettable, because if there was any way I could have kept him on, I would have done it. I had no choice.

Maurice Sheppard was fundamentally a bookkeeper and an accountant. I think he started with Harrah soon after he got out of the University of Nevada, and his whole life was devoted to Harrah's and to Bill Harrah. Shep had a soft-spoken way about him, and was not aggressive or extroverted. If Bill wanted to buy a piece of property or something of that kind, that was Shep's domain, and I would help him. I respected Shep, and I thought he did a lot of wonderful things for the company. He was very concerned about the image and success of Harrah's in the community.

Sheppard is the reason that Lloyd Dyer succeeded. Shep came to me after we'd worked with Lloyd awhile, and said, "I think Lloyd has a great deal of ability, and I'd like him to succeed in this company. Where should he fit?"

I said, "If Lloyd wants to succeed in this company, he's *got* to understand finance, so anything you can do to expose him to finance–I'm not talking about bookkeeping–will advance his career." That's the way that Sheppard tried to guide Lloyd, and tried to bring him up (I think he even made him vice president of finance), but it turned out that finance was not Lloyd's talent. Lloyd was an extrovert, a people person, and he was not going to be a financial engineer–he was going to manage a company by managing people.

Sheppard wanted to become president because he saw that the company was not moving the way it ought to; but Shep was the kind of a guy who would think for a month or two before he'd say something to Bill, and it might have been six months before he presented his case. (When Shep approached Bill, it would be in a voice so quiet that you couldn't hear him. He was concerned about trying to maintain a relationship without offending Bill, because Bill was easy to offend.) Shep tried to break that mold of "What does Bill want?" or "What does Bill think?", but he tried to do it privately. I suspect that anybody who had come in with a strong personality might have had trouble with Bill.

The minute Sheppard became president, it became a closed society at Harrah's. He moved into a small office, and instead of having the door open so the people who walked down the hall could step in, he kept his door almost closed. All of a sudden, here is the president of the company, walled off from easy communication with people. That was Sheppard's personality: he wanted to keep things inward and to himself. It didn't mean that he wasn't working; he was working very hard trying to under-stand the company. He worked hard on trying to improve the operating numbers of the company, and he was doing his very best, but in my opinion you cannot be president and leader and also be private. You've got to have your door open; you've got to have people feel free to come and talk with you. You've got to practice what in later years became known as "management by walking about." You should spend a lot of your time *being* with people instead of being introverted and away from them. So Sheppard's personal characteristics were such that I think he wounded himself.

Once you separated Harrah's management from the person of Bill Harrah–a difficult thing to do–you had to look at things differently. That separation occurred when Maurice Sheppard became president. Bill Harrah had been president in title, in name, and in deed, and Bob Ring had really just played the role. When Sheppard became president, Lloyd Dyer became an executive vice president, and in the history of Harrah's that particular team probably was the best management team that the company had, because they complemented each other. Both of them had not only the present but the future of Harrah's in mind, and they probably understood the strengths and weaknesses of the Harrah's people as well as any two persons could. Sheppard's dedication, analytical ability, and foresight–coupled with Lloyd's ability to lead people–made that particular period probably the most significant from the standpoint of bench strength and independent management of Harrah's. It was not as strong, in my opinion, when Lloyd became president . . . not that Lloyd was not a good president, but the contribution that Shep made to the company was significant, and I don't believe that his role was ever filled after he left office as president. Sheppard did *not* have the vision to see Harrah's growth into Atlantic City, but that's not to detract from his efforts to make Harrah's Reno and Harrah's Lake Tahoe successful.

Bill had standards of excellence that he wanted carried out, and he hired good people to do the various jobs. Rome Andreotti was a good man, but while there was no question about his ability to operate a casino, a lot of people at Harrah's hated him, because he was not skilled in interpersonal relationships. The stories would curl your hair . . . yet Rome was very competent in his particular field. Holmes Hendricksen was, and is, supreme in the entertainment field; Joe Fanelli was successful in food and beverage. The casino operation was pretty-well taken care of, and the finance and accounting departments functioned very well. What we had was a company that functioned.

Management's big fear was that they would make a suggestion that Bill would think was dumb. There might be an idea that made good sense, but it would sometimes take several months to think of a way to present the idea to Bill–to *ease* the idea in, so that it would come forth without being put out on the table and subject to, in effect, an immediate veto. I tried to loosen Bill up, and I told him that I thought his people were afraid of him, and it would be wonderful if he could encourage brainstorming sessions where people could sit around and say what they thought, even though it was cuckoo–let their ideas come out, without being criticized . . . and without being fired. [laughter] Bill's response to me was, "That's dumb." Bill's typical criticism of everything he disagreed with was that it was *dumb*: If he didn't think you were really good, he'd say, "You're dumb." (Bill did not have an extensive vocabulary.)

Bill had given the company leadership and vision, and when he stopped doing that, the company became static; but it continued to operate and function reasonably well because all of the pieces were in place and very centralized. Security, purchasing, food and beverage, finance and accounting, and construction were all in Reno. The various properties would operate, but all the support services and authority were centralized. This big dynamo of a company was going, and it functioned, but there was no planning to meet the future. Day after day everything seemed to go along the same. To quote Mark Curtis, "For four years we haven't stuck a stick in the ground. What's the matter with this company?" That was just because Bill had not said we were going to do anything.

Slot machines built Harrah's, and the machines were very important to Bill. We basically had the Pace machines, the mechanicals, because Rome Andreotti had an aversion to Bally machines for reasons that went beyond my comprehension. I think Rome may have thought there was something dishonest about Bally or Bally's representatives; also, Bally machines were new and different, and Rome was without question a traditionalist. (Although Rome would say that it was Bill Harrah who had an aversion to change, I knew Bill a hell of a lot better than that. Bill did not have an aversion to change.) Bill deferred to Rome's knowledge of slot machines and of the casino floor patron, and he believed in Rome's judgment with respect to their operation. Even though Bill used to read his daily statements, he never got into careful analysis of slot drop, slot hold, slot PC, slot presentation, et cetera.

McKenzie and Company were brought in to help reorganize the company in the early 1960s. Bill believed in hiring experts, and I thought McKenzie did a good job of restructuring the company, trying to get it going. The fellow who produced the reorganization study and recommendations stayed on in a planning capacity, and he wanted to stay with Harrah's. He was a dynamic individual, but he did not last, because he was the kind of guy who voiced his opinions. He abraded not only Bill Harrah, but he probably abraded the management structure that was in existence. The culture at Harrah's was such that management was simply not used to having ferment from beneath—thoughts bubbling up and so forth. The mold that Harrah's had created was that people worked strictly for Bill Harrah . . . Bill Harrah, the individual. Bill wanted to put his finger on each little piece; he called the shots.

The Arthur Little construction report that was commissioned in the early 1970s vastly criticized Bill Harrah's theories. Their analysis was that the Harrah's hotel at Lake Tahoe was ill-conceived, because the rooms would cost three times the industry average for a good hotel. Harrah's Tahoe rooms would cost $131,000 each, when you ought to be able to build a hotel room for $40,000 in those days. The Arthur Little report recommended that instead of building five hundred rooms at enormous cost, we should have built at least a thousand rooms for less money. A thousand rooms would have driven that much more business to the casino floor, and the company would have been that much more profitable. Within the company, the Arthur Little report became like a book that had been banned in Boston:

nobody was ever supposed to have a copy of the Arthur Little report. [laughter] There *were* surreptitiously-held copies in various places in the Harrah's organization, but it was like witchcraft–you weren't supposed to know about the Arthur Little report, and you were never, ever to refer to it.

Bill and I got along famously. We were very close friends; we had frequent candid and frank conversations about life, personalities, about the people who worked at Harrah's, about what Bill wanted, about what he saw. I didn't tell him how to run his business, and he didn't tell me how to practice law. He was brilliant, but eccentric, and he was *instinctively* a business genius, very right about so many things. In the beginning he was a perfectionist, although in later years he said, "I have found that I can't attain perfection." [laughter] Well, that's something that probably you and I knew in kindergarten.

Bill had a famous question that always put his employees on the defensive. When something was really goofy or wrong–"goofy" was one of Bill's words–he would ask the person involved, "Does it have to be this way?" Now, Bill meant *every word* in that question. Most of the time if you start soul-searching, you'll find that things are that way because you're lazy, or because somebody else hasn't done his homework, or because you are indifferent or haven't thought of it. Whatever the problem, you may find that it doesn't have to be that way–that things *can* be done the right way. And that's what Bill was trying to get across.

Where Bill's technique earlier in life had been to fix it, his technique later in life became to ask the question and let the officer or executive involved go through the digestion process of coming back and responding, because Bill *did* want an answer. He never threw out a question idly, and if you didn't answer him, he always remembered that. One time he asked Pat France a question that had to do with a parade of old automobiles in Carson City. As I recall, Bill said to Pat, "Why do we want to put this car in the parade?"

Pat's answer was, "Well, we did it last year." I thought he was going to get fired on the spot! In effect, Bill said, "That's the dumbest answer I've ever heard." Bill always got very upset over that kind of answer, which he thought was no answer at all.

Bill had a peculiar system: when he was out of town, and he wanted to know how things were going, he would be advised by code. Anyone else would pick up the phone and say, "How did things go?" and somebody would tell you. But for some reason, Bill wanted to be advised by code. One code was "Model T". I can't remember how the code worked, but everything had to be by using the letters in Model T. Communicating with Bill or having somebody send him information on the dailies in the code of the week was a great mystery at Harrah's, boy!

Another peculiarity was that executives couldn't go on vacation unless they reported in every day–every day you had to call in. That's not much of a vacation, but by God, they all loved it. Then there was the Pat France system of expense-account reporting. [laughter] Pat France and another fellow had an interesting system. They would fill their pockets with money when they went on a trip, and count themselves down; then when they came back from the trip, they'd count themselves down again. The difference was listed as expenses. [laughter]

We had two forms of financing at Harrah's: public financing, and a lot of private financing. We were able to raise approximately ten million dollars to build a Lake Tahoe hotel, but by the time Bill and Sherry and the South Shore architects got through with their designs for the first Lake Tahoe hotel, the cost ran to twenty-two mil, and nobody had twenty-two million dollars or a chance of getting it. So we abandoned that project and in 1969 completed the Reno hotel instead.

The Reno hotel was done with debt financing–very hard to put together in those days. We owed a substantial obligation to Art Smith at the First National Bank. (When Art left Las Vegas and came to Reno, I think there was rivalry between him and Parry Thomas in the banking world, and that may have motivated Art to put a strong effort into helping Harrah's get its financing.) We already had a financing package in place for ten million dollars, and after Art came to Reno, I reviewed that package with him, and admitted that it wasn't the best package in the world; but it was the best I could put together. Art said, "Let me help you put it all into one package instead of two." (We had a six and a four–six million dollars of lease financing with Boothe Leasing, a subsidiary of Greyhound, and four million out of American National Insurance in Galveston, Texas.) Art put it all together as a single ten million dollar bank financing package, and that was the way we built Harrah's Reno hotel.

In 1971 we took Harrah's public, and that was a dramatic and traumatic change, because Bill Harrah didn't want to go public. But we took it public in large measure because Bill personally needed money that he couldn't get from his salary or dividends to pay his accumulated debts. He just couldn't get the money–it wasn't there; it didn't exist. So we had a public offering of stock with a so-called piggyback or secondary (depending on whose lexicon you use) for Bill Harrah. (In other words, part of the stock that was being sold would go to benefit the company, and part would go to benefit Mr. Harrah, some of whose personal shares were being sold.) It was very difficult to get an underwriter and put that first public issue together–extremely difficult taking a gaming company public, particularly with the piggyback. I remember how hard we worked Wall Street, and everybody on Wall Street turned us down. Eventually, we started with a regional underwriter, Mitchum, Jones & Templeton.

Bill asked me over and over again what complications that public offering would bring into his life–what complications he would have as chairman of a company that had publicly-issued stock. Of course, this was something that we *had* to talk Bill into, because it was in the best interest of the company and in his best interest. I don't mean we conned him or deceived him, but rather we *comforted* him. We said, "Bill, maybe you couldn't live with partners; maybe you couldn't live with Warren Nelson or Virgil Smith as one of your partners, but you can live with a public company. A public company is going to enable us to plan for the future of Harrah's, and it will be in our long-term best interest." So Bill approved the concept.

Taking Harrah's public was a good thing for Bill, and it was a good thing for Harrah's. Harrah's had a pristine reputation, which it deserved–it really was a well-managed, well-organized company under Bill's leadership. A lot of Harrah's people used to say, "We're number one" (I don't think I ever said that), and Harrah's *was* the king of casinos in northern Nevada. Bill had a good company, and when we took it public, we were soon able to get the shares registered on the American stock exchange, and then eventually on the New York stock exchange. In fact, Harrah's was the first pure casino company ever to be listed on the New York stock exchange, which made us very proud. Harrah's was clean as a whistle, and the people in both stock exchanges swallowed all their remarks about the mafia and bad companies and so forth, and took Harrah's at face value. The listing on the stock exchanges was a coup from the Harrah point of view.

We had a second share offering before Bill died, and that was an offering of convertible debentures. That was again in substantial part motivated by trying to help Bill Harrah out with his personal financial problems. I'm not criticizing Bill–when I say that Bill had personal financial needs, I mean that Bill was spending money the way he wanted to spend it; and that was his privilege. To his credit, he did not raid the company and require it to pay him all sorts of ungodly sums–if he needed money, he sold a part of his interest in the company to get it. The fact that he sold shares probably is evidence of a straightforward approach of integrity toward his personal financial needs, rather than an attempt to find some way to bleed the company.

Bill really did treat the company with respect. Sure, he had his perks, but every corporate officer has perks. He had more perks than the other officers in Harrah's, but probably far fewer perks than most corporate executives today. You didn't see Bill Harrah paying himself substantial bonuses; you didn't see all the things you see in this corporate world today, which are shocking to me. Bill ran the business the old-fashioned way, where you stayed in the business every day and you tried to make money every day that you were in business.

Bill Harrah was constitutionally against committees and boards. The fundamental Harrah's philosophy that the officers abided by was, "What does Bill want?" This instead of striving for independent thought on how would you manage a company, and what direction the company should take. Although Bill used to go to various committee meetings, as well as board meetings, he told me (and the people at Harrah's knew) that he despised the meetings, but felt he had to go to them for formal purposes. He did not like to spend one minute in a meeting if he didn't have to. If a meeting was to be at ten o'clock, when Bill walked into the room, you didn't have to call Western Union; you could set your watch—you knew it was ten o'clock. It wasn't 10:01, and it wasn't 9:59; it was ten o'clock. Meetings were short and as direct as possible, and there was very little volunteering of anything in front of Bill Harrah. I could never convince him of the value of loosening his people up; Bill really didn't feel that way.

When we became a public company, even though we had public shareholders and were a very big company, Bill still pretty much wanted just to be Bill and not to go to meetings. So Harrah's had a minimum number of meetings, and the meetings were as limited as possible. There would be the financial review and some discussion . . . and then you could see Bill was getting nervous, and the meeting would adjourn.

I met Bob Maheu[1] for the first time when I flew to Washington, D.C. with Bill Harrah and Bob Ring for an IRS hearing. (At that time Harrah's had a Jet Commander, which, like all business jets of that day, didn't perform nearly as well as a Lear—but it was

[1] Robert Aime Maheu was an FBI agent during the Second World War, and later did work for the CIA. In the mid-1950s, when Maheu was operating an "investigative and problem solving" agency in Washington, he began getting assignments from Howard Hughes. Soon Maheu was receiving so much work from Hughes that he moved to Los Angeles, dropped his other clients, and devoted full time to the billionaire. When Hughes secretly moved into the Desert Inn in Las Vegas in 1966, he took Maheu with him, and made him his chief Nevada executive. For the next four years, until his dismissal in 1970, Maheu served as the reclusive Hughes's eyes, ears and voice.

nicer inside than a Lear.) Maheu had not come to Washington with us–he was there representing Howard Hughes. Del Webb was there at the hearing, and we offered him a ride back to the West Coast, but Del declined; Maheu accepted.

We all got out to Washington National, and no sooner did we get to the airport than Maheu had to go to a pay phone to call Howard Hughes. (He called him "Mr. Hughes".) You could see the slow burn begin in Bill, because he wanted to get in the airplane and go. (I could tell some stories about Bill getting in the airplane and going. He abandoned Bob Ring on one occasion. He would abandon anybody when he wanted to go, because it was time to go. But he didn't abandon Maheu, which surprised me.) Maheu stood in his phone booth for what seemed an eternity, and then he came to us with his importance, because Maheu always carried himself as though he was important.

We took off and flew for some time and then landed for fuel. Same thing: Maheu was on the telephone . . . calling Howard Hughes again, according to him. We waited and waited, while he had a long, animated conversation, and then we departed for somewhere in Texas, where Bill wanted to be dropped off on the way back. (I think there was a car show or an automobile auction or something, because he wouldn't go to Texas to eat chili or to see a Texan!)

The cabin of a Jet Commander is about the size of a dining-room table. Visualize the toilet facilities on the front right-hand side of the aircraft cabin–there was a potty seat behind the copilot. The potty on this airplane was a dry toilet, a pail or bucket, and I had never seen anybody use it, even though I had traveled in the plane a hell of a lot. Somewhere along the way to Texas, Maheu decided that he had to have a bowel movement, and using the potty didn't bother him at all. He took off his jacket, unbuttoned his pants, pulled them down, lifted the lid, sat down in front of all three of us, and evacuated. And it smelled! Of course, that didn't go over well with Bill Harrah, but Maheu didn't bat an eye . . . didn't so much as apologize! It was as though he were the king and could not do wrong; he could defecate in the court. Most of us would not have *dared* do that in front of Bill Harrah. Of course, none of us would have held Harrah's departure up for a phone call, either.

We dropped Bill off in Texas, and he was relieved to be out of the airplane. Off we flew to Las Vegas to drop off Maheu before going on to Reno. We landed at Hughes's facility; he had bought the FBO (fixed base operation) there on Highway 91–George Crockett's old Alamo Airways site, where the Hughes Aviation Services executive terminal is today. On the ground floor were the pilots' lounge and the customer lounge, and on the second floor was a bar and restaurant that had a little balcony from which you could look out over the airport. It was night when we landed and pulled up, and I don't believe I'd seen so many flashing lights in my life–spot lights, red lights, yellow lights . . . . It was as though all of the police and patrol cars in the world were out there to greet us. Obviously, Maheu had arranged an arrival. Cars pulled up, and we were taken inside, and Maheu said, "How would you fellows like a drink?" There hadn't been anything to drink on the airplane, so I said, "That would be great."

Bob Ring said, "Well, I can't drink." (Bob didn't drink because Bill Harrah didn't drink–that was a parrot situation. The minute Bill took his first drink after fifteen years on the wagon, Bob took a drink.) Maheu told them to open the upstairs area. They said, "Well, you know there's nothing up there, Mr. Maheu."

He said to us, "You fellows don't mind waiting a few minutes, do you?"

Well, I wanted to see what was going to happen, so I said, "No, we'll stay." (Bob was scared to death, because he knew we were doing something wrong.) [laughter]

Within minutes, ice, liquor, and food arrived from one of the Hughes hotels, and were carted upstairs, and all the lights turned on. In effect, we had a party–Maheu, Ring and Dixon . . . except Ring wouldn't touch any alcohol. We sat out on the balcony and watched the airplanes come in and land, and Maheu said, "This is why I'm in Nevada." In other words, "I could be in New York . . . . " We talked about where he'd been; we talked about his career, and so forth. This was a beautiful night: the sky was dark; the stars were bright; you could see the airplanes land; and we had all the service of room, food and beverage. It *was* a great life. It was probably ten-thirty or eleven o'clock at night before we broke up, and Bob and I went down the stairs and got in the airplane and came on in to Reno.

That had been a most interesting glimpse of Maheu's personality. He had said, "Mr. Hughes doesn't talk to anybody but me. He and I understand each other." But Maheu said he never saw Hughes in person; they just talked over the telephone. (If I were Howard Hughes, I wouldn't want that many phone calls, but I suppose that Howard didn't have anything else to do.) [laughter] I never met Hughes, either, but I met his reps, who said I gave Hughes bad vibes because I had brought too much attention to him with my work on getting his Husite assessment adjusted. I don't know anybody who ever did meet Howard Hughes personally, except, perhaps, the governor, Paul Laxalt . . . and, I suppose, Hughes's Mormon coterie. [laughter]

Bill Harrah was a rather unimportant person in Maheu's mind–Hughes was the only important person to him. Maheu's bread and butter, his source of power, was Howard Hughes, and just as Bill Harrah was the most important person in Bob Ring's life, Howard Hughes had to be the most important in Bob Maheu's life. Maheu was the public personification, the representative, of Howard Hughes. I'm satisfied that he spoke for Hughes, and every representation that I ever got from Bob Maheu was backed up. I met with him on a number of occasions with respect to Harrah's purchase and sale negotiations, as well as in respect to Nevada Resort Association matters and general casino matters, and I never found that Maheu spoke with forked tongue.

In the late 1960s, or perhaps 1970, Bill Harrah took seriously several offers of purchase from Howard Hughes, and signed a couple of letters of intent to sell. Bill was mesmerized by the idea that he could turn Harrah's into cash, but unfortunately he met with Maheu privately on these things, and as smart as Bill Harrah was, he was out-negotiated. As I recall, Bill signed a letter of intent to sell Harrah's, and the first deal with Hughes was for eleven million dollars, for crying out loud! I can't recall what was included in that transaction, but it was a raw deal, and we backed away from it. So Maheu came back, and he jumped the ante to thirty-five million, a pretty good jump. Bill said, "I'm going to take that," so we had a long discussion, the substance of which was, "Hey, you're getting a good price. You always wanted a lot of money, and you don't have any money because you're only getting paid two hundred thousand a year and a few free lunches to run Harrah's Club. But what would you do with the auto collection? And what about your airplanes?"

"Well," Bill thought, "maybe we ought to exclude the airplanes, and maybe we ought to exclude the automobile collection from the sale."

"Then how about Villa Harrah?"

"Well, maybe we ought to take that out of the sale." (Now, the sale was to be a package–a lock, stock and barrel transaction.)

Then we had to look at how Bill could keep Harrah's Automobile Collection, because it wasn't tax deductible. We started looking at the numbers, and you could see where we were going, so Bill gave me the assignment of canceling the transaction. It was very clear that he could not maintain his personal lifestyle, even if he had thirty-five million dollars, less the capital gains tax and so forth, which he would have had to pay. There he would have been, living at Rancharrah south of Reno, which he didn't entirely own. (Most of that property was owned by Harrah's Club, not by Bill Harrah.) So when he started looking at lifestyle and thinking, "What am I selling, and what am I going to do?" he became less mesmerized.

(Bill was *magnetically* attracted by those offers of cash from Howard Hughes, because he had never had that much money; but he didn't recognize how much of his lifestyle was being supported by Harrah's Club as a corporation–particularly the Harrah's Automobile Collection, which was a big-numbers operation. The same was true with Villa Harrah. You see, if he wanted to have a dinner, Harrah's would provide cooks, servants, and everything else. But if he had to reach into his pocket and hire them, it would be a totally different experience. That culture shock came to Bill as we considered this deal, and we unwound because it was not enough money.)

I was surprised that Bill hadn't gotten me out in front in the negotiations with Hughes and Maheu, but the bottom line was internal corporate politics. In my opinion there was no question that company management was–let's use a nice word–jealous of my relationship with Bill. I like Maurice Sheppard, but Sheppard wanted to be the central point at Harrah's, which is understandable. I think he was president of the company at that time, or due to be. (Maybe Bob Ring was president at the time, but Bob never ran anything; Bob was just a figurehead. Maurice was president for a year or so, and then it was felt necessary to replace him because some problems developed . . . we all know what the problems were. And I was instrumental in his replacement, which didn't do me any good in the company!) [laughter]

Bill and I sometimes talked about presidents and presidencies, as well as about what to do with Rome Andreotti. We talked about Bob Ring's performance as president of the company. Bob was highly respected, with many talents and a phenomenal memory, and he had a wonderful way of getting along with a customer, and great loyalty to Harrah's. But his approach to being president of Harrah's was, in effect, "What does Bill want?" Bob didn't take any initiative as president; he was more or less a figurehead. Bill Harrah was the real president of Harrah's, the commander-in-chief, and as Bob would say, "This is not Harrah's Club; it's *Bill* Harrah's Club." That was Bob's witticism about it, and he had wit.

Bill and I discussed succession, and his concern about Rome Andreotti. Rome was a good operator, but Bill said, "If I let him, he'd replace the rest rooms with slot machines." Bill wanted to have more public amenities, and Rome didn't perceive the need for them–Rome wanted more income generators, and that was a concern that Bill had in giving him a free hand. Rome would not recognize the importance of rest rooms, much less the importance of *beautifully clean* rest rooms.

Bill feared also that Rome was too loyal: "If I say, 'Rome, go that way,' he'll keep right on going that way, even if he walks straight through a wall. He doesn't know when to stop. He just *goes* until I make him stop." So those faults, if you want to call them that, disqualified Rome in Bill's mind as being president of the company.

We had lots of little problems because of Rome's devotion. Bill one time said, "You know, I don't like people who are overweight." Well, Rome went around firing anybody who he thought was fat or overweight. So I had to talk with him. I said, "For Christ's sake, what are you trying to do?"

"Bill doesn't like fat people."

"Well, I understand that, but that doesn't mean you've got to go through the club and fire every fat person. You have to *understand* that." I had to talk with Bill and Rome about it, because you can't run a business being cruel to your employees. (Bill was pretty critical about personal appearance, and there were a lot of things you couldn't do . . . you couldn't even have a beard. He wanted to have young, attractive people, and there was no question about that . . . but Rome would take on everything with a chain saw or an ax.)

Because Bill didn't like fat people, the fourth-floor conference room had a scale for the Harrah's officers. I had to laugh at all those poor bastards who worked for Harrah's. Every morning when they reported for work, one of the things they had to do was go to the conference room, step on the scale and make their calendar entry–the date and their weight. [laughter] You could look and see what Rome's weight was every day, what Sheppard's weight was every day, what Dyer's weight was every day, and so forth and so on.

Another interesting characteristic of Harrah's management people on the fourth floor was the number of magazines that they read. If there was a magazine of any kind that related even remotely to anything, they subscribed. Every executive had lots of stuff to read, as though they didn't have enough work to do. I never had time to sit around reading *Time* or *Fortune* while I was supposed to be working to accomplish something . . . but I suppose you could justify that from the standpoint of self-education. They didn't have any clear objective for those people–they had a presence, but they didn't have any programs.

One of my principles was that you always need to understand what you're trying to accomplish; your goals and objectives
always have to be kept in mind. At Harrah's, we did not have
really well-defined objectives. Harrah's created budgets every
year, and a great deal of work went into the budgetary process;
and they created a bonus program, and a great deal of work went
into their bonus thinking. But they did not, in my view, create a
program that gave defined goals or defined objectives to anyone.
They created a bonus program such that when bonuses were
given out–and they were not overly generous bonuses–there was
a great deal of subjectivity in giving them, rather than objective
measurement. The feeling was, "Well, he's a good guy; he ought
to get a pretty good bonus." Or, "He's not such a good guy, and
he won't get such a good bonus." So as a senior employee in the
bonus pool, you didn't say, "I've got certain things I've got to
accomplish this year if I want to earn my bonus."

A couple of years before Bill's death, it was clear that his
employees were chafing under his compensation programs. There
was a very minimal retirement program at Harrah's–I call it a
retirement program, but under the law it was a profit-sharing
program . . . except Bill didn't like the term profit-sharing.
(Profit-sharing programs were easier to make comply with labor
and tax laws than a retirement or pension fund. But although it
was a profit-sharing program, it was called Harrah's Retirement
Plan.) None of the executives were satisfied, and my recollection
is that they called in Booz Allen, Inc., to look at it. Booz made
some recommendations with respect to compensation and
retirement for executives, and they made some projections as to
what future salaries might be, but Bill was very disturbed over
the recommendations because they would increase corporate
costs, and they would provide corporate executives with a lot
more money than he thought they were worth. Bill was still back
in the Jimmy Contratto school of gambling, with the philosophy
that, "At five o'clock every day we're even. You got paid for being
here today; at five o'clock we're even." He firmly believed that.
He made exceptions in the case of some people, but not because
he felt obligated to . . . Red Farnsworth being one; he took care

of Red. There were a few people like that who Bill would take care of, but he had the five o'clock syndrome, and he firmly believed that if you didn't like your job, you shouldn't be there. He once said to me, "You must like being a lawyer, or you wouldn't be one. And the people who work here must like working here, or they wouldn't work here." Nearing the end of his life, Bill compromised and accepted some of the Booz Allen recommendations.

My becoming associated with Harrah's was the luck of the draw, I think. I had the good fortune of being at the right place at the right time . . . but you have to take advantage of your good fortune, and I worked hard to maintain the right kind of relationship with Bill. I worked hard at helping him in a way that he would accept. Most lawyers are rather dull people. That's a funny thing to say, and maybe I shouldn't paint with such a broad brush, but most lawyers would have had a difficult time relating to Bill, or vice versa. But I was able to have enough spontaneity, initiative, understanding of people, and perspective on business to relate to Bill in a way that made sense to him. I didn't sit in my office and wait for somebody to call up and say, "We've been sued. What do we do now?" I was proactive, not reactive, to use the buzz words that are so common today. I tried to bring Bill positive views, and took the initiative in talking to him so that he didn't have to call me. I'd call him and say, "I want to talk with you," and I would sit down and talk with him.

I built a relationship with Bill, and I was not afraid to talk with him, whereas some of his management were always afraid. Bill didn't like a lot of vacuous talk, so very early on during my meetings with him I was trying to find a way that I could talk with him that would be short, succinct, and to the point–not waste his time and not give him a lot of palaver. Before I would go to see him, I would think what it was that I wanted to discuss, and how to present it in a way that he could grasp quickly without a waste of his time.

As the years went by, we became more and more friendly. Even though I didn't have a lot of talk with Bill, it became easy, easy, easy. I could sit down and tell him straight from the shoulder how I felt about something, and I didn't have to worry about the way I presented it. Hell, he said no a *lot* times, like with the automobile collection or with charitable contributions or with community participation. There were just walls that Bill had in his mind, and you could not penetrate those walls. But over the years we built enough of a relationship that I could talk with him without being afraid of being fired. And even if I was fired, I was still going to live–I would still have bread and butter on the table, so I had a looser collar than most people.

[8]

Bill Harrah's Perks

BILL LOVED TO DRIVE AUTOMOBILES, but he was used to getting into a car that somebody else had prepared for him—had it cleaned and all running and sitting out front. He loved to go as fast as he could, and he loved to speed from Reno to Lake Tahoe in his Ferraris. When the Clear Creek grade from Carson City up to the south end of the lake was paved, but the curves left unbanked, he was so happy, because it made the curves more difficult to drive at high speed. That was delirious fun, and it brought him a great deal of joy. I've ridden with Bill on old 395 between Reno and Carson City, a two-lane highway, and if he got below ninety-eight miles an hour, he was having a bad time. He had the craze for speed. He built a "sleeper"—an ordinary-looking car which had really been highly modified by Los Angeles Engines, and then in his shop here. Bill loved to wait at a stop light and watch the person next to him edge forward, and he'd grin and beat him away from the light, and giggle and giggle. It made him so happy to beat somebody away from a sign or a signal. Or he would wait in one of his sleepers until someone tried to pass him on the highway, and then he would floor the automobile and go zooming around them—his day was made.

Nineteen forty-eight was the year Bill bought his first antique car, a 1911 Maxwell; and I think that 1948 was also the year he discovered Stanley, Idaho, located in the Sawtooth range, with gorgeous mountain backdrops and rivers. Back then, Stanley had a population of about forty, and most of them lived in tar-paper shacks; it looked like a Hoover Town,[1] but eventually Bill bought a little house there. In one day Bill could drive to Stanley, which had a little bar where he could drink. He loved to drive as fast as he could–he was psychologically *compelled*, I suspect, to drive fast–and the combination of his aversion to crowds, his wanting to get away from Reno, his desire to have a few nips, and his need to drive a car at high speed took him to Stanley.

(Bill was still drinking in his early days in Stanley. He stopped drinking in 1953 or 1954, and when he stopped drinking and started paying attention to his business, Harrah's Club began to prosper. That's when he made the decision that since things were going good in Reno, he would try to expand to Lake Tahoe by purchasing George's Gateway Club, which everybody thought was a crazy thing to do.)

Bob Cole was a hunting and fishing guide in Stanley, which means that he was like everybody else in Idaho–unemployed most of the time. [laughter] But it was a pretty good business, because you only worked during season . . . a laid-back way of life. Bill discovered Bob Cole, who was an absolute genius with rod and reel, with a gun, with everything. He was as fine an outdoorsman and guide as there was in the world, and he would take Bill fishing. (Bill didn't hunt; to my knowledge, he'd never hunted.) It occurred to Bill at one point in time, "This guy is so valuable that I better hold on to him." So he said to Bob, "Bob, I'd like to have you work for me full time. I'm going to give you a job." Bob asked Bill what it would entail, and Bill said he wanted him to be a guide, and then in his off seasons he could work at Lake Tahoe for Harrah's. It would mean a good income for Bob, and a good relationship, because these two guys got along. Bob understood Bill, and vice versa.

---

[1] During the Depression, the shack and tent communities erected by out-of-work men and homeless families were known as Hoover Towns, suggesting that former President Herbert Hoover was responsible for the Depression.

The story is that they struck a deal, and Bob was going to be an employee, so he said, "All right, Bill. I'll be over at four-thirty in the morning, and we're going to go out and catch salmon."

Bill said, "No, *seven* in the morning. You don't understand—you now work for me." [laughter]

From that start and from a lot of fishing done with Bob Cole, Bill did some floating down the Middle Fork of the Salmon River. In doing so, he spotted a property, which was then named the Middle Fork Lodge. It had a two-story building, which was the lodge; and it had a swimming pool fed by natural hot springs, and lots of land that was undeveloped—mostly hayfields, meadows and that sort of thing along Thomas Creek . . . a beautiful setting. When it turned out that the property might be for sale, Bill decided that he wanted to buy it. This was about 1966, and I was given the task of trying to acquire the property, which was owned by a fellow named Rex Lanham. Rex was a backcountry flyer, a contractor, a rancher—a man big in stature, big in view, big in vision, big in Idaho politics, and as down to earth as you could get. I don't think he knew what a suit and necktie were! He was part of the Idaho backcountry, but with big clout.

I talked with Rex about buying Middle Fork for Bill, following which Rex even went so far as to find his own lawyer, which was quite an event. But we had a problem, in that Rex had given an option to the Forest Service to buy the property. (He held title through the medium of an Idaho corporation. In other words, Middle Fork Lodge wasn't registered or deeded in the name of Rex Lanham; it was deeded in the name of a corporation, all of whose stock was owned by Rex.) Rex's position was that he'd given an option to the federal government, and he couldn't break the option. My position was Bill Harrah wanted the property, and I had to figure out how to get it. So I made a deal with Rex. He wanted, I think, $280,000. (That was the figure the government was going to pay.) I said, "All right. I'll make a deal with you: I'll buy the stock in your corporation. We don't have $280,000, but we'll give you $50,000 down, and we'll make annual payments. We'll own your corporation, and whether or not we can break the federal government's option will be *our* problem—but you will be gone; you'll be out of the picture."

Rex, who wanted the deal to go through private hands rather than the government, agreed. He didn't want to go back on his word, but he was a Barry Goldwater Republican who would do anything to keep the land away from the government, and in private hands . . . anything within his code of ethics. So we flew to Pocatello, Idaho, and opened an escrow, in which Lanham deposited his shares of stock in his corporation. We deposited a promissory note from Harrah's for the balance that was due, and we had an agreement of sale. And at that point Harrah's corporation owned the company that owned the Middle Fork Lodge.

Then I got ahold of Al Pagni, who was in our law firm (Vargas, Bartlett and Dixon) at that time. I thought the federal option could be broken, and I gave Al the job of doing the research and deciding whether or not we could break it. He came to the same conclusion that I had, so we put the federal government on notice that the option was voidable, and we were not going to honor it. We went through the usual red tape and bureaucratic procedure, but we prevailed; the federal government did not exercise the option. They also concluded that it had a fatal weakness in it, and they did not force the issue. So we continued to make the installment payments, and that's how Harrah's came to own the Middle Fork Lodge.

The Middle Fork Lodge was a great place. I flew up there shortly after the purchase, and I was surprised to see people already at work tearing down walls and rebuilding the lodge, enlarging it and changing it. As with everything else, once Bill owned it, he wanted it fixed his way. Once you start remodeling an old building, you take down a piece here and find a piece that has to be fixed. They started remodeling the building just a little bit, and rebuilt the entire lodge. [laughter] They made a very handsome property out of it, but it probably would have been easier to have started with dynamite and built from scratch.

In addition to the lodge, Bill built cabins for guests to live in. All of the original stuff at Middle Fork had been built out of native materials, but Bill wanted to build in a hurry, and so he bought prefabbed Lincoln-log type structures. He built maybe six or eight cabins, each with two single beds in them, heat, running water, and so forth.

When he finished his basic project, which was quite a construction feat, Bill had changed the nature of Middle Fork Lodge. Everything that went into Middle Fork had to be flown in. We started out with a Cessna 206 that I got from Reno Flying Service, and then we bought a DeHavilland Twin Otter. We flew in sand, gravel, concrete, nuts, bolts–every log, every stick of building material was flown in. The airport at Challis was used as a base, and it looked like a World War II staging area, with sandbag after sandbag stacked up, because Bill hauled in sand and gravel in order to make concrete. Every time you looked at a nail, every time you drank from a coffee cup, you knew that it had been flown in. Under the Harrah procedure, even all the food was flown from Reno, which didn't make any sense, but there was no purchasing arrangement in Idaho at the time. It was an enormous project that took years to build.

Bill invited an engineer friend of his–I should say an *acquaintance* of his, because that's really all Bill had–to visit Middle Fork Lodge when it was still in construction. After the visit, the engineer wrote a nice letter and said, "Dear Bill: Thank you so much. I enjoyed Middle Fork Lodge, bow-wow-wow-wow . . . . And let me tell you, I have a suggestion which will save you a lot of money. I've noticed that you're flying in sand and gravel. I've also noticed that the creek is full of sand and gravel, and all you'd have to do is dig the sand and gravel out of the creek, and you'd be spared all that expense of flying. You could do all your concrete work on site."

Instead of saying, "Thank you for the suggestion," Bill's reaction was, "I can't imagine anybody telling me how to run my business! I can't imagine this suggestion! Take his name off my list; I never want to see him again!" And that was the end of the engineer. Had it been me, even if I had preferred to fly in my sand and gravel, I would have written the guy, "Thanks for the helpful thought, but we're working on a different plan." Not Bill.

The publicity literature came to describe Middle Fork as important within the Harrah's organization–a retreat for management. It was said that Bill took people there for training, and for lower management it was a sign of accomplishment when you were finally invited to a Middle Fork retreat. I didn't look at it that way. Frankly, I looked on Middle Fork as a nuisance. [laughter] To me, it was a management *problem*–it was something that didn't fit into Harrah's; it didn't have any place in the company. Bill didn't even use it very often himself–if he was there two weeks a year, it would be a big year–and it was a drag on earnings, a tremendous expense.

Middle Fork had been a self-sustaining property when Lanham had it–that is, for fire in the kitchen, you just chopped wood and put it in the stove; you let the natural hot water heat the buildings; you let the Pelton wheel generate electricity. What Bill did was change it from a self-sustaining, primitive property into a maintenance nightmare which took many employees. We fenced the entire property–*acres*–with a beautiful wood fence. We had to maintain the Twin Otter and the 206 just to support the property, and we had to put fuel bladders in the Otter to haul diesel fuel to the lodge each week to generate electricity. (These were big loads of fuel to carry by air.) Then we had to have trucks to haul fuel from the nearby air strip across the river. Each step was eating up more cost.

There was an old suspension bridge across the river to get to the lodge, and we had to tear that down. Bill wanted to have a new suspension bridge that would be only wide enough to permit a Jeep to come across, because he didn't want any vehicle bigger than a Jeep on the property. (The first jeep on the property had been flown in in pieces by Lanham. He had cut it up, flown it in a piece at a time, and then welded and bolted it back together.) Lanham had the contract to build the bridge, and he tried to induce Bill to make the bridge wider; but just as with the engineer who suggested that Bill dig his own sand and gravel, Lanham's suggestion was denied. The bridge was built only wide enough for a Jeep to cross. It wasn't very long before Bill decided that he *had* to have a truck to get fuel from the air strip to the lodge, and he flew one in by helicopter. Once we had the truck, how could we get it back and forth from the airport to the lodge? We rebuild the bridge to make it wider as Lanham had suggested to begin with! [laughter] Again, every nut, every bolt . . . everything had to be flown in.

Bill built a huge barn (I don't know what the hell else you would call it) to display antique automobiles, and he flew in a few and put them inside this building. It was a wooden building with small windows, so you couldn't see inside, and you had to have access to it to know there were old cars in there. It had no relationship to Idaho or to the property at all, but Bill liked automobiles. He did restore a historic building on the land that was gorgeous, absolutely perfect. Bill also did a lot of positive things, and he would not permit tennis courts or any modern sort of development of the property, except for the automobile museum. However, he built a large administration building that was capable of running seminars for fifty or so people. Why, I'll never know . . . except for tax reasons.

Middle Fork was primarily a hunting and fishing camp. The fishing was not very good–catch and release in the Middle Fork of the Salmon River–but hunting was fair, and we were able to reserve all of the hunting rights for the lodge, instead of losing them to Idaho guides. This was a real political coup, and interesting, because Bill didn't hunt. In fact, outside of a few top executives, I don't think very many Harrah's employees ever got to go hunting and fishing. Some went there for seminars or retreats, which I didn't think was cost productive . . . fly people from Lake Tahoe to Middle Fork Lodge for a day or two seminar, and fly in all the food and beverage for them!

To run the property must have cost between one and two million dollars a year, negative on the earning side. Middle Fork Lodge was a voracious monster: it had its mouth open, and it required constant feeding. I could have understood it if Bill had said, "Hey, I love to use it, and I want to be there all the time." But if he put in two weeks a year, it would be big. It was just part of Bill's lifestyle–he didn't count cost the way you and I count cost.

Most of the people who worked at Middle Fork Lodge were not motivated people. It was like being in the military: it took them twice as long to do something as it should because they didn't have motivation. My son Drake went to Middle Fork to work around 1970, and I think the perception was that because he was my son, he wasn't going to carry his load. The truth of the matter is that he overwhelmed his supervisors, because when they gave him a project to do, he did it correctly, efficiently, and got it done so quickly that he was an exception to the rule. The other laborers and employees there were a little turned off, but the people in charge of the projects were excited. They'd never seen anybody dig as many fence holes as fast and straight, or get the irrigation furrows done so quickly. Drake was in his medium. He'd always been raised to be an honest boy–a hard-working guy, and straightforward–and he didn't know the meaning of the term "gold brick." I got quite a bit of feedback on the surprise of the people at Middle Fork at the job Drake was doing. Soon even the help began to like Drake, and he became kind of a shining star, even though he was simply a laborer on the lowest echelon. He got along with the people there well, and it was good for him and good for them.

Drake's tenure at Middle Fork continued for a good number of years, and his responsibilities increased. He took out hunting and fishing parties, and he became an assistant guide under Bob Cole, who was the head guide. Drake had his baptism of running into the legal system when he took a float party from Middle Fork to the Flying B downstream, and was apprehended by federal agents for taking a float party without a permit. He was simply following instructions, and I think that Bob Cole believed the instructions were correct–that they could float from private property to private property without having a license or permit. But it turned out that was wrong. It cost us some attorney fees, but we spared Drake a felony conviction. I don't think he even got a misdemeanor conviction, but he was endangered by that process and exposed to the court system. [laughter]

Drake continued to work at Middle Fork for close to ten years. In time he had an extensive outdoor life, most of it at Middle Fork, but some spent in Washington and Oregon. He concluded–rightly or wrongly–that he had matured enough at Middle Fork, and he began to drift a little bit. I had a ranch in Oregon, and about 1980 he came out of the mountains and began to run it.

One of the first things I did after Bill's death was shut down the Middle Fork Lodge operation, because I didn't think it was contributing. We hadn't had any luck with the tax laws, and we had not had any luck with star performers. You might say, "Gee, isn't this great? Your star entertainers would love to go up there," but it wasn't so. It took a peculiar person to enjoy Middle Fork Lodge. There was no TV, no radio, and it was quiet. There was a pool table and a card table and a ping-pong table, and you could walk or ride horseback, and those are all interesting things to people who *like* to do that sort of thing. But you'll find that your entertainers are really not into that, and boredom set in very soon. My experience was that if you invited an entertainer to Middle Fork Lodge, the first day he would say, "Isn't this wonderful?" The next day, boredom. If invited to the lodge again, he would politely decline because he had other things to do.

Perhaps second-tier Harrah's executives who were invited to participate in seminars felt honored to be recognized by getting to go to this privileged place. My own experience was that I could spend hours in the mountains . . . I could hike and walk, do all those things, and they were all rewarding to me; but I didn't see that as a cost-effective benefit for Harrah's employees. Had it been my choice, which it was not, I would have kept the property more self-sustaining and much closer to nature, and probably have been able to operate it for a hell of a lot less.

I was involved early on in the acquisition of properties–that is houses and lots–at Lake Tahoe, which later became the site of the Villa Harrah. We had an experience there that was similar to the one we'd had with Middle Fork: we bought a little lot to begin with; then pretty soon we bought half a dozen lots. Like Middle Fork, it grew into a monster that ate profits. (I suppose it's cruel to say monster, but it's true.) By buying surrounding lots, the property grew and grew, and Villa Harrah became a gorgeous property. Every water pipe, every electrical line, everything in the house was color coded. I mean, it was a dream . . . but a dream with only one bedroom.

In the so-called basement, the ground level, they created a huge dining room that would seat maybe one hundred people, and they had a kitchen to support it. But the *real* comfort of Villa Harrah was that it gave Bill a place of solitude and quiet, and to the best of my knowledge no one was ever allowed to stay there overnight except Bill Harrah.

I recall once asking Bill, "Couldn't Bob Ring stay there one night?" His answer was no. This, even though Bill probably didn't stay overnight at Villa Harrah ten nights out of a year. The entertainers couldn't stay either. Oh, no–off limits! I couldn't even get Bob Hope in there, though I personally asked Bill. Bill had a lot of eccentricities, and that was one of them. I always thought that was kind of too bad, but what the hell did he care about my opinion? It was too bad that somebody as close and dear to Bill as Bob Ring wasn't given the opportunity to stay there overnight just for the thrill of it.

Villa Harrah was a significant part of Harrah's, but it was one of the noncontributory parts. We added up the days spent up there for the Internal Revenue Service, because they got on Bill, saying that these properties were for his personal use. We started adding the days of his personal use at Middle Fork Lodge and at Villa Harrah, and you could put them in your hip pocket. With retreats at Middle Fork Lodge, there was some business use, and to a lesser extent that was true of Villa Harrah, but Bill's personal use of the property was very limited. He didn't ask, "Will these properties contribute to the successful operation of Harrah's?" He simply wanted the property to be there when he wanted to go there.

The same circumstances related to a house Bill owned in Stanley, except there he was dealing with his personal money instead of corporate money. He needed to add onto the house a little bit here and there, and then he kept trying to buy adjoining lots for privacy. (His house was poorly situated, behind a Quonset hut owned by the telephone company and a warehouse building–one of the least attractive sites I can imagine.) He also bought other properties in Stanley for reasons that some may find odd:

Bill got to Stanley one Friday evening, and called the hotel there (if you could call it that), and said, "Sherry and I want to come to dinner."

He was told, "Sorry, Mr. Harrah. We're closing the dining room at six-thirty." That irritated him; he couldn't get over it. So he decided to build a restaurant.

Bill had the same experience with motor fuel. The service station was going to close at night, and he wanted it kept open twenty-four hours a day. The guy said, "Hell, I can't keep a service station open twenty-four hours a day," so Bill bought all the service stations he could find in the area. I think he ended up with three; two of them were junk, but one of them still works.

I would venture to say that either of those events–that is, the late dinner or the late fueling–could have been accomplished by making an appointment, a reservation, or a phone call. [laughter] But part of Bill's personality that was difficult for other people to understand was that he could not communicate well; he would not speak. He *would* talk to me a little bit . . . I think more than any other person. But hell, I wouldn't tell Bill not to buy the restaurant in Stanley. If he wanted to buy the restaurant, he'd buy the restaurant; it was his money. It wasn't that he wouldn't listen to my advice; it was just that I was smart enough not to give it. If Bill wanted to buy a helmet in Timbuktu, I'd go get the helmet for him. I wasn't about to tell him how to spend his money, but I did try to keep him out of trouble.

One of the reasons I got along with Bill was, "I want to be able to get done what you want to get done; and at the same time to do it so that you're protected, so you're not hurt." Witness the acquisition of Middle Fork Lodge as a simple example. I think most lawyers, under the circumstances, would have gone to Bill and said, "Well, Rex Lanham has given an option, and the federal government doesn't want to sell, so we can't buy the property." I got along with Bill because I could get things done, and I could keep things not only technically legal, but safe. We didn't want problems–we wanted to be on firm, dry ground all the time. My response to Bill's challenge was, "You give me the problem; let me find the best way we can get this done."

After Harrah's bought the Beech Queen Air, their first airplane, Bill got to thinking, "I'd like to learn to fly." A pilot in the naval reserve, a highly respected guy with some personality, said to Bill, "I'll teach you how to fly." Bill thought that was going to be wonderful. He had this speed image, and the "ability-to-drive-a-car" image, and he liked the looks of airplanes. He and I sat down when he decided he was going to learn to fly, and the first thing he did was get a catalog of airplanes–new airplanes, pretty airplanes. Of course, the airplanes that he was going to learn to fly in would be fixed-gear airplanes, not retract-able–that's where you have to start–but he looked at speed fairings over the wheels of airplanes, and thought, "Well, I'd like to change the paint design on that, and maybe I'd like to change the shape of that speed fairing a little bit." He designed color schemes, new paint lines, new speed fairings, so forth, on airplanes which he didn't own. But he was imagining that he was going to acquire them in his new hobby, learning to fly.

Bill went out to the Swede at Reno Flying Service–Ray Engblom, who is long since dead–and got in the training airplane with an instructor. I think he might have had two or three lessons, but I could tell these lessons didn't give him the feeling that he really wanted. Because he was such a hot automobile driver, he thought he could be a hot pilot . . . yet, aviation wasn't giving him the sensation he wanted. The minute you're five hundred feet off the ground, you have the sensation of standing still–you don't have any sensation of speed in an airplane. So I think that the loss of sensation of speed (and the noise and racket) kind of made him doubtful about learning to fly. Plus he had a coordination problem: Bill was an extremely well-coordinated man in an automobile, but he was having problems learning to fly. There are a number of things that go into aviation that are different from the world of driving–you've got to rely upon vision, not the seat of your pants, and upon instrument presentation, so it's a learning process.

Here was Bill, full of enthusiasm about learning to fly, and the temperature of his interest began fading out. His instructor had to call him and say, "Come on, Bill, we've got to get out to the airport."

They went through a series of beginning lessons, and then the naval reserve called, and this particular pilot went down to San Diego and was killed in a mid-air collision in his naval reserve duty. And at that point, Bill stopped all interest in learning to fly. He quit. Of course, it was a sad loss, because the pilot was a friend of Bill's. Bill lost the incentive to learn to fly, and he never got in the seat of an airplane again, except as a passenger.

I believe that Bill got interested in racing hydroplanes about 1957 or 1958, and got out of boat racing around 1971. (His first racing boat was called *Tahoe Miss*.) When Harrah's was running racing boats, we had Everett Adams rebuilding our Allison engines. Bill Stead, the local hero, was also soon employed by Bill. Stead lasted for about two years at Harrah's, working in public relations, but his real job was the racing boats, and he hired a guy down at Orange County Airport to boost the engines by water injection. When Harrah's parted ways with Stead, there was tremendous confusion. Out at Stead's ranch there were hundreds of parts for racing boats and engines, but nobody in Harrah's had run any inventory on who owned what. Bill Stead said, "Everything out here is mine." Harrah said, "Everything out there is ours." So we had one of the damnedest controversies you have ever seen over who owned what and who owned even the injector for the engines! It ended up in litigation, and it was very bitter, but simple inventory control could have handled it. Unfortunately, Bill Stead got killed in a plane accident in Florida in 1966, and that ended the litigation. Nobody wanted to see it end that way.

One time, Danny Kaye came to Reno in a Lear Jet. Danny took Bill on a demo flight, because Bill had never been on a Lear. Bill came back and said to me, "Wow! I can't believe it! Things come up so fast. They come up faster than you think they do."

Well, that was just like putting bait out there! The next thing we knew was that Harrah's had to have a jet aircraft. Shep was involved in this decision, and there was a debate over whether we *should* get a jet. After that, we had to decide on what type. Should we get a Lear Jet? What's good and what's bad about them? My recollection is that Harry Volpi was opposed to a Lear Jet, because the early Lears, the 24s and 23s particularly, were airplanes that could get ahead of the pilot pretty easily. (Harry Volpi was the guru of aviation for Harrah's. He had been in construction and maintenance for the Harrah's Club properties, but he eventually ended up in the restoration shop at HAC, primarily on the aviation side of things–that was his strength, and Bill really relied upon him. Harry was responsible for rebuilding "The City of Reno", the Ford Trimotor which was on display for many years at HAC; and he was the guy who recommended the purchase of Harrah's first Beech Queen Air, and later, when Beech changed from piston engines to turboprops, the first model King Air, the A-90.)

In any event, numbers of candidate jet aircraft were laid out for Bill, and the recommendation finally was to purchase a Jet Commander for a couple of reasons. One was that with its mid-wing, passengers had greater visibility. And, without question, the cabin was more comfortable than that of a Lear Jet. Even though it did not have the rocket-like performance of the Lear–it wouldn't climb like a Lear; it was a bigger airplane; it was slower, more clumsy–the safety issue that Volpi put forth, plus the cabin comfort issue, finally made Bill decide on the Jet Commander.

Bill had a habit: he wore his wristwatch on his right arm, which is not unique for a southpaw. When we flew, his right hand would come out, and his big watch would come with it. He would look at it, and then he'd reach in his pocket, take out a notebook, and write down the exact time of takeoff of the aircraft. He would also write down the time of landing, so he knew how long he'd been in the air on any given flight. He always asked the pilots before take-off, "How long is the flight?" and he was always checking reality against what they'd told him.

Harrah's Jet Commander came without thrust reversers, and a jet aircraft without thrust reversers rolls down the runway at a pretty high speed. Hell, I've landed Lears in Reno that have taken ten thousand feet to stop when thrust reversers didn't work; that's two miles! Normally, when pilots make a standard landing they let the aircraft roll, because otherwise the brakes burn out in a hurry. (They'll roll five to seven thousand feet with light braking before there's a turnoff at the Reno airport.) But Bill, with his watch and so forth . . . maybe we'd bypass the high-speed turnoff, and we'd go out to the second turnoff before we could turn to come back to Harrah's hangar. Finally, that got to Bill, and he said, "I want to land *shorter* than that."

The pilots would say, "Well, Mr. Harrah, this aircraft doesn't have any thrust reversers. It has only brakes." But Bill's rule was to make the first turn. The bottom line was that when you landed Harrah's Jet Commander, you went against all of your instincts: you stomped on the brakes; you gave it *maximum* braking. [laughter] Nothing is wrong with that, except that the brakes weren't designed to give maximum braking every time you landed. It got to the point where we required new brakes every seven trips because the pilots had to stand on the binders so hard and so tight. But it made Bill so happy! Here he was landing and making the first turnoff, and he grinned from ear to ear. It didn't bother him in the slightest that every seven such excursions meant new brakes! I don't know what the cost was for Harrah's, but I know what the cost is on my Cheyenne today, and a new brake on either side is three thousand dollars. You're talking heavy-duty expense when you're talking about aircraft braking. But it was another way to indulge Bill.

As time progressed, Bill became more and more withdrawn from his company and from the public. Not too many years went by before he built into the bottom of Harrah's Hotel, behind the Steak House, a private dining room, big enough to seat perhaps twenty people. Access to it was out of the bank building, down a fire escape, across a bridge, across Douglass Alley, through a door, down a couple more flights of stairs and into the basement where the Steak House was. That way we didn't have to walk through the casino; we could go strictly unnoticed from Bill's office through this circuitous labyrinth, and into the private dining room. Bill said he felt so much better having lunch there, because that way nobody bothered him; he didn't want to be bothered with people saying hello to him. The older he got and the more time went by, the more he wanted to insure his privacy, and he was reasonably successful in that venture. I don't recall a single instance in which Bill ate in a public Harrah's restaurant in Reno after the private dining room was built.

At Lake Tahoe, I don't think he ate anywhere but at Villa Harrah. He would spend many hours at Harrah's Automobile Collection, so we had the same situation there: we had a little private dining room. If I had lunch with him at HAC, we had lunch in the private room, and of course he spent his evenings at HAC.

Bill loved anything that had to do with automobiles, and he had a big leather briefcase that he would stuff with automobile magazines. He usually left the office by four o'clock, and would go out to Rancharrah, where dinner was at six o'clock sharp. After dinner, he would go to HAC and stay until ten or eleven o'clock at night, just walking around his cars. In later years HAC was his passion. All the parts that were bought for restoring his automobiles were on display tables, so that when Bill drove into HAC and parked his car in his private garage, he would walk in through the door, and there would be display tables with the various parts that someone had bought somewhere for him. Bill would look over the parts–pistons, carburetors, connecting rods, spark plugs, whatever–and then once he had seen them, they were taken away and put in inventory. [laughter]

One of the sad problems with HAC was that after Bill's death, I found we had no cataloged inventory. I mean, what was there was there, but you didn't know if there were ten spark plugs or a thousand spark plugs. I'll never know how they operated that place. I was never able to find an inventory at HAC, and I think I probably could have stolen several engines and three or four automobiles out of the place, and no one would ever have missed them. HAC was Bill's domain; Harrah's Club did not intrude.

It was said that Harrah's was the General Motors of the industry, and Mark Curtis and others were very proud of Harrah's controls, but they didn't bring those controls out to HAC; that was strictly off-limits. The people who ran Harrah's Club, ran only Harrah's Club. The people who ran HAC were pretty much mechanics and old car buffs, and there was never, in my observation, any skilled management at HAC.

Lee Jellison was the general manager at HAC. Lee was a fine person, a mechanic in Sacramento that Bill had run into and said, "Boy, I sure like your work. Come on up to Reno and work for me." So Lee Jellison came up, and he ran HAC, and one of the things he loved to do was get in an old car and drive around, or get on a motorcycle and ride around the yard and grin from ear to ear. He was happy being around all the cars, and Bill was happy having Lee there. Lee certainly understood the art of being a mechanic and an automobile restorer, but he did not understand the art of inventory control or management.

Bill's last planning act was to build his new auto museum out on the I-80 property, for which we acquired substantial acreage. It took Lloyd Dyer several years with the help of Ted Mattson, a local realtor, to acquire an old dairy farm and bakery and several other properties, and do the assemblage. Various people in the company tried to plan how to build the so-called "Harrah's World" out there, but those were all exercises in futility, because there was going to be no Harrah's World unless Bill Harrah wanted it. The dream of Harrah's World was weird, anyhow—it was, "Maybe if we acquired enough property, we could run a railroad train around the perimeter of the property, because Bill has an old train at the HAC." You can imagine trying to run an old train from the museum around out there! You couldn't have kept that train together for two hours, let alone years, even if we could assemble the train and put it out there. [laughter]

The purpose was to create a showcase for the automobile collection, so before Bill died he commissioned a design for a hotel-casino on that property to exhibit automobiles. It was to be a very small casino, a small number of hotel rooms, and *five hundred* automobiles on display in a beautiful showcase; and it was pretty clear that the casino would not be big and profitable enough to support the property or the project. I was at one of the last board meetings that Bill ever attended, when they presented the model for the property and for the new development on I-80 with the HAC museum. The board authorized the expenditure of forty-five million dollars—an unheard-of sum in those days—to build this hotel-casino-museum. Nobody *dared* to sit down and pencil out the loss or the cost; nobody *dared* to come up with a projection. I never heard anybody say, "It's going to cost forty-five million dollars, and the projected losses are going to be X, Y, Z per year." Everybody knew it was going to lose money, but the question was "What does Bill want?" Bill wanted the museum, so the board authorized that project. [laughter]

I think the first thing I did as chairman of Harrah's after Bill died was to cancel that project. It would have been disaster for the company. The company had no money; the company's earnings were in decline; and Bill had substantial personal debt besides the estate taxes to pay. I would not even have taken on that venture if Bill had *lived*, except that the question before the board was not, "Is this a good idea?"

[9]

Tropicana and Showboat

IN 1964 I GOT A CALL FROM BILL HARRIGAN, a major share-holder in the Tropicana in Las Vegas. He wanted some advice on how you buy out dissident directors when a company isn't doing what it should do, and so forth. I went to Las Vegas and lived in the hotel for a month, and worked with Harrigan, and met with the board of directors, and we scared them. The board had hired another Reno lawyer to represent them, and I kind of walked on him a little bit . . . I have fun doing that now and then. [laughter] In effect, we wrote them some letters that said, "If you don't do this, you've got some legal problems, because we are going to sue you." Shortly thereafter the board of directors acquiesced in all of our demands. The result was that when we resolved the Harrigan matter and got that behind us, the Tropicana called up and said, "Hey, we like what you did so well we want you to become our lawyer. Come on down here." [laughter]

The Tropicana was then the Tiffany of the Strip. It was a typical Las Vegas Strip hotel, which meant it was a series of low-rise buildings attached together. It gradually expanded and had two showrooms–the main showroom for the Folies Bergere, and the Blue Room for individual acts. It also had the first gourmet restaurant, as I recall, in Las Vegas, and a coffee shop that served excellent Jewish food. This was important to the Tropicana, because it had a large Jewish clientele from Chicago.

There was a handful of owners at the time I got involved with the Tropicana, and it was managed by J. K. Houssels, Sr., who started gambling in Las Vegas in 1931. Houssels was an engineer who had come to Las Vegas about the time Boulder Dam was being contemplated, but he stayed and became a gambler on Fremont Street. Everyone in Las Vegas knew Kell. He had been an investor in the Tropicana, and had had a minor interest in it, as far as I know, when it first opened about 1957. But the Tropicana had lots of problems, and to save it, Kell simply dug in his own pocket and put out the cash. The history is clear–he put in the bankroll and got the company running, which is something that couldn't happen today with all the controls that exist. And Kell had an old-time gambler's loyalty to his partners–he wasn't like a lot of people in the gambling business today. He treated his partners fair and square, and they sat on the board.

Kell would come to work at the Trop at eight o'clock in the morning; you could set your clock by it. At five o'clock p.m., he would walk out, but by seven o'clock he'd be back, and he would be there until eleven or eleven-thirty at night; then he'd go home. Lots of casino owners and operators used to work similar schedules. (Jimmy Contratto did the same thing over at the Cal-Neva.) The old timers in the casino business ran hands-on casinos. Joe Kelley, down at the Showboat . . . you could bank on it–you'd go there in the morning, and Joe would be in his office or on the floor. You would go there at night, and Joe would be there. The people who ran these joints *lived* in the joints. I lived with them a lot, and I spent a lot of evenings with Kell and a lot of daytimes, too. On occasion, I even counted money in casinos, and I felt privileged to do that. I was with Kell when he put in the first TV monitors I had ever seen in the state: we would sit in his office and try to monitor the games. (I've monitored games through binoculars, and I've monitored games from catwalks . . . and I wish my eyes were better. But I thought that the early TV monitoring was horrible. I couldn't make sense of what I was seeing.)

Kell had monthly board meetings, and early in 1965 I started sitting in on them. A hotel-casino's legal problems are many: You have the sheriff coming out to see you; somebody wants a political contribution; you find that the cigarette machines don't work; the furrier is going to build a competing fur shop in another hotel-casino in violation of his lease . . . . Or the casino isn't handling its money right; or the markers aren't paid; or Jon Peters set the hair of a famous performer and demands payment from the Tropicana of twelve thousand dollars . . . . There are just myriad legal problems that come up. Eventually you become close enough to the companies so you become a board member as well. Being a board member, you get to help decide policy, and you get a lot better insight into where the company is going. Then you begin to select other people to do a lot of the hands-on legal work.

The Tropicana began to decline over the years–people in the Tropicana may argue with me over that, but I thought it was declining because it was not putting back into the property the capital reinvestment that needed to be made on an annual basis. Instead, it was taking its earnings to buy out dissidents or dissatisfied shareholders. That had started in 1964, and the terms of repurchase were rather onerous on the company. In effect, the situation was that if there was a partner who said, "Hey, I can't get along with you guys anymore; I want out," then Houssels would try to find a way to buy him out. That was kind of the code of the West. The way they found to buy him out was to have the company repurchase or redeem his shares, so over the period between 1964 and 1968 capital was being devoted very substantially to the repurchase of shares of partners who wanted out. I use the word "partners" loosely–I mean shareholders who wanted out before the company was eventually sold to Carl Pohlad, who controlled, among other things, Texas International Airlines, the Minnesota Twins, and the Marquette National Bank in Minneapolis. We sold the Tropicana to Carl Pohlad in 1968. It had gradually lost its elite customer base as new properties like Caesar's, for example, were built.

About the time that I started with the Tropicana I became involved with the Showboat, because J. K. Houssels (senior and junior) were also involved in the Showboat. The Showboat was a similar situation, but at the other end of the spectrum. It was not the Tiffany of the Strip, but catered to local Las Vegas people. It had a large bowling alley, and in effect dealt with the common man. The Showboat was on the Boulder Highway, a very tough location, and it had to succeed by marketing to a different person. Although it was a corporation, it was owned by a half dozen or more partners, and it was run with monthly meetings at which the owners were present.

Going to every Showboat board meeting and listening to the partners talk and eventually becoming a member of the board was educational. I learned how a different company serving a different clientele worked and functioned. At the Showboat we were not buying out dissident partners–we were trying to continue the company and make it succeed, and while I was on the board, we built a hotel tower. That hotel tower is still in use today, and I am proud of that facility, even though it was built on a strict budget and was not built to be deluxe. The hotel rooms there surely need refurbishing today, but the basic facility makes those rooms functional and successful.

When I first went to the Showboat, all it had was a series of low-rise motel rooms around in back. Probably some of them had been built in Bill Moore's time. Moore, who was given great credit for the creation of the Showboat, was famous in the early days because he was a member of the Nevada Tax Commission, which was responsible for issuing gaming licenses and making sure that gaming taxes were paid. He was the so-called owner of the Last Frontier, and it was the pride of Las Vegas that Bill Moore was wearing both hats–that he was a licensed operator at the Frontier as well as being a member of the licensing authority. Bill gradually fell from grace and succumbed to drink. Mr. Houssels, Sr., who had the Las Vegas Club, as I recall, and the El Cortez, then came out and took ownership of the Showboat.

At Showboat board meetings, we'd run up and down the figures in detail: "Why is per off in a pit? Why is this? Why is that?" However, we didn't bring up personnel issues. The Showboat was run under the tight thumb of Joe Kelley, and he didn't want any of his people to come up and talk to the board.

[laughter] Even though the Houssels family dominated both the Trop and the Boat, the Showboat was operated differently in that respect.

Today in the Showboat organization we have something we call MBO–Management By Objective. We have objectives that have different weights, and as a member of the compensation committee, I periodically review the performance of the senior executives and top management of the company–how they are accomplishing their objectives. (It's up to these four or five top officers to evaluate the people down below.) We have felt in the Showboat that there is room for some subjective evaluation, because we're dealing with human beings, although the principal measures that we have are certainly objective measurements. With respect to the chairman's and president's roles in each of the Showboat subsidiaries, we have a quantum which allows for a subjective evaluation element. There are certain things that are just resistant to being measured in dollars-and-cents terms; otherwise, you could just manage by computer. There should always be an element of subjective judgment, even in a system which says, "If you can't count it, it doesn't count."

In the late 1960s I started serving on the boards of directors of some casinos. (When I was with little companies, like the Cal-Neva, I had served on the board, but I'm talking about public companies, such as the Showboat, the Tropicana and Harrah's–real boards of directors instead of nominal boards of directors.) I didn't get on a board without first being counsel, and sometimes being a secretary or something in a corporation, which seemed to be an appropriate place for somebody like me. The transition was simply from counsel and secretary to being on a board, and there wasn't a crystal clear line of demarcation. Becoming a board member was a promotion, and certainly well received, but it was kind of accidental:

In a conversation one day in 1968, J. K. Houssels, Sr., said, "You know, I've been thinking about appointing another member to the Showboat board of directors, and all of a sudden I thought, 'Why isn't Mead Dixon on the board?'" He said, "Why aren't you on the board?"

I said, "You never asked me."

He said, "Well, you ought to be on the board. You're here all the time; you're here at the meetings. Will you come on the board?"

I said, "Sure." That's how I got on the board at the Showboat.

Shortly after that I got on the board of the Tropicana, but there were no landmark changes in my relationship with either company. As a board member I was probably more free in expressing a view at a board meeting than I would be simply as a lawyer, but I always got along with these guys . . . and with Bill Harrah. When Harrah's went public we had to create a board. I knew Ralph Phillips, who was one of the founders of Dean Witter, so I put him on the Harrah's board. I told Bill, "Here's what your board ought to be: a, b, c, d," and I didn't put my name forward as a board member, although I could have. (I didn't ever ask to be put on a board.) The consequence was that I didn't go on the Harrah's board until 1975, and then it was one of those light bulb ideas of Bill's–the same thing that Houssels had said: "Hey, how come you're not on the board?"

"You didn't ask me."

Board meetings varied by company and management style. The Tropicana and Showboat (or the Boat, as people called it) groups liked to meet monthly with their boards, and they liked to have management detail–minutiae–brought up, such as, "Is this a good advertising program? Shall we spend three hundred thousand dollars enlarging the refrigeration in the kitchen?" In other words, there was a really close relationship between operations and the board. Both of those companies were dominated by the Houssels style of management, which was, in effect, "Let's sit down here and decide what's going on with the company, what we should do next, and whether we should have four towels or three towels in a room." Now, this was in addition to a financial review, and both of those Las Vegas properties had detailed financial reports and detailed discussion and analysis of the reports right down to daily operations during each meeting.

If I owned a hotel, and I was there every day running it and watching it, I would "get the cost screwed down pretty good," to use Joe Kelley's language. That's what comes from hands-on management. You're there every day, so you know if you've got an excess janitor or an excess porter; you know if you've got the tables over-scheduled, too many dealers there; or you've got too many tables spread and no customers. The old Nevada style was store-style: you didn't think you needed the modern, corporate techniques of planning and conception, because you were running the place every day just like you were running a service station. But when these places get pretty big, that old style doesn't always work.

Old man Houssels ("Senior," we used to call him) had two sayings: "If it ain't broke, don't fix it;" and "Don't tinker with a fine watch." That meant, "Just leave everything alone. Everything is going just the way I like it. I don't see any problems. We'll just go on day to day," and that's what we did. Our problems, from the board point of view, were not planning problems. Our problems were making sure that the accounts and operating details were right, rather than the big picture of: "Where is the company going? What are we going to do five years from now? Are we grooming the right people? Do we have the right systems aboard?"

Neither the Showboat nor Tropicana had as sophisticated an operation as Harrah's. They did not have adequate bonus programs, to the best of my recollection, and the Showboat did not even have a budget. I resigned from the Showboat board in 1978 after Bill Harrah's death. My full-time obligations at Harrah's, with the Harrah estate and with Harrah's as a company, left no time to deal with the Showboat.

In 1987 I was on the Showboat board again, a second time around, and I became aggressive because they were running that company with no budget . . . whereas I was used to planning and thinking. Budgeting is part of the process, but it's not a substitute for planning; you need a combination. As I watched Showboat's earnings continuing to drop, year after year, I had to put the question to Joe Kelley, "What is your plan, Mr. Chairman? What will you present to the board? What is your financial projection for next year?" I decided I had to agitate and I did. I put all my effort into improving the management process at Showboat, and I think it has paid off.

[10]

Harrah's Merges with Holiday Inns

IN THE LAST SIX YEARS OF HIS LIFE, Bill wasn't interested in the growth of Harrah's, and if Bill wasn't interested, things didn't go forward. (He probably knew that with his aneurysm he had a terminal illness.) Bill was interested in his matrimonial adventures, and I *know* that he had a focus on what he wanted to do as an individual–but he was not focusing on "How can I make Harrah's grow? What is the future of the company?" He had stopped that. He had his venture in Stanley, Idaho, and his automobile collection, which dominated his life . . . and he was trying to straighten out his domestic life, which was usually in turmoil, although the last four years he stayed married to Verna, which gave him some peace and happiness. And Harrah's club . . . I won't call it a cash cow, but the business was generating reasonable money, a little better profit each year. The place was clean, and Bill made sure that Bob Ring and Rome Andreotti were around and kept all the light bulbs burning; but he had no interest in expanding to Las Vegas or taking on a new challenge.

I had some serious problems with Bill that I couldn't correct. For example, automobiles. Bill had sixteen automobiles assigned to him–company motor pool–but he didn't own a single automobile in his own name; he didn't have a title to a car. Why would he buy a car? The company provided him with sixteen of them. I said, "Bill, for Christ's sake, you ought to own one car! (In today's life, with the Mike Milkens–the junk bond king who was convicted of violating the SEC code–and all today's perks, it would mean nothing having sixteen automobiles, but back then it would.) I said, "That's the kind of thing you get in trouble with if we go public and somebody starts inquiring."

Bill's salary from Harrah's was very minimal. We kept increasing it as fast as we could in later years, but for years he was making seventy-five thousand a year, then a hundred thousand a year, and, when we went public, two hundred thousand a year. Eventually, shortly before he died, his salary peaked at about three hundred and seventy-five thousand dollars. His total annual income, salary and stock, was under three million dollars at the time of his death–probably closer to two million. Finally we pledged 50 percent of his Harrah's stock with Chase Manhattan Bank for a twenty-five million dollar loan. I remember the people at Chase saying, "Boy, this Mr. Harrah must really be smart. He wants to borrow twenty-five million dollars; he's really got some ideas for the company." He had *no* ideas for the company. He wanted to borrow the money so he could enlarge Stanley, Idaho, and so he could travel around the world and take care of his personal lifestyle, which is exactly what he did. There wasn't one quarter of that money that went into any plan for the company.

I didn't know Bill was going to die. He had planned to go on to New York after seeing his physicians at the Mayo Clinic at the end of June, 1978. Nonetheless, just before he went to Mayo the last time, he had me prepare a codicil to his will.

I got a call from Rochester, Minnesota, probably from Bob Hudgens, saying Bill had had surgery, and the operation had not gone well. So I got on a plane and went there immediately and met with the doctors. (I can't say I met with Bill; I was with Bill, but he was a quivering, shaking body lying on a table and dying.) Mayo Clinic was kind enough to allow me to look at all of Bill's medical records, and I went through them from the day he had started at the Mayo Clinic to the day of his death. The records revealed that Bill not only had had the aneurysm six years earlier, but that follow-up examinations had indicated that he was likely to have *another* aneurysm. He had a very serious health problem, but he had not disclosed it to anyone at Harrah's, and you can pretty much say that for the last six years of his life, after the repair of his first aneurysm, Bill knew that he was living on borrowed time. That accounts for his change in life-style–he decided to enjoy Harrah's and enjoy life, borrow money, spend money, go into debt, play with Stanley, Idaho, and, in effect, buy lots of automobiles and have fun rather than build Harrah's future.

When Bill Harrah died on June 30, 1978, he had $500,000 in life insurance that was payable to the company. George Drews, the chief financial officer of the company, said, "Book the $500,000 on the last day of the fiscal year." We were on a July 1-June 30 fiscal year, so that helped our earnings picture for the year . . . otherwise we would have been down more. George laughed about booking that extra $500,000, which supported the company's declining earnings, and it became kind of an in-house joke: they said, "In his last act, Bill tried to help the company."

After Bill died I came back to Reno and tried to figure out what to do next with the company, which was my responsibility because I was the executor of Bill's estate, which was almost entirely stock in Harrah's! [laughter] He also had some shares of stock in Stanharrah (his Stanley, Idaho, property), which we had put in a Nevada corporation, and he had his Rancharrah property out on South Virginia Street. Of course, 50 percent of Bill's Harrah's stock was pledged to Chase Manhattan Bank for a twenty-five million dollar personal note, but fortunately only about thirteen million had been drawn down, so we didn't have the whole twenty-five million to pay.

I had to determine what to do with the company, and how to pay Bill's personal debts and estate taxes without any money, and how to establish the necessary trusts for his widow and his children. Now, all of that didn't happen instantaneously–you try to look at the terrain before you start walking through it. I spent a couple of nights in the mountains with a sleeping bag and backpack, thinking about it, because I didn't want to make a mistake, and I didn't want to have any personal selfishness or Dixon goals stand in the way of the overall objective. The vacuum that was created by Bill's death left a company that was now, in effect, leaderless, and I had to think about the impact of that on the future of the company from the perspective of the employees, management, the community, and the financial community. It was clear that we would need to have access to the financial community at some point, and to do that you had to have a company that had the appearance, at least, of a well-oiled machine, of a functioning company. [laughter]

I could not accomplish what was needed from my law office five or six blocks away from Harrah's, communicating by telephone; and I could not simply allow Harrah's management to run the company and make decisions: while they knew how to operate, I didn't think they had the big picture . . . and I had to work with the big picture. I knew something about the strengths and weaknesses of Harrah's as a company, and something about the casino industry fitting into the community and business worlds, so I held a meeting of the board of directors and I asked that I be elected chairman of the board . . . which I was. The voting members who were Harrah's management people would have been Lloyd Dyer and Rome Andreotti (I don't recall Bob Ring *ever* being at a board meeting, so he must not have been a member of that board), but the directors who were the important ones to me were the outside directors: Frances Crumley, Art Smith, Ralph Phillips, and myself. (I may have missed one or two people.)

I did not want to become a target. I wanted to be a leader and to get things done, but I was very much aware that my taking over Bill's position as chairman would be misunderstood, and that it might cause animosity or hard feelings within the company. So I wanted to be extremely delicate in dealing with Harrah's management, the board, and the Harrah's community. I had to use finesse, and my approach was to substitute the Harrah's board of directors for Bill Harrah, rather than substituting Mead Dixon for Bill Harrah. This meant that we would have monthly meetings of the board rather than the customary quarterly meetings. The monthly meetings would discuss more management, vision, goal and detail problems than had been the past practice. In other words, I wanted the board to be the governing body of Harrah's, and to participate in making decisions. That way, the focus would not be on "Mead Dixon says this," but that the board of directors says that this is what we're doing. You know, anybody could come in with the voting power–and I had the voting power–and simply say, "This is what I want, fellas, and I'm the boss." I wanted to avoid that kind of confrontation, and I wanted to elevate the status of Harrah's board members from simple robots to participants who could see where the company was going. I mean, I wanted to utilize their abilities–they were all intelligent people. I wanted to create a team, and I think I accomplished that.

The next thing I wanted to do was create a perception that there would be no changes in Harrah's–that there was an excellent management team in place that had been well-groomed by Bill Harrah; that it was the best management in the state of Nevada; and that it would continue unabated. To further this perception, I asked Lloyd Dyer, who was president of the company, to become chief executive officer. Well, that diminished my apparent outsider's role and increased Lloyd's apparent role. In fact, however, the decisions that were being made about the future of the company were decisions that lay within my purview. This helped reinforce the image of Harrah's as continuing with no changes after Bill's death, although there were and *had* to be changes after Bill's death for many, many reasons. The company had built into itself some of the problems you see in Washington, D.C., today–a few too many perks. I think management knew that, but it's something they had grown up with, so . . . .

Once I got established as chairman, we had an overview of the company at board meetings and discussions. There were some pet things I needed to stop, but I had support. I stopped the forty-five million dollar project to build a casino/automobile museum out on I-80 . . . killed it dead. But if I'd sat still and let things coast, that project would have gone on. Another general philosophical change was that we were going to buy no more automobiles for Harrah's Automobile Collection, and we were going to get that operation under control.

Then we took a look at Middle Fork Lodge. It may sound unimportant, but Middle Fork Lodge was costing somewhere between one and two million dollars a year to operate. From a standpoint of contributing value to the company, it was worthless. Besides being worthless, it was a temptation, in the sense that Harrah's officers–and Bill had encouraged this, of course–could get in Harrah's airplane and go to Middle Fork Lodge and go elk hunting. The company would pay for the elk-hunting trip, and air transportation back and forth, and for the operation of the lodge. It made no sense to me; it was sending the wrong message to management. So I came to the conclusion that we had to stop the operation of Middle Fork Lodge in order to save a million dollars or more a year. It's an easy way to earn money, isn't it, by stopping spending?

So we began shutting down Middle Fork Lodge. We hired helicopters and began pulling the antique automobiles out. We brought out the art collection, which was very disappointing–the Charles Russells and so forth that had been purchased for Middle Fork Lodge were not as valuable or as attractive in the real world as they seemed at the time they were bought. They were genuine, but they were really not first-caliber art. After all this, I curtailed the operation of Middle Fork Lodge to a caretaker status; we didn't send officers up anymore.

We also took a look at many other nickel-and-dime things, such as Harrah's air force, which I never did *fully* get under control. Harrah's air force was employing a total of twenty-eight people, but it really didn't contribute anything to the bottom line of the company, as far as I could determine. Now, that was petty stuff, excepting as it set a *tone* for management. My idea was to tell management that I wanted them to focus upon the success of the company, and not upon its frills or frivolities. I don't know why we ever needed the air force, anyway–we had four airplanes! We had two to support Middle Fork Lodge, and we had two jet aircraft, and there just wasn't any reason in my opinion to have two jet aircraft. After all, during Bill's lifetime we only had a property at Harrah's Tahoe and a property in Reno, and you can't use jet aircraft to go there. We did employ the jet aircraft for some customer use and for some entertainer use, flying entertainers back and forth, but we probably could have very well gotten along with a single aircraft; and as it eventuated, today they don't have *any* aircraft, and the company works fine.

We had under construction at the time an expansion across Center Street, and the so-called Harrah's garage and Harrah's office building further out on Rock Street. They were projects that you might or might not have gone forward with, but they were really aimed at operation and increasing the capacity of the company; in other words, they weren't just toys. So those projects continued.

This was a period of getting into the saddle, getting used to what was happening, and starting to have all of the daily reports come to my desk. Unfortunately, just then Bob Ring moved into Bill Harrah's old office; he just kind of moved in–that was part of the inside intrigue in the company. I went in to Bill's office, and there was Bob Ring sitting there! Bob is the nicest guy in the world, and I think he may have felt uncomfortable, but was I going to have an office at Harrah's, or was I going to be given a closet and play their game? So I had to say, "I'm sorry, Bob, but I want you to move out. We'll create an office for you that's substantial and fits you, but this is the office that was the chairman's office; and since I'm the chairman, I'm going to occupy it."

Bob dearly loved Bill Harrah, and he said, "Can I have his desk?"

I said, "You can have every bit of his furniture–orange chairs, blue chairs and all." That made Bob extremely happy, and we created the office next door to mine for him. We moved Bill's furniture into it, including his desk, which was a thin plank that spread out, and his orange chairs and so forth. It seemed to make Bob very happy.

I put in my kind of office furniture, not Bill Harrah's kind. Bill's furniture was flamboyant, and I wanted to give a different message. I wanted to give a message of my personality and my role in the company, so I brought in a traditional brown desk, and traditional, conventional chairs, and established those . . . and I created a conference area. I'd been very successful in the practice of law in having a small conference table in my office so that clients didn't have to sit in front of my desk and look at me behind it, and be separated. So I created a conference area in my Harrah's office, so if we had three or four people to meet, we'd all sit down at the table and talk. That way I wasn't a lord sitting behind a desk, giving orders; I was part of a *team*.

During the process of having one-on-one interviews with the officers of the company, I learned that there were some areas that were troublesome: an unacceptable personnel system, unacceptable planning in the company, an unacceptable slot system, and an unacceptable management information system (MIS). We were also weak in marketing, but we had a reputation for being an excellent company, and we had to keep that reputation out there in front.

Our management information systems (the security programs and the accounting programs and the reports, and so forth) were really quite antiquated. Bill Archer had created the systems, and pretty much done so by programming them his way with patchwork here and there . . . nobody could really understand the programs, except him. [laughter] They were all done on an *ad hoc* basis, and were regarded by the independent accountants as being unacceptably weak. When we attempted to make the necessary corrections, we found that we didn't have any organized systems. It was just whatever Bill Archer wanted to create, he created; and if he should die, we were really going to be, in George Bush's terms, in deep doo-doo. Well, Archer did die, of course, so I had a totally unacceptable MIS system.

At the same time that I was trying to strengthen the company, I was faced with the obligations that I had with respect to Bill's estate and the estate taxes. I had to marshal his assets and find some way of dealing with this, but I knew that if there were any appearance of financial weakness, it would handicap me in negotiating any transaction that would bail the estate out of its problems. Bill had left substantial debt, and left his stock in hock . . . but he left no money, and I was faced with a pending cash crunch when the estate tax came due. We couldn't just go to the company and say, "Give us a lot of money!" because the company didn't have the money. Even if it had, I don't know how I could have gotten it out except by declaring a dividend, or maybe selling or buying something. [laughter] Also, we had other shareholders to think of, because at about this time there were substantial conversions of the outstanding subordinated debentures, and Bill's ownership in the company began to dilute itself down to somewhere close to 70 percent. I couldn't, in good conscience, come up with a deal that would not treat other shareholders *in pari passu*. The way I did it was this: the principal shareholders of the company would be either Bill's estate, or, after the administration of the estate, the trusts that he created for his heirs. In broad perspective, approximately half of his estate (or half of his stock) was in a trust to benefit his widow, Verna, and the other half was in a trust to benefit his two minor children. The controllers of his trusts would be, in effect, the controlling shareholders of the company.

I could see that the heirs would want to run Harrah's the way Bill had always run it, and they would probably want to have personal involvement in management decisions. That suggested that in the long run trying to be a fiduciary executor and one of three fiduciary trustees, and yet manage Harrah's and be in charge of it, was going to be impossible–or at least exceedingly uncomfortable. So I thought that the best thing I could do would be to dispose of Harrah's–to negotiate an acquisition merger into some larger company, so that Harrah's would be properly managed and the long-term asset that the heirs had would be highly marketable shares of stock in a successful company.

I used the firm of Dean Witter as my investment counsel, in large part because Ralph Phillips was on our board. (I had brought him in to Harrah's as a friend.) Phillips was a founding partner, with Dean Witter, of Dean Witter, Inc., in 1927, and he was a highly intelligent man, the soul of integrity, and very comfortable to work with. From Dean Witter we needed some appraisal of Harrah's and Harrah's stock for estate tax purposes, but principally I wanted them to help me identify potential merger candidates. Then, ultimately, I would want Dean Witter to give me advice and recommendations as to the fairness of any terms that I might be able to negotiate in a merger.

In the beginning the rest of the board did not know about my concept of needing to merge, but I told the accountants that if they wanted to continue to be accountants for Harrah's, they should stop scratching out numbers trying to leverage this out for the family, because that was not the course of action I was going to take. Of course, the accountants were really trying to be creative, and they were concerned that we would have some obligations coming up, which I can understand. They had the concept, which was pretty much written into Bill's will, that we would continue the company without change and operate it for the benefit basically of the Harrah family. But in my opinion, that was unworkable, and I didn't want to have a lot of people sitting around and pushing their pencils trying to come up with that concept. "And I don't want to hear anybody raise that issue again," I said.

With the help of John Sande of Vargas, Bartlett & Dixon we identified ten or eleven major United States companies that appeared to be desirable and potential merger candidates. John, of course, was my stalwart, my principal strength, in working with the estate. Phil Satre did a lot, too–at that time he was still with the law firm–but my recollection is that it was John Sande that I worked with in identifying these major companies, reviewing their financial statements, and reviewing their history, as if *we* were making an investment in *them*. Dean Witter made the calls to the companies, asking them whether or not they would have a merger discussion, and got turned down by every one.

Holiday Inns was a company that I threw into the mix, not a company that Dean Witter had selected or recommended. Quite frankly, Dean Witter said, "Holiday Inns is not really a prime company. We think there are some problems in that company that you need to be careful of." But Holiday Inns was a *potential* merger candidate. My recollection is that I personally called Kemmons Wilson, who was then chairman of Holiday Inns, and asked him if I could visit with him and discuss Harrah's as a potential merger candidate. He said yes. I can't remember where the first meeting took place, but I think I flew to Chicago in August of 1978, and met in the O'Hare Hilton with three or four people from Holiday Inns as they were passing through on their way back to Memphis. We had a general discussion, and they asked me a lot of questions about the casino business, because at this time Holiday was interested (with Lou Walter) in a venture in Atlantic City. I answered the questions directly and straight from the shoulder.

I came back to Reno either that night or the next day, and then made arrangements again with Kemmons Wilson and in September or October flew to Memphis, where I looked at the Holiday Inns operation and made the acquaintance of the various people who were their movers and shakers. So the Holiday Inns discussions began, but there was no merger agreement early on, and no inclination to merge early on. It was a matter of, "Who are you, and who am I, and what's the future? Is there room for Holiday Inns in the gaming business? Is Harrah's too big for Holiday Inns? Is there a synergy between the two companies? Is there some kind of future role that they could play together?" Of course, at this time I wasn't sure that Holiday Inns was the only candidate out there . . . but I kept getting turned down by other companies.

At the time that I began to talk with them, there was some discomfort among the Holiday Inns board members with respect to the proposed merger, as well as with getting into the casino business with Lou Walter in Atlantic City. Holiday was part of the Deep South–the Christian South–and there was a long period of time when all Holiday Inns board meetings were opened with a prayer. Holiday Inns was an organization that had grown up around Kemmons Wilson and his group of friends, and they were all reasonably conservative and religious people. But there was change brewing at Holiday when I started my merger discussions, and eventually there were some resignations of senior executives because of the casino gaming issue . . . one of the most senior being the president of the company. That gave me encouragement and hope to continue in my discussions.

The focus of my discussions shifted from Kemmons Wilson over to Roy Winegardner, and then from Roy Winegardner primarily to Mike Rose, who had been a lawyer for Roy. (At this time Mike was president of the hotel side of Holiday Inns. Mike was quite clearly not only the protégé of Roy Winegardner, but his heir apparent, even though Roy was just coming into his ascendancy and just becoming chairman of Holiday.) I got along well with Mike Rose. He was tough and he had an incisive mind; he had a tremendous analytical ability, far superior to mine. He was skilled in numbers, financial statements, and corporate organization, and I think Mike knew that a merger between Harrah's and Holiday would be good for the long-range future of Holiday, because already their hotel system was becoming very tired. They were dealing with many franchise operators, and the quality of their properties was becoming impaired by the passage of time and by the economics of the industry, which was something I didn't recognize. I didn't know anything about the Holiday Inns system, except that I thought it was the best motel system in the country.

There was always an interest on the part of Holiday to help create a merger that would work, but there were financial problems. There was a limit to what Holiday Inns could pay for Harrah's, and there was a limit on the value that Harrah's would have. I wasn't really privy to the Holiday evaluation of Harrah's long-range value, but I knew what I wanted for Harrah's stock, and what I thought the value of Harrah's as a company was. If it was a straight merger, Harrah's would have been worth probably 25 percent of the total value of the merged companies, and Holiday was understandably nervous about letting Harrah's become too strong in the stock-owning or guidance process of Holiday Inns. So we tailored a merger that would not give Harrah's that much weight in the Holiday Inns system . . . but that meant that there had to be some *cash* put up by Holiday. I didn't want Harrah's to run Holiday Inns, but I did want it to have a voice on the board, because so much Holiday Inns stock would be held by the Harrah estate.

In early 1979 we got very close to a merger with Holiday, but were unable to consummate a transaction, so we did something different: Harrah's and Holiday entered into an agreement that all future casino expansions would be joint ventures, except those that were already underway or planned–the Holiday Inns acquisition of a minority interest in the Holiday Center Strip in Las Vegas; the Holiday Marina project with Lou Walter in Atlantic City; and the proposed Harrah's Atlantic City hotel. We agreed that any future casino expansion by either company would be done only through the joint venture. From the Harrah's point of view, there was some advantage to the joint venture, because Holiday Inns was a major company with a strong position on the stock exchange, and with access to financing *far* beyond what Harrah's ever had. (We had still not completely gotten rid of the casino gaming stigma, so that financing for casino expansion or construction by a company such as Harrah's was limited.)

So we now had a contractual joint venture, which was like a headlock–they couldn't expand in the casino business unless they took us in; we couldn't expand in the casino business unless we took them in. Theoretically that would mean that if I found a wonderful casino expansion, and could convince Holiday of its importance, we'd have the Holiday Inns team working with us, and we'd a have a good team. On the other hand, if they found a good casino expansion, they could go nowhere without talking to us, which would also help us. It seemed to me that there were business advantages there; it seemed to me also that it made Harrah's that much more visible to the New York financial markets.

Another value to the joint venture arrangement was that it kept contact between Harrah's and Holiday alive. Both of us knew that we wanted more than the joint venture arrangement; both of us knew that downstream it would be logical for us to merge. If we had the joint venture arrangement with Holiday, who else could Holiday merge with? Could they run in and make a deal with Caesar's Palace? They couldn't. They were locked out of the business, and couldn't make a deal with any other casino operator. So if Holiday wanted to grow in the casino business, they only had one way to grow, and that was with Harrah's.

In the fall of 1979 we reached an agreement on merger, but it came apart because the stock of Holiday Inns fell. When you negotiate a merger where stocks, debentures or securities are involved, you have to make all of your transactions contingent upon the securities staying within a trading range or value until the merger goes through. Holiday Inns' stock changed in value to the point that the merger transaction wouldn't work.

We negotiated and renegotiated, and over a period of time finally were able to get a transaction that stuck together and worked. We submitted it to the shareholders of both companies, and my recollection is that it was February 28, 1980, when we finally put the merger together with a formal vote of shareholders. The merger was a done deal, and as of March 1, 1980, Harrah's was part of the Holiday Inns organization.

Two of us from Harrah's were put on the Holiday Inns board. I was one member, and Art Smith, who was then chairman of First National Bank of Nevada, was the other. In this transitory period, Art and I were able to keep the Holiday Inns board cognizant of Harrah's and the Harrah's point of view. Art Smith did a very good job that way. He is a gregarious, outgoing person, and he established personal relationships with the members of the Holiday Inns board, and was really a good Harrah's representative . . . if you can say that, because we were really one company. Of course, what we wanted was a smooth transition so that Harrah's would become an integral part of Holiday Inns, but we had to go through the culture shock that came with being part of Holiday. I think perhaps a two-way culture shock–we were used to doing things in one way and Holiday was used to doing things in another way, and we had to bring the two companies together in a system. It took a while, but we did that. I guess I could say like Paul Harvey, "And that's the rest of the story."

Holiday paid somewhere close to three hundred million dollars in the merger. Prior to the merger, we engaged the Merrill Lynch firm to represent the interests of the public shareholders, with Dean Witter representing the Harrah estate. The entire merger transaction was reviewed independently by both of these investment banking firms, and they had to be satisfied that the public shareholders' interests were represented as well as those of the estate. You could argue there was a conflict of interest between the estate and the public, but there really wasn't, as long as both got the same. You couldn't make a sweetheart deal–you couldn't sell too cheaply to Holiday, and in effect force the public shareholders to surrender their shares too cheaply. If anything, the estate took some of the short end of it to make the transaction go together, because at the last minute the estate had to take a promissory note in partial payment: the way the financial markets were at the time, Holiday simply couldn't come up with all of the cash that was required–or they didn't want to. Whenever there was a doubt, the estate would step up and meet those doubts, so the public was always treated favorably in the merger.

We got half cash and half convertible debentures, which had an interest rate. The public shareholders got convertible debentures that were freely tradable and not restricted, whereas the converts that Harrah's estate received had many restrictions upon them that were insisted upon by Holiday. That way Harrah's would not, simply by the mass of its convertible debentures, be able to do something unfair to Holiday Inns or something that Holiday Inns didn't want to be done. We had restrictions on the resale, restrictions on registration, and so forth, but I thought all of the restrictions were reasonable from the estate point of view. (The estate couldn't trade its converts if it wanted to, and that turned into a tax case which is still in litigation. It's on appeal now, but I think we won most of our issues as to whether or not the estate's convertibles were worth as much as the public converts. We said they were not because of the restrictions on them.)

I had decided to pursue the merger because it was in the best long-run financial interest of the heirs of Bill Harrah. Sure, it would have been fun for me to have maintained Harrah's as a stand-alone company and exercise my power–and I had plenty of power–to run the company. I could have been the boss and had a long career in seeing what I could do experimenting with Harrah's. I would have liked to have the chance to prove myself as a successful casino operator, but my decision was to do what was in the best interest of the beneficiaries of Bill Harrah's will–and that's what I did. I took a lot of heat for merging Harrah's with Holiday Inns, but this was not a popularity contest, and I wasn't trying to please all the people of Reno. I was trying to do the right thing for the beneficiaries, and that's what I did.

[11]

After the Merger

NO MATTER HOW MUCH we had talked about the relationship of the two companies before the merger, the reality after the merger was just a little different . . . as I suppose any marriage is. We were trying to bring together two totally different corporate cultures and businesses, but the differences were not quite as apparent to me before the merger as after it. Remember, Holiday Inns was in the business of renting hotel rooms, and Harrah's was not in that business; and the marketing of casino customers is a lot different from trying to sell a Holiday Inn hotel room to a business or vacation traveler. Holiday was shocked to learn the amount of money that Harrah's would invest in a hotel suite or in upgrading a Harrah's property. When we at Harrah's would talk about eight or ten thousand dollars to refurbish a small suite, we thought that was not enough money . . . but we were trying to be budget conscious to maintain a good relationship with Holiday. I recall very clearly when Holiday responded that they could furnish an entire Holiday Inn room for fifteen hundred dollars. They couldn't understand how we could spend eight thousand dollars in a refurbishment.

After the merger, lots of people came from Holiday Inns headquarters in Memphis to Reno, and I had the feeling that some of them were people that Memphis was very happy to get rid of . . . and eventually, Reno probably got rid of them, too! [laughter] But it was an evolutionary process, with no ill will and no effort at machination or cunning that I could ever see–Mike

Rose would have gone through the roof had he suspected that people were acting for the wrong motives . . . maybe he sent too many people down, or maybe his people sent too many people down; but whatever they did, they did with the best of intentions. There *were* culture clashes: a lot of Harrah's people were spoiled, living in the Bill Harrah culture, and, of course, a lot of people from Memphis came here without understanding the gaming business. I'm sure that each side felt smarter than the other.

Immediately after the merger, Holiday Inns asked for the resignation of George Drews. That did not surprise me, because George was Harrah's chief financial officer, a vulnerable position in any merger. And I knew that finance would be of interest to Holiday, because Holiday was uncomfortable with the planning function at Harrah's . . . as was I. Nonetheless, although I had expected to lose the board of directors, or a great many members of the board, I had hoped to retain the Harrah's operating team . . . but that was not to be. (George Drews was replaced immediately, so he went over to Si Redd, and Si gave him the job of running Sircoma. George became their president, and ran Sircoma for a number of years prior to its transition into IGT, with Matthewson and that group.) The big surprise was that Holiday requested the resignation of Lloyd Dyer. Lloyd was president at that time, and in the light of hindsight I guess I can see that they wanted a Holiday Inn person in that position–Dick Goeglein was sent out to take over that function.

My role between 1980 and 1986 was one of maintaining a Harrah's presence on the Holiday Inns board, and bringing my Harrah's experience to the Holiday management. When Holiday started taking control of Harrah's by sending their people in, I had a *reasonable* reservoir of knowledge and experience that was of value to Holiday. If Holiday had simply walked in and said good-bye to everybody at Harrah's, "We're going to start running this," I think they would have had a more difficult time than they did.

I was there as chairman; Richard Goeglein–they used to call him Dick Goeglein in those days–was there as president, and he and I worked closely together. Our offices were side by side, and we met and planned the future of the company together. I think I was of value to Goeglein; I know Goeglein was of value to me. I was able to introduce him to the players at Harrah's–explain the background of the company, who the people were in the community, and that sort of thing. And Dick was a quick learner.

We had not gotten an effective computer system in place at Harrah's during Bill's lifetime–management information system is the correct term. I first ran into MIS systems in the Tropicana when Carl Pohlad took over in 1968. Carl is a heavy hitter. He came into the Tropicana, and he could see that we had problems, so he brought in Arthur Anderson with MIS. That was my first exposure to management information systems, and I tried to export that knowledge to Harrah's, but I was never really successful. Finally our accounting firm got so concerned over lack of information and inadequacy of control that they said, "If things continue, we're not going to be able to sign a certificate next year." That led to one of the worst fiascos I've ever seen, and it was because I was not used to MIS people–they're all strange.

After Bill Harrah's death, I had employed our accounting firm to establish adequate controls and MIS procedures, a program that was going to cost millions of dollars. But when we merged with Holiday, Holiday said, "Dixon, you're doing all the wrong things. Alexander Grant & Co. doesn't know what it's doing with MIS; we're going to send up our MIS people." So a lot of MIS people from Memphis came up and said, "You're buying the wrong equipment. You're putting in the wrong systems. We're going to spend more millions of dollars, and we're going to connect you to the Memphis mainframes." [laughter] So we went through that procedure and got that established. Then they changed MIS personnel in Memphis, and whoever they brought in said, "The people we sent you were wrong. We've got to do Harrah's MIS system all over again. They've given you all the wrong information, and you have everything connected to the wrong kind of equipment. All the programs are wrong." Within a few years we went through several MIS systems at Harrah's, trying to get it under control. And big bucks!

Every company needs a budget. Pre-merger, I was given a copy of a business plan that Holiday prepared for Harrah's, and I was amazed that they could turn out such a plan and budget so quickly. They were intelligently and very carefully done. Holiday would take a projected budget for the upcoming year and call that the business plan for that year. Then we'd try to project the planning process out for a period of years, allowing for inflation, planning for "out" years, taking into account what marketing felt it could produce as changes in revenues occurred. In other words, Holiday made projections–not simply one-year budgets–and these were based upon alternatives. But the farther out you plan, the wilder the guesses get. We could get out to ten years in projections, but we could only hope we were aware of the coming changes in the business world, demographics, politics, and personnel and payroll. (Harrah's had never done that kind of thing; they just looked at one year at a time, period. At Harrah's it was simply a process in which all of the people would sit down and say, "OK, I did this, thus, and such last year, and for this year it's going to cost me X and Y and Z." The year's budget was put together, but it didn't allow you to think ahead to where the company might be going. I had many pre-merger discussions with Mike Rose, telling him that I was very concerned about the lack of planning at Harrah's, and the *inability* of Harrah's to plan.)

Mike skillfully executed corporate planning, but I will not say that Holiday devoted the kind of capital commitment to the corporation that I would prefer. I think they over-leveraged the company. After the merger, Holiday started out in fear of the 1980s, which I didn't fear. (I didn't know the eighties were going to be the strange Ronald Reagan years that they turned out to be, the years of corporate mergers and takeovers and acquisitions.) Holiday was reasonably fiscally sound and not over-leveraged, but to some extent the company post-merger worked in a different direction, with a drive on Holiday Inns' part to leverage the company so highly that it would not be a merger target. They eventually, after my departure, went into negative equity, and you can't leverage *more* than going into negative equity. They created a company in which the shareholders had no equity, and the debts outweighed the assets . . . or at least that was the balance sheet result. (Of course, I was not privy to the things that took place beyond my tenure, which ended in 1986.)

At Harrah's in the Holiday system there was an attempt made by the Holiday human resources people to measure employee performance and create a matrix, which took into consideration a number of factors. That evolved over a period of years. The process was guided in part by a fellow named Maurice Mascarenhas, who was a so-called guru of management style that Holiday brought in. He was a highly intelligent guy, and I think he tried to push everyone a little bit over the line. You'd say, "Maurice, you're crazy," but you couldn't argue with him.

Maurice had a couple of principles that were exceedingly interesting—and I've heard him talk about them enough times that I *know* they were his principles! [laughter] He started with the premise that whatever number of employees you have, you have 10 percent too many. Another of Maurice's fundamentals was that he didn't say that people had goals or objectives—they had KRAs: Key Result Areas. Everyone was to review and establish his KRAs on an annual basis, and have his KRAs approved. The KRAs then carried with them a so-called action plan. For example, John Doe would have four to six Key Result Areas that he was to accomplish within a given year, and he would have to develop an action plan which would enumerate the steps he would take to accomplish these key results on a timetable. Then there would be a quarterly review with the executive or employee about whether or not he was accomplishing the goals. (I didn't have much problem with this, because I was not included in it.) [laughter] The concept was that your bonus program was going to be measured against your objective evaluation. You were going to be evaluated both on the financial results of your particular department or area of responsibility, and on the overall performance of the company, and the matrix was divided by class of employee.

Another of the Maurice Mascarenhas principles was, "If you can't count it, it doesn't count." [laughter] I think that there should probably have been more room for subjective judgment than Maurice would approve, but, on the other hand, there was a distinct advantage in having measurable goals or objectives, and I think the Holiday concept was pretty much a correct concept: to try to get measurable standards.

Harrah's was stuck with–and in love with–its old-fashioned mechanical slot machines. I remember coming back from Las Vegas and telling Rome that we ought to get dollar carousels, but Rome would never go for them. First, they were Bally machines, and second, he thought they made too much noise. I had lots of conversations with Rome about slot machines and slot machine management, but while Bill was still alive I could never penetrate. After Bill's death I had more authority, so I again started asking questions. I asked the fellow who was running Harrah's casino floor, "What slot machines do you have, and where? What's your floor plan? What's your per? How are you doing?"

"I don't know," would be the usual answer.

So I talked to Rome. He said, "We can't let those fellows know. They don't know what the PC ought to be on any machine, because that's confidential; that's secret. Only three people know that information–me, Bob Ring and Bud Garaventa."

My question was, "How can they manage? How can they be responsible for a slot pit or a casino floor if they have no control over the location of machines, and don't know what the machine is supposed to be doing?"

Then I went to finance and accounting: "How do you run your audit?"

"We don't run the audits, because it's all secret. We don't know anything about the slot machines. All we know is so much money comes in, and so much money goes out, period."

Can you imagine running two gaming casinos and not having the fellow in charge of each casino understanding his slot pers? I can't. But that was the way it was, and that information was thought to be too dangerous—"Our competitors will find out our combinations; our competitors will find out the secret of our slots' success." There is no question that slot machines were the foundation of Harrah's business, and that Harrah's had a good casino. My only question was, how could I be responsible for it if I didn't understand it, and why was all this kept so secret?

That was the state of Harrah's management pre-merger—very difficult to live with. I *instructed* that it be changed, but it was just like trying to move the Taj Mahal! [laughter] We finally got finance and accounting involved, but we had culture shock.

When we opened the Center Street casino in 1980, I decided that we were going to put in some modern machines, but Andreotti said, "Bill would never allow it, and it's going to be over my dead body."

So I said, "As you elect," and we put Bally's machines in the Center Street casino.

After that, we started tracking—we started trying to get a slot control system. That was one of the most difficult projects that I have ever seen, and there were a *lot* of difficult projects at Harrah's. We didn't want to hard-wire and computerize every-thing like they tried to do at the Flamingo, but I wanted some rudiments. One of the arguments that we always got was, "You can meter the machines, but the meters aren't accurate." Well, they're a hell of a lot more accurate than having zero! But I could never get that message sold. When you have as many machines as Harrah's did, you need to have some control, but it took years to accomplish anything. No matter what you did, there was resistance to it from the casino floor or from gaming management or from the computer scientists. But I was ignorant enough to think there ought to be a way to get it done, even if it was not perfect, and eventually it was accomplished.

We had a lot of discussions about slot machines, and Rome finally decided that it was in fact true that Bally was getting ahead of us. But the conclusion was that we at Harrah's would build a slot machine, instead of ever having a Bally. In the mid-1970s we started a project out at HAC (Harrah's Auto Collection) to build a slot machine. That project went on and on and on.

The idea was to create an electronic machine that would present mechanical reels in the traditional fashion, with an up-to-date case, so that the public would believe they were pulling a Harrah's slot machine with the same feel–the same pull of the handle, the same handle pressure, and the same reel release; the same clunk, clunk, clunk reel stop that you got through the old Pace mechanicals. Our concept was that people would never be satisfied with anything except a machine that simulated exactly what they were used to: the feel of the Pace machine; the feel that if you pull a handle with a certain degree of strength, or with a certain motion, you can affect the payoff outcome. We wanted people to believe they were still dealing with a *mechanical* machine–the computer brain was not to be part of this thing's appeal; nobody was to know about it.

We worked on that machine for as many as three years. I saw presentation models of the machine put up, and believe me, I was *sold* on a Harrah's slot machine, because here were people who knew what they were doing: Bill Harrah, Rome Andreotti, Bud Garaventa, Lloyd Dyer, Maurice Sheppard . . . . (I'm wiser today than I was then.) We continued to work on it, and finally we got a pretty good machine, but it wasn't quite right. Then Bill died, and here we had a slot machine, and I can't tell you how many thousands of dollars' worth of power and time and so forth were in it. We sat down with our consulting firm, Booz Allen and Hamilton, and said, "Here's our problem: We've got a slot machine that's been pretty well developed, and it isn't coming through; it's not complete. Here's how many dollars we've spent. What will we do with this machine?" (Now, this is post-merger.) The conclusion was that we had invested enough money in the machine; that it would be desirable to continue it to completion, but that we did not have adequate internal resources with which to do that.

(To get the whole picture: the Bally machine was changing all the time; the Japanese were beginning to come on line with machines; Mills Jennings is trying to get you on the phone–they wanted to come up with a new machine . . . . We were in a period of ferment in the growth of the slot machine industry, and Harrah's was still sitting there with those old mechanical Paces!

There were no dollar carousels, no banging, no noise; you couldn't put in five coins and play five coins through a machine. You were sitting there putting in a nickel or a quarter at a time.)

By 1982, when we eventually got the Harrah machine so we thought it would work, it was going to cost more money to produce it than to buy good competitive machinery . . . and the technology of slot machines had passed us by. So we scrapped the project. The result was we had spent a lot of money, and we failed.

Si Redd had been the Bally distributor for the state of Nevada, and he was one of the greatest salesmen in the world–really a great salesman. His company, Sircoma, was building video slot machines here in Reno. (That company is now IGT [International Game Technology], probably the foremost manufacturer of video slot machines in the country today.) When Harrah's slot machine began to slow down, we took a look at buying Sircoma. The machines were interesting, because the reels would come down the video screen as you see them today . . . perhaps not quite the sophistication you see today. We went out and took a look at Sircoma and the cost of buying it for Harrah's. At Si Redd's plant, I saw all of these empty cases– housings–out back in the warehouse. It turned out that what Si needed for his video slot machines was a cathode ray tube–he needed a television screen. He was acquiring screens to put into his slot machines by buying televisions, throwing away the cabinets, receivers and controls, and keeping the boob tubes. [laughter] I took one look at that, and I thought, "What an opportunity there would be here just to buy the tubes instead." But I guess Si's numbers were strong enough that he hadn't bothered to find a contractor to provide the tubes. There was such a tremendous markup on his slots–I think he was getting in excess of six thousand dollars for a relatively simple machine with a CRT–that he could afford to buy televisions, keep the tubes, and throw the rest away.

We had first looked at Sircoma before the merger with Holiday, but we did not have enough money then: I needed what cash we had to meet estate tax deadlines in the event the merger should fail. After the merger, we again took a look at Sircoma and the price that Si wanted for it, and tried to figure out what we should do. We decided we wanted to buy Sircoma, but first we had to present our proposal to Holiday management in Memphis, because it was well beyond Harrah's authority to do anything about it. Well, the presentation went nowhere, and I think perhaps Holiday was right in a sense. They said that two things were wrong: purchasing Sircoma would be deviating from our principal business, which was running a casino; and we didn't have the management depth to run over there and take charge of manufacturing video slot machines. So we dropped the project. (In hindsight, we made the wrong decision. Look at IGT today.)

There was no question that the automobile collection was an asset that Bill had expected to be sold or disposed of after his death, but there was a great public outcry that it should not be sold. Holiday Inns felt that they couldn't afford to have that much capital tied up in automobiles sitting in John Dermody's warehouse, or the Pacific Fruit Express warehouse, and Holiday Inns was right about that. Here were thirty million to thirty-five million dollars' worth of automobiles that were not producing a quarter, and they were costing a lot of money to hold, with interest rates running as high as 20 percent in the Jimmy Carter years. It would be insane to think that Holiday Inns or anybody else would let thirty million dollars in assets sit there idly. I mean, that's not the real world! You probably would have been subject to a shareholder's suit for mismanagement if you sat on thirty-five million dollars' worth of nonproductive automobiles and did nothing.

What were we going to do? We had a situation where Nevada said, "Bill Harrah is a great man; he would never want this collection broken up." But Bill had the power of the pen: all he had to do was sign his name, and we could have preserved the collection . . . but he didn't. We could have created a charitable foundation and had the collection be in it and not part of Harrah's, but Bill wanted it part of Harrah's because Harrah's had the stream of income to support the collection. I don't know how the Internal Revenue Service viewed it, but by the time the collection reached the magnitude and value that it did, the business purpose at best was questionable, and from the Holiday Inn point of view, it had *no* business purpose. So Holiday said, "We're going to start liquidating the collection."

Frankly, I had some disagreements with Holiday with respect to some of the people they brought in to analyze and put in charge of the collection. Holiday was acting in good faith, but they put a fellow named Joel Finn in charge, and I had a lawsuit pending against Joel Finn for fraud. In my opinion, it was an absolute, slam-bang, cold-turkey case. I had evidence that Finn sold a car to the automobile collection, representing it as the authentic Vanderbilt Cup Racer. It turned out that the car had been constructed out of spare parts, and instead of an automobile engine, it had a marine engine out of a fishing boat! Harrah's had a problem with putting Finn in charge of the collection, because that meant dismissing the suit for fraud against him, and that was painful to me and to many of us at Harrah's. We fought this out with Holiday, but lost. It was tough, very tough to digest.

Even though Holiday was doing the best it could, the public outcry at the potential loss of the collection was great. I had calls from all over to save the collection: from United States senators from other states; from Dave Thomas, the chairman of Wendy's; from the governor of Nevada; and from the mayor of Reno. And I had lots of calls from local business people. We said, "Fine, we'll save the collection. Will anybody donate money to help us?" My recollection is that after public meetings and discussions and every effort, we got cash and pledges amounting to sixty thousand dollars, which was not enough.

So Holiday Inns began liquidating the collection, knowing that it was an unpopular thing to do, but realizing that it had to be done. We were able to retain maybe two hundred cars in the Harrah Automobile Collection, thanks to the generosity of Holiday, and we've got nine or ten million dollars in bond issue debt for the museum building that houses them. If we had fifteen hundred cars (the original number), we might be facing a fifty-million dollar bond issue debt. Hell, we can't even pay the nine million.

After we merged with Holiday Inns, we had an opportunity to expand gaming operations into Australia. This was because Harrah's had worked for so many years to build the necessary legal infrastructure, both in Australia and in Nevada. I had spent a lot of time in Australia in the 1970s, because Bill had become interested in the possibility of gaming over there. He had met a fellow in Melbourne who said, "You ought to look into gaming in Australia, because everybody here likes to gamble." So that became the challenge.

Now, Lloyd Dyer had talked with Governor O'Callaghan, and told him, "We're going to take a look at gaming in Australia. Do you have any objection to that?" (This is hearsay on my part, because I did not hear it from the governor; I heard it from Dyer.) "No," the governor said. "That's far enough away that I don't really care. If you fellows were going to try to start a casino in Mexico, I would object, but if you want to go to Australia, hell, we don't care."

I went to Australia and spent a lot of time there building a consortium from the ground up, realizing that we had to do more than just get movers and shakers: we had to get government clearance. At that time there was no legal casino in Australia–down in Tasmania, yes, but not in Australia. I met with all the government people in Canberra, Melbourne, Sydney, Brisbane, and Perth. I met with the movers, the shakers, and the leaders, and I put together a group comprised of the L. J. Hooker Company and Ansett Airlines . . . Sir Reginald Ansett and Harrah's, trying to put together a casino venture. [laughter] (For a while we played with Travelodge and that group; Southern Pacific Corporation was another big Asia rim organization.) Sir Reginald Ansett was really great, and Keith Campbell ran Hooker's. Both were top-notch guys; we were in with first-class people.

We moved along, even looking for casino sites, and I met some illegal gamblers in Sydney. I met with lots of government people, treasury people, and we talked about the legalization of gambling–what would be required, and whether Harrah's could bring money in and out of the state. We looked at whether we could become investors, and how much Harrah's could own under Australian law; then we formed Harrah's Pty., Ltd., a proprietary corporation, and registered in all of the states of Australia so that we would reserve the name "Harrah's".

This Australia thing took years to put together–it wasn't done instantaneously. At some point I got a letter from Pete Echeverria[1] which, in effect, said, "Dear Mead: I resent your attempt to establish gambling in Australia on behalf of Harrah's. You're doing something improper by trying to bring gambling to these people when it's not legal there." Well, I was shocked to receive that letter. I realized that we had some political problems with operating a Harrah's casino outside the state of Nevada, but Australia was so far away that I thought we could get enough holy water to do it, in light of the O'Callaghan conversation with Dyer. As it eventuated, we were stonewalled–I mean *absolutely*. I had a number of meetings with Pete Echeverria, and he said, "I'm not going to allow you to go outside the state of Nevada; and furthermore, I don't think Harrah's should spend any money that it earned in Nevada outside of Nevada."

I said, "Pete, how can you feel that way or think that way?"

He says, "We're going to control it by regulation. You can't spend any money outside the state of Nevada."

I said, "Hell, it's our money; we can spend it where we please!"

Well, we had that kind of argument, and then I met with Governor O'Callaghan. We had some problems, because O'Callaghan fundamentally did not like Harrah's. (He and Chuck Munson had gotten into a match with each other at some point in time.) When I met with O'Callaghan with respect to this foreign gaming issue, he stood up for Echeverria.[2] So I had a problem: "What the hell am I going to do?"

---

[1] Peter Echeverria was a member of the Nevada Gaming Policy Committee, 1975-76, and 1977-78.

[2] In the vernacular of Nevada casino gaming regulation, any extension of a Nevada gaming operation beyond the borders of the state was "foreign" gaming.

(Pete wanted to keep Nevada green, and so did O'Callaghan: that was their term, not mine–"Keep Nevada green." The grounds of their opposition were that it was in the financial interest of the state of Nevada to keep gambling suppressed everywhere else, and not let operators go outside the state without forfeiting their Nevada licenses. Echeverria's theory was that we had to spend all of our money in Nevada . . . . I still don't understand the sheepherder with that one!)

We filed an application with the Gaming Policy Board to try to change the rules and regulations that prohibited Nevada operators from foreign gaming. I was in Carson City at the hearing, and the governor was sitting up there with Echeverria, William Weinberger, and the other participants on the board. All of the vibes and all the signals were wrong–I knew we were going to get turned down, but we made our best presentation. Barron Hilton was sitting in the back of the room. We'd never had a conversation about this matter at all, but he could sense, like everybody else, that we were going to get a denial. He stood up, and bless him (because this was not like Barron), he said, "Governor, I'm Barron Hilton of the Hilton Hotel Company, and I'd like to express my views."

"Yes, Mr. Hilton."

He said, "Hilton Hotel Corporation, bow-wow-wow . . . big company, outside the state of Nevada . . . . " He said, "I have just committed to a seventy-five-million-dollar project in New Orleans with partners and investors, and there is a strong possibility that gaming will be made legal in New Orleans. I think it's unfair to me, it's unfair to Hilton Hotels Corporation, and it's certainly unfair to investors who put that magnitude of money into this wonderful project to find that if gaming is made legal in New Orleans, they are prohibited by the state of Nevada from engaging in the business. That's not the way to play ball. That's not the way the world is." And you could watch O'Callaghan change his mind. He listened to Barron; he thought about it. Echeverria was ready to make the motion of denial, but O'Callaghan leaned over and whispered something to Pete, and the motion that emerged was they would take the matter under consideration. But they didn't *deny* our application to change the rules prohibiting Nevada companies from going to foreign gaming.

I walked out, and I thanked Barron, because now we really had a shot. So where did we go from here? Echeverria decided that this matter was such a hot potato that it should be referred to the legislature, so that's what he recommended, and that's what O'Callaghan did.

We had a series of hearings, and I *knew* that we had to win. We hired a Los Angeles law firm to do legal research relating to the interstate commerce constitutional issue. Finally, we were able to convince the state authorities that since their opposition to foreign gaming was based upon economic consideration–which was clearly unconstitutional–that they could not stand. What the state had to do then was say, "We have no objection to you going into foreign gaming as long as the foreign jurisdiction is properly *regulated*."[1] Everybody thought at that time that New Jersey was going to be so corrupt that it couldn't properly regulate gambling, and therefore Nevada gamblers were not going to be able to go to New Jersey. And expansion by Nevada operators into New Jersey concerned the Gaming Policy Board a hell of a lot more than our expressed interest in Australia.

(I've always felt that the guys from New Jersey were treated by Nevada as though they came from a crooked state. Nevada was saying, "We know all about regulation, and you don't know anything about it; and we're not going to let our gamblers expand into New Jersey because you guys don't regulate properly." It's my opinion that part of the eventual stringency and over-regulation of gambling in New Jersey was due to the taunting by Governor O'Callaghan, Peter Echeverria, and others in Nevada government. Echeverria said, "It took forty years of gambling experience for Nevada to get where it is." So New Jersey, in effect, said, "You tell us we can't regulate gambling. We're going to show you; we're going to get tighter regulations than you've got!" What the governor needed to understand was that Nevada

[1] Nevada Foreign Gaming Act, 1977.

had to mind Nevada's business and keep Nevada's casinos running straight, level and clean. Think about the purposes of gaming regulation: to keep criminal elements out of gambling; to assure that all taxes are paid; and to assure that the customer isn't cheated. But O'Callaghan and Echeverria really believed that by locking up the gambling casinos, denying them the right to expand outside the state without losing their Nevada licenses, they could prevent casinos from spreading around the country. Well, you might lock up the corporation, but you can't lock up the employees. [laughter] There was an emigration from Las Vegas into Atlantic City; I saw it. They got lots of employees from Nevada.

New Jersey has its problems primarily because in a state like that, you have to start so big–you have to open a joint with four thousand employees. That's a lot different than opening a joint with twenty-five employees, and nobody in Nevada had that experience. It was a shock to open from ground zero with three thousand to four thousand employees, all on day number one. So even though the regulatory objections were overruled, entry into Atlantic City was difficult.)

By the time licensed gaming casino companies got permission from Nevada in 1977 to operate outside the state, we were well established in Australia with friends . . . but gambling had not yet been made legal in Australia. I was over there in February of 1978 with Bill, and what he really wanted to do was drive in one of those old car treks through the Australian countryside. He didn't care at that time whether or not we engaged in gambling in Australia, but I'm satisfied that if Bill had lived (or if we had not sold Harrah's), we would be in business in Australia today.

This is the way it eventuated after Bill died and we merged with Holiday Inns: Australia decided to legalize gaming in Queensland at Surfer's Paradise, which was the Miami Beach of Australia. It had been made famous by its mayor, Sir Bruce Small, who was the first guy to ride a bicycle from coast to coast and dip its wheels in the water on each side of Australia. ("Think big; vote Small," was his slogan.) Queensland finally decided to allow a casino, and in Australia they do it differently than they do in Nevada: parliament gives a charter to a casino company. (You don't go down and apply for a gaming license; you get an act of parliament that enables you to go into the casino business, and gives you protection, and so forth.) The first thing that happened was that the people involved–Jupiter's group from Australia–came to Harrah's in Reno. They said, "We know your company, and we want you to come with us."

Now our tree was bearing the fruit of all of this groundwork. But by this time we were a subsidiary of Holiday Inns, and the Holiday point of view was "Sure, we'll go in on this gaming venture, but we won't put a quarter in it–not penny number one." So Harrah's, through Richard Goeglein, responded, "We're the premier gaming company in the world. Do you want us? We'll come, but we won't put in a penny, and we want X percent of the operation; we want Y percent of this; we want . . . " and so forth and so on.

The demands were clearly unreasonable on Harrah's part, so Jupiter said, "Sorry. We really want you, Harrah's, but we can't make this deal." And the deal went to Hilton; I think Barron put up ten mil. Hilton's Conrad Hotel system is now established in Surfer's Paradise. It's been a very successful venture, and it could have been a Harrah's venture. That's where we would have been as a result of all of our groundwork had Holiday Inns been willing to put in even a little equity.

I had this problem with Holiday a number of times. Every time we tried to do something, any participant would say, "You got to put up something besides your name. You don't have to put up all the money, but you got to have something at risk. We want to be in pari passu; we want you to lose money if we lose money." In other words, you might only have to put ten million dollars (as the Hilton did) in a three hundred million dollar project, but you've got to put in something . . . and we couldn't get that something past Memphis. Holiday Inns was basically a no-equity participant. You could get in any kind of venture, but . . . .

We had guys assigned to try and build hotels. We wanted a hotel in New York–we were thinking about building some hotels with Harrah's name on them, on the theory that it would generate business the same way Hilton does. Came up with deal after potential deal. But if you take a no-equity, no capital, no-risk stance, you come up with a goose egg, and that's as far as I was ever able to get with the Holiday Inn people: "Anytime you can come up with a good deal that doesn't cost us a penny, and we can make a lot of money on it and have no risk of loss, then we go ahead." [laughter]

Today Harrah's is doing everything it can to get established in Australia under Phil Satre's leadership. I have none of the details, but there's about to be a new casino awarded in Brisbane, and Harrah's is head-to-head with Hilton on the short list for that new casino.

Charles Franklin was house counsel for Harrah's, but after the merger he was going to leave the company. I wanted somebody from our law firm to come over to Harrah's, because a good house counsel was important for growth. I asked Phil Satre to come to Harrah's. Initially, I had only considered making him secretary of the company and moving things slowly, but I thought about it and thought about it, and I brought him in. In effect, I said, "Phil, there is a career opportunity here for you. You come over here as house counsel and as secretary, you learn something about the company, and you can become president of this company with your skills and ability. If you'll come, I'm going to make a statement about you: I will give you the title of vice president in the very beginning," . . . which was against Harrah's religion, you know. Well, Phil was reluctant to come–it was a big move, but he finally said OK. So we made the announcement: Phil Satre, vice president, general counsel, and secretary of the company.

Phil took over that role and filled it *admirably*. He learned more about Harrah's operations than I will ever know! He was in his thirties, and he was aggressive, ambitious, and talented. Without question, he was the right man for the job, and we had made the right selection. You could say, "Phil, will you take care of it?" and he took care of it! You never had to have a sleepless

night with Phil; if he was to do something, you knew it was going
to get done. There are not many people like that.

Phil just did so much work. I don't know how he carried the
load that he carried, but you can see where he is today: he's
gone all the way up the ladder; he's been able to operate five
gaming casinos, and he devotes hours and hours of time to travel,
and now he's the chief operating officer of the Promus Corporation. He has the organized mind to be able to handle his obligations and his opportunities, and he's got enough of an analytical
mind to see how he wants Harrah's positioned. And I'm sure he
knows how he wants the hotel divisions of Promus Corporation
positioned.

I induced Phil to come to Harrah's with the encouragement
that he had the right stuff, and that he would become president,
but in those days I didn't envision him becoming president of
Holiday Inns; I only envisioned him becoming president of
Harrah's. He was the kind of person that Harrah's needed–much
stronger, and, in my opinion, much more competent than the
people already on board. But this is not to say that he could
shoot craps or deal Twenty-One. There's a lot of difference
between a guy who is a casino manager or floor man (a guy who
understands the games, as Rome did), and a fellow who can run
the overall business.

I can't begin to tell you the count, but before Phil Satre
became president there had been more and more people in
Harrah's corporate central headquarters, many coming in from
Memphis. I felt that often people were sent in to us by Memphis
in order to get them out of the way of the Holiday Inns system.
[laughter] Rather than saying to them, "Say, old buddy, you're
really not the guy we want in this function," I think Holiday may
have been saying, "Oh, by the way, why don't you go to our
Harrah's subsidiary and see if you can make it there?" Now,
that's a little bit unfair, but there was a suspicion that some of
the folks who were sent out from Memphis were sent out for
corporate political reasons rather than because they were the
best guys out of the box. It was not long, however, before we had
a lot of talented people from Memphis . . . and some not so

talented. Lots of them exhibited great polish and great aplomb, but they still had to learn that it was the casino business and not the hotel business. Phil Satre was able to dramatically reduce the number of people in Harrah's corporate headquarters. He laid off two or three hundred people in one fell swoop, and there was some public outcry.

As soon as Phil became president of Harrah's, he began to mold it in his style. The outcome is the Harrah's that you see today: each property is a stand-alone property. Decentralization was part of Phil's change in management technique–making the company (to use the expression that is used over and over) lean and mean. He put responsibility on each property for its own functioning, so each had somebody in charge of the casino floor and was able to develop what we used to call a VPGM (Vice President and General Manager; now they're called presidents or vice presidents). Each casino was able to develop someone as its general manager who had the necessary strengths and talents, and who was given the responsibility of running his own shop and managing his own budget. That was the Satre concept, as I understand it, and it was a clear break from the past. That pretty much marked the end of old Harrah's.

We were perhaps unique at Harrah's in that we had no employment contracts. Bill Harrah did not believe in them, so there were none during Bill's tenure, and after he died I had the fiduciary obligation not to clutter up any merger transaction with the issuance of golden parachutes or employment contracts to Harrah's employees (that would have diminished our ability to negotiate a merger), and nobody at Harrah's asked me for any. We assumed that the guys at Harrah's would stand or fall on their own merits, and that was just about the way it was.

Bob Ring stayed with the company until his retirement, and he continued to have an office at Harrah's after, even though he was simply on his retirement compensation and was not active. Bob was vice chairman of the company, but that was pretty much an honorable title. (It may have been vice chairman emeritus, something of that kind.) Bob had a lot of strengths, a lot of personality. The employees loved him, and the customers

loved him, but he had no management role at all. He was kind of
Mr. Outside, meaning he was Mr. Public. He maintained that role
as long as he was physically able, and he was always welcome at
Harrah's and at his office.

Rome Andreotti remained with Harrah's until he died. Rome
had friends and enemies, as we all do, but his friends and
enemies were perhaps more sharply defined. Either you liked
Rome or you hated him, but Rome was without question loyal to
Bill Harrah and loyal to Harrah's. His strengths were his knowledge of gaming and his belief in all that he had done in all of his
years of gaming at Harrah's. He was respected in the gaming
community, and Las Vegas old-timers would always say, "How is
Rome doing?" He was known in the casino industry by people
who were hands-on on the gambling floor.

Rome maintained his role until he died. After all, neither I
nor anyone from Holiday had any degree of competence in how
to run casino games; how to keep cheating down; how the casino
floor should look; how casino employees should be trained. Rome
had those skills. During Bill's lifetime, Rome had always been
involved in the budgeting process, but that function moved away
from him after Bill died.

Rome contracted cancer (which ultimately caused his death
in 1984), but as he got sicker he continued to work. He would go
to Atlantic City on a regular basis, and go through the casino and
satisfy himself that Harrah's procedures were being followed,
working with the people on the casino floor there. Rome was an
anomaly in a sense, in that he was central and Harrah's was not
a centralized operation anymore.

I had been in a position pre-merger, while I controlled
Harrah's, to give myself a golden parachute or an employment
contract, but I did not do that. Whatever chances were there to
take, I took, and I was privileged–I think I use that word
correctly–to stay on board and remain a part of the organization
until I became overage in grade. Holiday had a provision
requiring retirement from its board at age sixty-five, but I
reached sixty-five and continued beyond that for a few
months–in other words, somebody didn't come out with an ax

and chop my head off like a chicken in a henhouse. I went a few months past that into the year 1986, when they were kind enough to give a retirement party for me in Reno, and I was able to have a lot of my friends attend. It was significant for me to have a clean separation from the company, and it was done in good taste, but from that point on I've been a free agent.

[12]

Harrah's and Holiday Do Atlantic City

WHEN I BECAME CHAIRMAN OF THE BOARD, I wanted Harrah's to be a successful company, and it seemed to me that the most significant opportunity for us was an Atlantic City opportunity. It seemed to me that to miss the boat in Atlantic City would be a mistake. (To go from Reno into Las Vegas would have been the wrong move at that time.) We were deplorably late in getting into Atlantic City, but we did move there. Sheppard had gone back there in 1977 to review it for Bill, and he had reported that, "Atlantic City is terrible; it's an awful place; it's not going to succeed," and that was the end of Bill Harrah's interest in Atlantic City.

After Bill died, I made Lloyd Dyer CEO of Harrah's, but I decided to take control of the operation of the company. One of the first things I did was hike my body to Atlantic City to *see* it. (As I recall, I took Lloyd and Art Smith with me). Resorts International was going gangbusters, and I'd already decided that we had to be there, but we didn't have any property, and we didn't have any political clout, and we didn't know anything.

Atlantic City was over-age and gray; it was a little hick town: forty thousand unemployed people, the town was closing down, and there weren't many talents there. As far as the infrastructure, the political system and the legal system, it was nothing. But I had some pretty heavy-hitting friends in Philadelphia, and I got ahold of one, and I said, "I want you to help me get acquainted in Atlantic City and help me with property acquisition and legal matters."

I assigned two people to Atlantic City. One of the guys was Mert Smith, who was the VP/General Manager of Harrah's Reno. I knew he was unhappy with Rome Andreotti–Rome's style of management was thumbs on top of the head, and Mert didn't like that. I asked Rome, and he said, "Mert is competent, Mert knows gaming, and Mert can run a casino." So I asked Mert if he'd like to go to Atlantic City, and he leaped like a trout after a mayfly. He said he'd love to go. I also got Chuck Munson.

Chuck Munson should have been one of Harrah's cherished assets, in my opinion, but Sheppard had banished him to Harrah's hangar. Here was this very skilled guy, very outgoing–a community relations guy. Chuck was one of the best lobbyists we ever had . . . in fact, one of the best lobbyists I ever saw. He could get along with anybody, and had a high IQ and a good personality. But when Sheppard became president of Harrah's, he put Chuck in a humiliating position, in my opinion: he put him out at Harrah's hangar, sitting out at the airport in a little office, with not much to do. Sheppard had a policy of starving people out, like Andy Iratcabal, who was secretary-treasurer. Sheppard's way to get rid of Andy was to route him out. Less and less paper began going by Andy's desk; less and less information came to him. Finally, he sat there, dried up, with *nothing* coming in to him. [laughter] Andy said, "What am I going to do? Nobody talks to me; nobody sends me any work–I just sit here!"

I said, "Well, there's a strong message there, Andy, isn't there?"

Sheppard did the same thing with Chuck–he sent him out to the hangar. [laughter] One of the first things I did was to get Chuck out of the hangar. I brought him back downtown, where he belonged, to give him some dignity, and he became an asset to the company, a real asset. Then when I decided about the Atlantic City team, I asked Chuck to go. I got Mert as an operator, and Chuck for community relations and politics.

Steve Wynn was beating the bushes assembling property for the Golden Nugget in Atlantic City. Harrah's also made a full effort to try to find a location there during the late summer and fall of 1978. I sent Chuck and Mert to Atlantic City and put them up in HoJo's–Howard Johnson's, which later became Caesar's–and they lived there. I got this fellow from Philadelphia helping me with the legal aspects of it, and I got a broker who was the right guy to have on the real estate side in Atlantic City. I walked Atlantic City; I drove Atlantic City; and I met with the planners. A terrible job of planning had been done by Atlantic City for casinos. There was a restricted number of hotel-casino sites, and, as I recall, you could have about one acre to build a hotel-casino–which is totally ridiculous. Eventually, in the spring of 1979, we found two adjoining pieces of property that were available, but were outside the planning area. One property belonged to a group of rabbis.

We paid Ed Kline, the owner of the larger parcel, five hundred thousand toward its purchase on the condition that it be included in casino zoning, and we got an option from the rabbis for their adjoining parcel. Kline was a contractor and a heavyweight in the community, but matters dragged on and on, and we could not seem to get a resolution of the issue. We kept hearing, "It won't be long now; everything is going to go all right. We're going to get the proper zoning."

I finally went to a meeting on site with Kline and his people. Walking in, I felt very much in command of my personal resources, which I generally do anyhow [laughter], and I faced him eyeball-to-eyeball and said, "It's time to fish or cut bait." I used those words as sternly as I could, because I was going to go after him and break his neck–one way or another I wanted my money or the land. When the zoning change was denied, we had to sue to get our money back, and that put us back to square one! Here we are in Atlantic City, desperately trying to get started, and no property.

Right across from the Kline property was the proposed MGM site. I made a phone call to Fred Benninger (MGM) and said, "I'd like to talk with you about your site in Atlantic City," and I flew to Vegas and met with Fred and Barron Hilton and Kirk

Kerkorian at the MGM. I felt that we had something substantial to bring to the table: Harrah's was a class act, and if we could transport that Harrah's class and put it in this three-ring circus with MGM and Hilton, we would create a destination area that would have great marketing appeal. I knew that the properties were tight, and we might end up with a squeeze on acreage, but I thought we could go ahead and assemble the land and put together a joint venture. We agreed to that in principle, but we didn't have a contract—we just had a handshake. Our idea was that we would make the land acquisitions, divide the cost three ways, and in effect shake dice for who got which third of the property.

So we started. Benninger thought he was a hell of a negotiator . . . and he was. He started making acquisitions, but we got stuck with some city property in there, and some people said they would never sell to our consortium. I even hired lawyers out of New York to beat the bushes for land, and eventually a property came up for public auction. After becoming chairman of Harrah's, I had taken my name off the Vargas, Bartlett and Dixon office, but I put Phil Satre (of that firm) to work to complete the assemblage of the Atlantic City property. Phil did most of this deal with the help of Larry Orloff, who was a consummate lawyer. We were able to acquire the last piece of property by using a "straw man" that Orloff put up. (A straw man is somebody who is not who he purports to be. Let's put it this way: Harrah's wanted to buy that property to fill out the joint venture, but had we tried to buy the property in our name, I'm sure the price would have been exorbitant. So an individual from New York or New Jersey was contracted to bid, and he bought it for us, but that was not disclosed. In other words, he was purchasing for an undisclosed principal.)

With the property acquired, each of us—that is, Hilton, MGM and Harrah's—had its own design team go to work, and we had a parcel-selection process. I can't remember whether Harrah's had the first parcel going in or the middle parcel, but I know that Benninger of MGM was very happy to get the parcel that was closest to the bay. He had decided to bring up to the bay the replica of the *Bounty* from the movie, *Mutiny on the Bounty*, which MGM owned and which was sitting down in Florida. He wanted that boat to be part of his attraction in building there.

We started designing a Harrah's hotel-casino for this site and running cost estimates, and ours came to two hundred million dollars. I felt that was more than Harrah's should commit to the project, and wanted to reduce our commitment to one hundred and eighty million. I wasn't Steve Wynn. (Steve Wynn has told me many times that his goal was to emulate Bill Harrah. He thought Bill Harrah was the finest casino operator he'd ever seen. In the Golden Nugget and in his Mirage project, he tried to take Bill Harrah's principles forward, and I think he probably has–Steve has put into his projects a lot of the excellence that Bill Harrah tried to put into his. But Steve is outgoing, exciting and daring–lots of things that Bill Harrah wasn't.)

We worked hard to get rid of excess expense in the development of this project, with a five-hundred room hotel and the amenities that the Casino Control Commission would require–public areas, and so forth. We wanted a certain type of casino and a display of some antique automobiles, all within the one hundred and eighty million dollar budget. But it all came to nothing . . . . In October of 1979 we had come close to a merger agreement with Holiday, but it failed because their stock fell out of the collar, and when Harrah's eventually did merge with Holiday in February of 1980, we had a problem: since we were now one company, we couldn't go ahead and build a Harrah's hotel that was across the boulevard from a competing Holiday property–it just wouldn't make sense. So we had to sit down with Hilton and with MGM and say, "We want out." And they were gracious enough to let us out–Benninger and Barron Hilton were first-class individuals on that. It meant more cost to them, or finding a third partner, or them trying to renegotiate the parcel size or the licensing authority so that two properties could be built, but we got out of it. After the 1980 MGM fire in Las Vegas, MGM could not go ahead in Atlantic City, so they sold their half of the land to the Golden Nugget, which already owned two other sites in Atlantic City. Hilton built a beautiful hotel on its half of the property, but when Hilton failed in its licensing attempt, Barron sold the hotel to Donald Trump.

At the time that we were trying to work a venture with Hilton and MGM, I had a condominium at 9600 Atlantic Avenue–suite 1604, overlooking the ocean. It wasn't a big condo, but it was my home away from home. I don't mean this with a Cheshire-cat grin, but I will never forget standing at the little bar in that condominium when Mike Rose came to visit me. Mike and I got along very well in those days; we had a lot of communication back and forth. He came to visit me with respect to Holiday beginning their Holiday Inn Marina project, and us beginning our project. There was no realistic hope at that time of a merger with Holiday Inns. We'd had some preliminary discussions, but it was just too big a bite for Holiday to handle, and I was floating around with Harrah's, trying to figure out the future of the company. When I told Mike what I was trying to do, trying to get our cost down, he reached into his coat pocket and said, "Look at this." He brought out a card with some numbers neatly typed on it, and it showed that they would be able to build their Marina casino-hotel for fifty-five million dollars, I think. Mike said, "Here is our cost estimate, and we never miss a budget by more than 5 percent."

I looked at that, and I thought, "Dixon, you've got something to learn! *How* can these people do it?" Now, I'd been through this cost of building before; I'd shopped New York for cheap contractors and cheap building construction, and I'd been through all that business of trying to get financing to build Harrah's hotels before Harrah's had any hotels. I'd had some success, but I never was able to get a contractor to build at a price that I wanted. I looked at those figures, and I couldn't believe it! But I had to believe Rose, because here was a guy who was the president of the hotel division of Holiday Inns, and this was his bible, and he said, "That's our experience."

Lou Walter was in the Marina joint venture with Holiday, and the project was not a happy one: the cost went through the allocated fifty-five million dollars faster than granola though a goose! I still recall the screams in Memphis (this was after Harrah's merged with Holiday) when the project went through one hundred and forty-four million dollars. Now, this is Dixon's view–it might not be accurate, because not all of the workings or operations of Holiday were ever known to me–but my perception was that this fifty-five million dollar estimate was something that was done by the hotel design department in-house at Holiday Inns. My recollection is that the architect who designed the project was paid twenty-five thousand dollars, whereas Harrah's was talking architectural fees in the neighborhood of a million and a half to two million *minimum*, and another million or so for interior design–we had some heavy money laid into that part of it.

So here you have a project that was designed by a Memphis architect who had never been in Atlantic City–never been in a casino, as far as I know–and as it turned out, the engineering was done by a Nevada engineer who had no license . . . or if he had a license, it had been revoked. So the building was not exactly what you wanted. [laughter] The costs were a lot more than we wanted, especially when the property had defects . . . that's the nicest way I can put it; smile when you say it–defects. If the man in the room next door to you received a letter from his girlfriend, you could hear him open it! The sound would go right through the wall. But I won't get into it, because Dixon and Holiday looked at things differently.

Eventually, in November of 1980, Harrah's/Holiday got in the property and started operating (as Harrah's Marina), and it became successful, but there was nothing easy about it. We had to spend millions more on the property to keep it from sinking into the bay, because it was inadequate in its foundations; and the convention area would not support the events that we wanted to put in it; and the laundry wouldn't function. It was a project that had so many faults that if it were politics, you would impeach the people who were in charge of it. I think the fault was in Holiday's system of fragmenting management into compartments and departments where each got a bonus for production below budget . . . which essentially meant screwing the other department.

The weakness in the Holiday Inn system, according to the Dixon perception, was the compartmentalization of every function: the guys who did the architecture and design in Memphis had a goal, which was to do as cheap a job as they could–get some plans drawn up and out of their office at a minimum of expense. And each fellow who was in charge of something else had the same kind of goal. Everybody accomplished his goal, but nobody accomplished the overall coordination of the picture. The guy who was responsible for the architecture and design had no responsibility for the function, so if he could cut something out, he'd cut something out. That's a gratuitous observation on my part, and I better stay away from that and not declare myself an expert; but if you ever wanted to see a property that was built inadequately, with functional conflicts, the Marina is a classic example.

Holiday Inns' goal was to build to dollars, where Harrah's goal was to build for quality. A simple example of this: the Casino Control Commission disapproved the Holiday Inn rooms in the Marina, because they weren't big enough to meet minimum standards. This was a subject of tremendous concern in Memphis; Memphis resented being told that they had to make their rooms bigger. But that's the rule in Atlantic City–you have to have four hundred and fifty square feet, (or whatever it was) per room. Typically, Holiday rooms are two feet narrower than standard hotel rooms, which generally are built to a fourteen-foot width. (Holiday always built to twelve feet.) That extra two feet was, in effect, money in the bank. That's what they tried to do in Atlantic City, and the Casino Control Commission, or Department of Gaming Enforcement–whoever the regulatory authorities were–put the brakes on and said, "Uh-uh. This project will not fly."

Roy Winegardner came up with a solution . . . after he chewed up a few cigars. (Roy was a good guy–a tough, rough plumber who became a multimillionaire and very successful, and managed to salvage Holiday Inns when it was kind of going sixty different directions under the loose management of Kemmons Wilson.) Roy started with the principle that no bureaucrat was going to tell him how to build a room. What he did was move the exterior walls out four feet, which added the required square footage to the room. In other words, he lengthened the rooms, instead of making the rooms wider as had been wanted. It was the cheapest solution. Where Roy and I came to a parting of the

ways was that that was *all* that he would do to meet the square
footage requirement. He didn't utilize that additional space
beneficially, so that you continued to have a bathroom that was
too small. I won't say it was the typical Holiday Inn bathroom,
where you step out of the tub and your foot goes in the toilet,
but it was close to that . . . with Greyhound bus terminal toilet
seats instead of seat covers.

The closet space in the Holiday Marina was, in my opinion,
a disgraceful use of space (the cloak rack measured only eighteen
inches in a twenty-four inch closet), but I couldn't get them to
enlarge the closets. I thought if we moved the wall out four feet,
we could add a couple of feet to the closet space, but
Winegardner said it wasn't necessary because people only stay
one night. I said, "Well, what if the wife has a fur coat? It'll fill
the whole closet."

He said, "We have no trouble at Holiday Inns," and that
ended that discussion. I mean, I wasn't the commander in chief;
I was pretty much an errand boy.

The numbers show Harrah's Marina is fantastically successful, but it was sad that we couldn't have utilized that extra four
feet by enlarging the bathroom and closet space a little, creating
a nicer room. And we later had to go through all the rooms and
increase the soundproofing. In later years, Phil Satre made many
improvements in the Atlantic City property, and we spent a lot
of money improving the rooms' decor from plain vanilla, where
everything was painted brown–a typical Holiday Inns theory. We
made some strides, but it was an educational experience, both
for me and for Holiday. Going in, Holiday was very strong on
cookie-cutter building, and very strong on limiting its capital
investment and room volumes. And Winegardner was used to a
place where a night auditor would also run the hotel–in other
words, a one-man operation at night.

I had given a talk to Holiday Inns' people pre-merger, in
which I said that Harrah's have hotel rooms, but we're not in the
hotel business; we have restaurants, but we're not in the
restaurant business; we have bars, but we're not in the bar
business. Our business is running a casino, so everything we do
has to support that. But Winegardner and others walked through

Harrah's Tahoe and reported to me that we had far too much food storage, far too much of this, far too much of that. Roy refused to understand the volume of people that we had to deal with at peak periods on a daily basis–feeding seventeen thousand people a day! I don't think the entire Holiday Inns *system* would feed seventeen thousand people in a day. It was very difficult for them to understand the amount of back-of-the-house space that we needed for support, and the operations we needed to run a casino in comparison to a Holiday Inn.

In Atlantic City, because of the Holiday policy, we didn't have enough back-of-house for anything, and had to do lots of off-site work. They were simply coming from a different culture, a different background, and they also were not listening. I meant what I said when I told them, "We're not in the hotel business and we're not in the restaurant business," and so forth. But that message did not get through with sufficient clarity.

During the merger, I knew that we had some problems; we had some disagreements on the Holiday Inns board as to whether or not it was appropriate for them to become involved in casino operations. I knew there were some culture differences, but I felt our relationships were basically good. Mike Rose was very warm, very interested, very analytical–a brilliant man. And Roy Winegardner was a hard-driving guy. But I didn't think that Winegardner was going to be so dogmatic in his approach to construction costs, and what you give a customer, and I didn't recognize that Mike Rose was going to be so oriented to financial analysis–Rose allowed that to be the driver in his life, rather than recognizing Harrah's to be a mover and shaker in hotel-casinos. At the same time, I didn't recognize that Harrah's had so little to offer in the big world.

Harrah's knew something about operating casinos, but Harrah's was extremely naive in the larger world, because Bill Harrah's management style was limited in its talents and in its depth. I didn't fully perceive the limitations that we had, nor did I understand how the end system worked, and one of the culture shocks that came post-merger was that you might be talking to somebody *very* senior at Holiday Inns one day, and the next day the guy was gone! This was moving chairs for corporate consideration, which was something new to me; I hadn't seen that many moving chairs. (This was before the days of the golden parachutes and substantial rewards to executive officers.) I thought I was reasonably learned and sophisticated, so part of my culture shock was that there was no permanence in Holiday Inns; that people would come and go with greater rapidity than I would want if it were my company.

Pre-merger we bought from Resorts International a parcel of land on the boardwalk in a joint venture with Holiday. As I recall, we paid twenty-four million dollars for the parcel, and Holiday and Harrah's each came up with 50 percent. I remember trying to acquire additional property; I remember razing the structures that were there, and having trouble with the neighbors. Again, Phil Satre was a very significant figure in moving this project forward. José Torres, as I recall, was the Holiday Inns liaison. José was a rising star in the Holiday group, and a competent guy, I thought; but Phil was lead man for Harrah's on that project, and we got to the point where we thought we would be able to build a Harrah's hotel-casino on the boardwalk with a lot of the amenities that Harrah's wanted.

We were at the contract point, when who should rear his ugly head but Donald Trump? Donald had his public relations organs beating the drums in Atlantic City, and somehow Mike Rose became attracted to Donald Trump. Mike had a meeting with Donald, and when he came back, in substance he said–and this is not even a paraphrase–"I feel more comfortable with Donald Trump than I do with Harrah's, so we're going to make a deal with Trump; We're going to be fifty-fifty partners. Trump has twenty-five million dollars in equity in his project, and we're going to take the fifty million dollars that we would have put into the Harrah's project, and put it into the Trump project." That was the end of that discussion, and that closed the opportunity to build a Harrah's Hotel. Donald's project turned out to be nothing but a fiasco, with litigation and hard feelings and an impossible relationship between Trump and Mike Rose. It was not only a clash of egos–if you're trying to deal with Trump, you realize that you are on a *fast* track.

We had so many problems with Donald and with the deal; it started out bad and got worse. Donald was to get a bonus for bringing construction in under projected costs, so you can be damned sure that he *was* going to bring it in under projected costs. I think if he had had to omit the kitchens, he would have done so in order to bring it in under projected costs and get his bonus. Our Harrah's people tried to participate in the design of that project–we tried to talk Donald into putting in an adequate number of elevators, and tried to get an adequate showroom, but we couldn't even get him to provide a service elevator . . . and all the entertainment and so forth was on the sixth floor.

We said–this is illustrious–"Suppose we want to put an automobile on stage or a grand piano; how do we get it there?"

Donald's response in effect was, "Put it on the escalator."

We couldn't even get Trump to punch a hole in the wall so we could lift something up with an outside crane to put it into the showroom, because Donald was going to bring the project in under cost to get his multimillion-dollar bonus . . . which he did.

One of the weaknesses of this project was the name: Trump Plaza. That's what it's called today; that's where it ended up. It was going to be Harrah's at Trump Plaza, but we couldn't even agree on the name of the property. Harrah's at Trump Plaza had no parking, and even Donald was smart enough to recognize that he had to acquire land for parking. My recollection is that the land was going to cost ten million dollars, and when Trump called upon Holiday for participation, Roy Winegardner almost ate some of his cigars, because here was money that Roy had not counted on. Donald's response was, "Don't come up with a quarter, but I'm going to charge for every car that parks on that land; and it's going to be a lot of money." That convinced Winegardner that Holiday had to go in on some kind of partnership with Trump on acquiring the land for parking.

When the ultimate dissolution of the joint venture came about, this particular piece of land was the subject of adult, serious litigation. As I recall, Trump claimed that he owned the land, and that Holiday had no participation in it, which was flat-out not true. In the fragmentation of the relationship before the parking garage was built, Robert Trump called me and said, "Mead, I think your operating people are trying to put one over on us. They think we ought to build a parking garage on this property."

I said, "Well, so do I."

He said, "No, your operating people don't know what they're talking about. That's just an excuse for your lack of command. You don't need a parking garage, and your operating people are steering you wrong, so we're going to have a controversy over this."

Well, the end of that relationship came in litigation, but I'm not the fellow to talk about it; I had no part in it. I do know that the termination of the partnership was a good thing from the Harrah's point of view, entirely apart from the Donald Trump aspect of it. It was clearly a difficult period for Harrah's: Harrah's had the Marina project, and it was dividing its energies between the Trump Plaza and Marina projects, and there weren't really sufficient resources available to do a good job in both.

The Trump Plaza was, in theory, the silk-stocking property, so that your best customers from Harrah's Marina would all want to go to Harrah's at Trump Plaza. Or if they didn't want to go to Harrah's at Trump Plaza, you were persuaded to *send* them over there, because Donald wanted that to be the showcase property. But I'm not satisfied that the Trump Plaza *was* a showcase property. I think it was a hype . . . property with the Trump name on it. I've stayed in some of the rooms in that property, and didn't feel that they were any better than an ordinary New York hotel room. I've never stayed in the luxury suites that were on the top floor, but the ordinary hotel rooms were *quite* ordinary . . . and it was inconvenient to ride up and down on the escalators for so many floors; and the restaurants were ill conceived; and there was no advantage taken of the view over the ocean. You'd stay in rooms that *could* have an ocean view, or in public rooms or public areas that could have an ocean view, but you had no ocean view. It was a New York project hustled onto a very small site, and it had to be thumb-nailed; everything was vertical. Trump Plaza wasn't a luxury property: it was a hype property because the Trump name was on it, and that's where people wanted to go.

If you were running a Marina property, did you want to see your best customers go over to the Trump Plaza? You sure didn't, especially when you weren't sole owner of the project. You start thinking about running two very closely-connected casinos in the same town, and you wonder how you'll manage such a situation. (Harrah's tried to run our Reno and Tahoe properties individually, and not bleed from one to the other. I suppose we could say our better customers wanted to go to Harrah's Tahoe, but the Reno and Tahoe properties were distinctly different. They were marketed and positioned differently, whereas Harrah's Marina in Atlantic City and Trump Plaza were to a certain extent competing for the same customer.)

In the end (1986) Donald bought Holiday Inns out of Trump Plaza, pretty much at cost, and paid the buy-out on a slow note. (That's Norman Biltz's term. It means, "I'll pay you when I can," I guess.) That was something that I had nothing to do with, and know little about, but in my opinion everybody felt better after that relationship was dissolved and they no longer had to put up with Donald. After that, we no longer had the constraint on the Marina property that we couldn't improve it or change it, because we might be in competition with Trump Plaza. So it was a healthy solution, a healthy divorce. (I won't say that anybody was satisfied with the financial settlement, but from the standpoint of management it sure clarified the Harrah position in Atlantic City and gave us a lot more breathing room.)

From the beginning, I did not think we should have gone into the project; I had a very, very strong aversion to the deal. I wanted to take the money and build a Harrah's project, instead of taking fifty million dollars and ending up with half a project. I wanted 100 percent; I wanted the property that I felt was the *right* property, instead of what I saw as a property that would be very difficult and expensive to operate. I had such an aversion to the Trump property that I closed that project out of my mind as much as I could.

Darrell Luery, who is now chief operating officer of Bally's Vegas and Reno, was a marketing fellow sent out from Memphis by Holiday to take care of Harrah's marketing. Darrell was bright and persuasive, and he was able to persuade Goeglein that he could develop Harrah's at Trump Plaza as the CEO. Interesting, since it was Luery's first dabble in operations; in fact, it was the first time, to my knowledge, that he got out of a room where they cut advertisements and marketing programs.

One of Darrell's great innovations was that you walk down Center Street in Reno and encounter bare footprints in yellow on the walk. The footprints go down the walk, and all of a sudden they turn into Harrah's! I wondered, "What in the hell is going on here?"

Darrell says, "Oh, that's a great idea. Everybody's going to follow those footprints and walk right into Harrah's." Well, that's *his* marketing, and I won't comment further . . . .

We went back to Atlantic City, pre-opening, and Darrell had big hoopla put on with all the employees, and so-called "tremendous" employee enthusiasm for the pre-opening event. Then came the opening of Trump Plaza, which was a *total* disaster. When Trump Plaza opened, we didn't even have the cages completed. I sat on the floor in one of the cages, counting money with no place to put it; no boxes to put the money in–no drawers, no shelves. It was the strangest experience. I'd been all through the property, through the man traps, through this and that, but I was also in the back of the house where they were still trying to put things together while the property opened. My recollection is that the Division of Gaming Enforcement shut down the operation, even the slot machines, on the theory that Harrah's at Trump Plaza was not competent or prepared to run slot machines, let alone table games. So the whole project came to a screeching halt . . . and there was some justification in Donald Trump getting mad. Here's Donald with his pride, his name, his premier property opening, and Harrah's–a supposed winner in the casino business–couldn't even get the casino open and run slot machines. That was a significant disaster! I don't know how it came about; Phil Satre probably knows much better than I why it failed, because he was getting hands-on involved in the management of the company at that time.

The casino world is not static. If you look at the Las Vegas Strip of 1947, with the kind of customer that you had, and then look at the Strip today, just a glance will tell you you're dealing with a totally different market. You're dealing with tour and travel markets; you're dealing with people in sandals and shorts and halters or something instead of women in fine clothing. Instead of Cadillacs, you've got people arriving by bus. The casino industry has changed, so I'm not sure that you can take what Bill Harrah did–which was genuine leather, live flowers (no plastic plants), and lots of luxury–and successfully transport that to 1992.

In today's casino world, competition is tougher, and the customer is different. I didn't personally understand the Atlantic City market. If we stop and look at the Atlantic City market–it was different from the market that we had in Nevada. In Nevada, people come and stay awhile, but Atlantic City is a bus market, the so-called day tripper's market. I believe you could satisfactorily run a casino in Atlantic City with no rooms at all if you just ran the day trippers in and out, in and out.

So the subject of rooms has to be thought through. Fred Benninger had the right philosophy: hotel rooms are to drive business to the casino floor. Five hundred rooms are not going to drive enough business to the casino floor to keep your joint open, so now you want to start talking philosophy: what do you do with those rooms? What you really need in Atlantic City are rooms that are going to hold the *best* customers. To that extent, I think the Harrah philosophy of building better rooms would be some help; but I'm not sure that Bill Harrah's philosophy of excellence would make a hell of a lot of difference in the bottom line at Atlantic City.

Licensing in Atlantic City meant carrying all of the detail that New Jersey required; and that wasn't the big end of it. The big end was meeting Joe Lordi, who was the first chairman of the Casino Control Commission. I've had success meeting people

one-on-one, but I'll never forget meeting Joe at the top of the
Holiday Inn in Atlantic City. (He would corroborate this if he
were alive.) We met in the bar at the top of the Holiday, perhaps
as late as ten o'clock at night. What a dynamic person he was!
We started drinking whiskey together, and we had a lot of fun
talking shoulder-to-shoulder, and went eyeball-to-highball . . .
which would probably make the New Jersey authorities wince.
But I wanted to meet him–he was the top of the box; he was the
guy who was really developing gaming in Atlantic City. I wanted
him to know me, and I wanted to know him. I don't mean to
imply that I wanted to influence him improperly; I just wanted
to talk to him from the standpoint of being a guy in charge of a
company that wants to come to Atlantic City, and it was a very
interesting evening. That stood me in good stead later on,
because as Harrah's went through its various procedures, we had
to meet Lordi and the commission, and I had confidence in the
guy as a straight shooter. I think he had confidence in me, too,
knowing that I wasn't going to come in and lie to him or mislead
him. There is no substitute for being able to make contact.

Just offhand, I did not have any other personal relationships
with members of the Casino Control Commission, although I did
meet with them formally on various occasions. I always thought
that I was able to communicate with them pretty well in
hearings, but they were a very skittish group–they wouldn't even
meet in Atlantic City because they didn't want to get that close
to gaming. They had their offices in Trenton. Peculiar!

Later on, as Harrah's began to get its license, we ran into
some problems, which Phil Satre handled very skillfully. There
was a question over the integrity of Harrah's in Nevada–among
other things, it had to do with prostitution. (There may have
been some other issues, but prostitution was the most sensitive
one.) You have to recognize that in Nevada, that sort of thing was
present in the casino world. I mean, the casino world wasn't a
church; it was a real world out there, and there were hookers in
the real world. There was a question about whether Harrah's
spent money on female companionship for customers, and it was
an issue that was very serious. So Phil Satre wrote what he called

a "white paper"–I liked the name–and it successfully addressed the issue. I give Phil credit for the admirable job he did in presenting the real Harrah's picture to New Jersey, enabling us to get a gaming license despite the adversarial position that the DGE took toward Harrah's.

There's no question that Harrah's had some problems from its operations in Nevada. We weren't the only company that had them, but when you hold yourself out as being the world's finest gaming company, and then you find a skeleton in the closet, it's all the more dismaying.

[13]

Gaming Regulation and Expansion

PARRY THOMAS WAS THE MOVER AND SHAKER in making corporate gaming a reality in the late 1960s. He became the most significant banker in Nevada–Valley Bank of Nevada in Las Vegas–when he began to arrange financing for Strip casinos; and to develop the Strip, it seemed clear to Parry that you had to license corporations. When Parry put that thought forward, and began building political pressure toward changing Nevada statutes to permit corporate gaming, Bill Harrah was opposed to him. Parry had made a lot of money for himself, become a well-to-do man, and that always bothered Bill Harrah, who thought a banker should work for a salary and not make money . . . a matter of philosophy. [laughter] Bill also objected to Parry's position because Parry used the Teamsters as a primary source of financing, and Bill Harrah didn't want anything to do with the Teamsters or anybody who associated with them. Finally, Bill perceived corporate gaming as a threat to individual owners like himself.

I thought corporate gaming made sense, and I had a number of conversations with Bill about it. After working it out with him, I testified on a couple of occasions, and had a lot of personal conversations with legislators with respect to licensing corporations. I could see nothing wrong with licensing a corporation; in fact, Harrah's Club *was* a corporation. Title to all the property of Harrah's was in the name of Harrah's Club, a corporation, including title to the automobiles, the gaming equipment, and the land. But Harrah's Club did not hold a gaming license. The gaming licensee was William F. Harrah. It didn't make a whole lot of sense to me.

We started to agree in principle with Parry's idea that corporations should have a license, but Bill Swackhamer, who then was a legislator, was concerned that if Nevada licensed corporations, they would sell a lot of stock and swindle the public. I tried to explain to him that Nevada casinos were not going to be hot stock market projects as long as gambling was limited to the state of Nevada, because people buy stock in growth companies. Anyway, we weren't suggesting selling stock to the public; we were simply going to approve corporate licensing.

With the help of Parry Thomas and Jack Diehl, we finally succeeded in drafting legislation allowing corporate gaming. The corporations that were permitted to hold gaming licenses were strictly non-public corporations: every shareholder had to be investigated, and every shareholder had to be licensable or licensed, but the casino license could be issued in the name of the corporation.

About this time (but in advance of legalizing corporate gaming), the Hilton Corporation was set to come to Nevada. Everyone wanted Hilton to come in, and an exception to the licensing statutes was drawn up under Paul Laxalt, so that Hilton could be licensed before public companies in general were allowed in. (Of course, the Del Webb Corporation was already in the gaming business in Nevada under the Del Webb lease fiction. The concept was that the Del Webb Corporation owned a property—owned the Sahara, for example—but the corporation leased the gaming operation to a group of its inside executive officers. On paper, the executive officers were the gaming licensees—they held the gaming license, not the Del Webb Corporation—so technically no corporate license was needed or granted. However, the terms of their lease were such that all revenues from the operation of gaming were paid to the corporation. It was the same as allowing the corporation to be the operator, and it was a complete fiction.)

When the I joined the Showboat board, I got a gaming
license. I had no trouble at all getting licensed, but if it had been
ten years earlier I might have felt bad about it. There was a long
period of time when I could have participated in the casino
industry, but this would have required a casino license, which I
did not want, because licensed gamblers were not very well
respected. There were lots of lawyers and lots of members of the
public who looked upon gamblers as inherently being crooks. Bill
Graham, for example, was looked upon that way.[1] Lots of
gamblers had come in from outside the state of Nevada–Moe
Dalitz,[2] for example–even though they had previously been
involved in illegal gambling. There were rumors of connections
with the Purple Gang in Detroit, bust-out operations in Hot
Springs, and so on. Many of these people had bad reputations,
unsavory backgrounds. It was believed they had paid off law
enforcement people, bribed public officials . . . and of course it
was undeniable they had engaged in illegal gambling outside
Nevada. So on the whole, a gaming license was not an honor–it
was almost a badge of dishonor in the early years. Therefore, one
of the things that you wanted to do as a lawyer was to avoid
being on a gaming license, because you didn't want to be a
licensed gambler with all of those bums.

Obviously, there were exceptions, but there was a general
reluctance on the part of lawyers to become gaming licensees.
The dichotomy was funny. As a lawyer, you wanted to have
successful clients, like Harolds Club or the Golden Hotel or
whatever, but you didn't want to become thought of as a gaming

[1] William Graham and James McKay owned the Bank Club in Reno. In 1938
they were convicted of mail fraud charges, and served some time in a federal
penitentiary. With the support of Sen. Patrick McCarran, they received a full
pardon from President Harry Truman in 1950.

[2] Morris B. Dalitz headed the Cleveland group that acquired 75 percent of the
Desert Inn in 1948. His group also eventually purchased the Stardust. Said to be
a member of a crime syndicate, Dalitz was alleged to have operated illegal
gambling clubs in Ohio and Kentucky before moving to Las Vegas. In the 1960s
the federal government put great pressure on Nevada to rid the casino gambling
industry of old-timers with reputations like Dalitz's.

operator–you wanted to be thought of more as a professional man, so you kept a separation. There's really nothing wrong with that; in fact it is kind of inherent in the practice of law that a lawyer retains his independence and separates himself from his client.

Gamblers were a world apart . . . they certainly were in Reno, anyway. People in the gambling business in Reno were not really part of upper-crust Reno society, but with the eventual acceptance of gambling as a legitimate business, and with the entry of people of respectability into it, it became OK to be licensed.

The gambling business evolved from requiring no licensing, to the ministerial issuance of licenses by the Tax Commission, then to the rules of the Gaming Control Board, which required background investigation, fingerprints, mug shots, personal history and all of those things. That was the gradual evolution of gaming.

I had a philosophical problem with the harshness with which the regulators and the legislature treated the industry. I've been there when applicants or their lawyers said, "You can regulate us; you can do anything you want to us. We're at your mercy; we have no rights. We accept the fact that we are a privileged industry, and because we're privileged, you can do anything you want to us." I can understand the gamblers having that attitude, because they had come from states where gambling was illegal, but I have a hard time understanding why all of the lawyers bought into that. That must have been part of the guilty conscience about allowing gambling in the first place. So there was a firm belief that the Gaming Control Board could do anything it wanted to to gamblers, including revoking their licenses without due process.

In 1955, when the board tried to revoke Marion Hicks's[1] license at the Thunderbird, everybody thought sure as hell that

[1] Marion Hicks, in partnership with attorney Cliff Jones, bought land on the Strip in 1948 and constructed the Thunderbird. In the 1950s Hicks and Jones expanded and brought in new partners, including Jake Kozloff, whose participation led to revocation of the casino's license by the Nevada Tax Commission.

was going to happen, because gamblers had no rights; but Judge Merwyn Brown refused to uphold the revocation. This was a matter of tremendous consternation and concern to the regulators: how could a mere judge prevent either the tax commission or the control board from revoking a license?

Judge Brown was a gutsy little bastard, and I liked him; he was a maverick! I don't know why he ruled in Hicks's favor . . . whether it was out of courage, or whether Hicks paid him a lot of money. [laughter] (I shouldn't say that about Merwyn Brown, but there was a rumor that Hicks must have bought the judge.) Brown made a rationalization, as I recall (and it was sustained in the Nevada Supreme Court) that there are two different standards: that is, upon the application for a license, there may be a denial without any apparent reason; but Hicks had been granted a license, and once that was done, there had to be some hearing and some cause, some due process, before the license could be revoked. You can't just simply call up the guy and say, "Your license is revoked, period." The court made that distinction, and Hicks continued to run the Thunderbird.

I have a philosophical problem with the whole concept of the regulation of gambling. Why do you regulate gambling, and what's the theory of its regulation? New Jersey, of course, has departed from any theory that I can possibly think of in its regulation of gambling, and to some extent Nevada has tended to do that–to be a busybody in the regulation of gambling. As I see it, gambling regulation should be different from the regulation of other businesses, because *gambling* is different from other businesses. Banks, savings and loans, and the aviation industry are regulated in some respects, but the gambling industry is regulated pretty much with high-handed officiousness. (This might not be true today, but it certainly was in the past.)

It currently takes over a year and a great deal of inconvenience to get a gaming license in Nevada, and I think it's going to be a long time before the process changes. We still have a public perception here that puts casino operators at a disadvantage, and politicians follow public perception rather than logic. [laughter] Politicians don't often make decisions that are hard or clear or rational–they make decisions based upon their perception of public opinion. I can turn on the radio, and people are calling in to talk shows and saying, "We don't want any more gamblers in town, and the casinos are making too much money, and we ought to increase their taxes . . . . " You hear great emotional shouts like that from the public, and I don't think that the legislative climate exists to simplify procedures in Nevada.

But economics is going to govern things, in any event. Why would you want to build a substantial casino in Nevada, in view of the current economic situation in the state and in view of the uncertainty of gaming even outside the state? Nevada casinos were successful because casino gaming was confined to the state for so long. Nevada would never have been able to build its great gaming resorts if gaming had been allowed in every state, even on a limited basis; and if there was only one state that sold liquor in the United States, you'd see great resorts built in *that* state.

Don Carano of the Eldorado was quoted in the newspaper recently as saying there was no investment money available for northern Nevada casinos because Reno was not regarded as a competitive location anymore. I think that's probably generally true, but Reno has always been simply a regional market; it has never been the resort destination that Las Vegas is. If Oregon goes into slot machines, or whatever they're doing up there, maybe the people won't drive down to Reno for that kind of gambling, but they will still go to Las Vegas because of the *mass* and the appeal that Las Vegas has. The town is different, without question.

There's going to be a shakeout on the Strip, with the new competition down there: Project X, Treasure Island, and the MGM theme park. I'm not sure the traffic will grow enough to fill over ten thousand new hotel rooms in those three properties, together with the recently-built Mirage and Excalibur. You're going to see some fallout of properties that have become obsolete in Las Vegas. There already are bankruptcies, and I think there are going to be more failures and some doors closed, at least until all of the debt is wrung out of those properties that are not very successful today. Obviously, one of the least-successful operations is the Aladdin. But there are a large number of properties not making money in Las Vegas, and they're going to be hurting.

The issue is fundamental economics. Steve Perskie, the chairman of the Casino Control Commission in Atlantic City, is convinced that there are not going to be any new casinos built in Atlantic City–that Atlantic City is probably built out right where it is. His big goal is to try to induce the casino industry that already exists to build more hotel rooms, in order to create a more stable destination market and make Atlantic City less dependent upon day-trip traffic. Perskie's perception is based on the fact that now casino gaming is no longer simply Nevada and New Jersey–it's the world.

Casinos are here to stay; whether or not they are going to make any money is the question. We are becoming a service-economy society. The United States is no longer making bricks and mortar and steel; we're no longer principally an industrial nation; we're becoming an information nation in which services are important. But where do casinos fit into our world? Take a poor SOB who lives in the city–he works all day, and he goes home to his little flat. He can't go outside, because he'll get mugged; or if there's nobody to mug him, there's nothing out there but cigarette butts and trash and lots of cars. What is he going to do? Is the average Joe going to go to the seashore and swim? Is he going to go hike in the mountains? He's going to go where there is something that fascinates him, and that's pulling the handle on a slot machine and losing or winning some money. Or he'll play the card games or video poker or Twenty-one. He becomes a participant, not a couch potato; he gets some excitement in his life, and that's a very real thing. I believe for that reason we have gotten over the moral hump of this–that's why millions of people come to Nevada and Atlantic City every year. With that moral issue behind us, casino gaming offers a tremendous emotional outlet.

It was discovered by the casino industry–and I suspect by others–that Indian tribes, as sovereign states, were beginning to run their own bingo games, and were beginning to dabble in casino gambling. As a result, there was a move to get federal legislation to regulate Indian gaming. Such legislation was passed several years ago[1] to the effect that Indian gaming could take any one of three classes: Class One, as I recall, was traditional Indian gambling . . . whatever the hell that means! Class Two was simple games, bingo being the principal one, so that if bingo were permitted in any state, then Indians could go ahead and run bingo games in that state. (Most states had churches, predominantly Catholic churches, that had always had charitable bingo–maybe a thousand dollars a week. That being the case, Indians were free in those states to engage in bingo and games in that classification.) Class Three is fundamentally full casino gaming, and that has to be negotiated under a compact with the state, which can grant or withhold authority for Class Three games to Indians within the limitations imposed by the Indian Gaming Act.

The result has been that everywhere you go you see Indian bingo on Indian reservations, and increasingly you see Indian casinos. There is a new Indian casino in Connecticut that's been the subject of tremendous controversy, and Minnesota presently is operating fourteen Indian casinos. I think there are twenty-four full-fledged Indian casinos operating in the United States at this point, and there are probably another fifty under discussion for development.

The Indians themselves have had relatively little experience in operating casinos, and the consequence is, at least in these early days, that most of the Indians (even in bingo) have contracted with experienced people who have been in the casino

---

[1] The Indian Gaming Regulatory Act, passed in 1988, has as its principal thrust the control and regulation of the spread of casino gaming on federal Indian reservations. To that end the act established within the Department of the Interior a National Indian Gaming Commission with fairly broad powers, and spelled out a variety of restrictions on gaming, including a requirement that Tribes enter into compacts with the states within whose borders Indian casinos were to operate.

business or the bingo business elsewhere to come in and run the Indian casinos and get them started. So there have been joint ventures or partnerships in many early Indian casinos, in which the Indians' principal participation is to provide the reservation on which the games can be conducted, and to share in the earnings or profits. I see transition coming in that. You're seeing Indian bingo on remote reservation sites, and you are beginning to see full-fledged casinos that are actually operated by the Indians. The signs that you see are, "Why go to Las Vegas? Come to the Broken Arrow Casino instead. We've got it all!" You see those signs around the country, wherever there is an Indian casino. What you're seeing is growing acceptance throughout the United States of casino gambling, and I think Indian casinos are contributing to that.

No question, the presence of Indian casinos is going to accelerate the casino movement, and my initial reaction to their establishment was, "Watch out! If other states see how successful the Indian casinos are, they are going to legalize casino gaming within their borders, because they can't sit still and let the Indians make all the money and the state receive nothing in taxation." (I think Steve Wynn has also expressed that view.) But if states legalize gaming, and impose a tax on it, the legal, state-licensed gaming casinos will have more favorable locations than the Indian reservations. Arguably, we could have Indian casinos in Nevada, but their locations would be disadvantaged. There are no Indian reservations that I know of on the Strip in Las Vegas or in downtown Las Vegas. There's an Indian reservation [Reno-Sparks Indian Colony] in Reno near the freeway, but I haven't seen any proliferation of Indian casinos in Nevada.

If states change their laws and/or regulations after Indian casinos are already established, then we're going to see conflicts like the ones we have with salmon fishing on the Columbia River and other expressions of Indian rights or sovereignty. The battle of Wounded Knee won't amount to a hill of beans compared to trying to close an Indian casino or create gaming regulations that make Indian casinos uncompetitive. I suspect that those states that have any significant development of Indian casinos are going to have serious problems if there is an attempt to license non-

Indian casinos in more favorable locations. You can't give the Indians casinos on remote reservations, then bust them out by giving gaming licenses to others near population centers.

[14]

Epilogue

THERE WAS A RULE IN HOLIDAY INNS that you had to retire at age sixty-five, but I had my sixty-sixth birthday before I severed my relationship in 1986. I had done all I could in the transition (from Harrah's as an independent company, to Harrah's as a part of Holiday Inns), and I was without question becoming supernumerary the last year that I was there. Following retirement from Holiday, I had no contractual arrangement with anybody for anything, so I came out and tried to reconstruct my life and find out where I was going–not in any tragic sense; but every time you make a change, it's a change. Vargas and Bartlett, my old law firm, was kind enough to give me office space, so I had a reintroduction to the office, and saw my old friends and associates.

I was the executor of the Harrah estate, which was a big responsibility and was time consuming. The problems of executor were increasing with our tax cases–some *very* heavy problems were coming on. I was also asked to come back on the Showboat board. I did so in 1986 or 1987, and I assisted the Showboat in getting its licensing in Atlantic City, because I had a degree of credibility with the Atlantic City Casino Control Commission and a lot of know-how in the licensing procedure. I'd always been able to persuade those people that I was a straight-up, straight-shooter guy; and if I told them two and two were four, they'd say four is the number. I helped the Showboat with its weaknesses, getting licensed, and I testified in support of J. K. Houssels, Jr., and later in support of Jackie Gaughan. I arranged for Larry

Orloff to represent Jackie and get him licensed in Atlantic City, and I think that my support of both of those fellows was of significance in getting them approved in Atlantic City: not only supporting them in testimony, but helping Gregory Nasky and his group plan the strategy for their presentations–what they were going to say, what they were going to do–and I gave them the lustre of integrity and credibility. (I was accepted by some of the most antagonistic regulators you've ever seen, because I had a track record in New Jersey as well as in Nevada . . . and that was part of how the Showboat got started in Atlantic City.)

I think that I was able to make a major contribution to the growth of Showboat because of the baptism that I had gone through at Harrah's. I had thought I was pretty smart, but my experience with Holiday gave me a broader scope of understanding. [laughter] Consequently, I was able to look at Showboat and see its weaknesses in management and organization–it had been a little company, hands on, that did not know how to get big. Despite illness that caused me to miss meetings, I was able to guide the company so that it finally got direction and organization, and I know Showboat appreciated my help. The programs and changes in management that I was able to orchestrate have paid off, and the company's on the road to success.

Maybe I had too much of a universal approach to the law, and I never really became a tight, narrowly-defined specialist. Actually, I'm not sure that Bruce Thompson or George Vargas ever became tight, carefully defined specialists, either–certainly not the way we see it today, anyway. If you go to the Vargas firm today, you will see people who do nothing but very specific kinds of law, and that's it. I can go to someone up there who practices some specialty, and ask him a general question, and he thinks I'm talking Greek to him. In the practice of law today I see a high degree of efficiency and productivity in very narrow areas, but it takes away flexibility, and it may take away your initiative to think you can do *anything*. It's the "I can do anything" kind of attitude that leads you to take on broader challenges. The broadness of my experience as a lawyer, and my interest in the

people who were my clients, enabled me to develop *some* degree
of management talent and leadership.

I had lots of trouble personally (and I think we did as a law
firm) with young lawyers who had come out of law school and
never really understood the full work ethic. It's harder to pass
inferior work in the real world–where machine guns are aimed at
you and there's barbed wire out there–than it is in the academic
structure. When you are in the real world, you're playing for
keeps.

I've come down to the office and worked lots of Sundays. If
you don't get your work out of the way, and it hangs over you,
you're ruined, because when you have stacks of unfinished work
you get nervous. The more nervous you get, the less capable you
are of performing the job ahead of you, and the more impatient
you are with people. You become a different kind of person. It is
absolutely clear to me that if you are in control of your work and
are getting things done, you get in control of yourself and in
control of the relationships you live with–whether it's your
relationship with your family or your relationship with your
clients. There's no substitute for feeling that everything is OK,
and that you've got time to be yourself as well as keep on
working.

I found the courtroom experience to be easier for me than
the legal paper world from the standpoint of strain, preparation,
and communication. The paper world of corporate planning,
documentation, long and complex contracts, securities transactions, and so forth was fun, but was also a burden. You are trying
to reduce to written form something that's very specific, and as
an individual practitioner, you are competing against big
organizations with great resources that charge clients thousands
of dollars for paper product. You can't put out paper product on
a competitive level without having the same great resources
unless you work twice as hard, butt glued to a chair, paper on
the desk.

But the courtroom was different. A courtroom is where you
get immediate response–what you say is being heard; you can

almost feel the feedback from the judge or the jury or opposing counsel. You can extemporize; you can express yourself a little more loosely, because no one expects the spoken word to be the same as the written word. You get a result, and you get it now! It doesn't mean that you don't have to prepare or that you don't have to understand judges and juries and jury instructions, but as courts evolve, more and more of that stuff is becoming what I would call boiler plate. I always found that courtroom practice was easy, and even though I didn't have a lot of it, I had a pretty good track record with it. It was easier because you could use your brain; and it was gratifying because you got a quick result. The immediacy was rewarding.

The entire legal system today is under examination. Can the ordinary working stiff afford a lawyer? Of course not! Can even a well-to-do person afford a lawyer? Hardly. It's worse than medicine! One of the problems with law is that a lawyer may give an honest opinion and be right, but the adversary system in the practice of law makes everything subject to adversarial examination. If I have appendicitis, and a doctor says I do, and I then go to another doctor and ask him if I have appendicitis, he is also going to say yes. But the legal system is not structured that way. Nothing that you put out in the legal arena can simply be on the basis of its substance. You say, "I believe in this," and everybody who reads it may agree, but if there is the slightest legal loophole, as in the Forest Service option to buy Middle Fork Lodge . . . if there is the slightest way to whittle it down or break it off, somebody is going to find a way to do it.

There are two ways to do work for the client you represent: you just do sloppy work so it looks good on paper, but might leave space for somebody to get around; or you try to cover all the bases. If you try to cover all the bases, you run the risk of becoming a "Philadelphia lawyer." The art, the key to success, is to learn to write well, and to use words so accurately and succinctly that you can cover all the bases with a minimum of them. That was always my goal–to cover all the bases without having a document that was sixty-five pages full of whereases, heretofores, and thereafters. I tried to avoid as much of the conventional legal language and construction as possible; I tried to write documents and contracts that you could understand. For example, it was customary for lawyers to begin a complaint something like, "Comes now John Doe, plaintiff named in the above entitled case and for cause of action against Richard Roe, the defendant named above, and does hereby allege, state, and bow-wow-wow . . . . " That kind of lawyer, the old-fashioned kind, would have about four or five lines before he would get down to what he started to say. I developed a different system. The first line of mine was "Plaintiff alleges," and then I started paragraph one. I cut out all of the historic Blackstone B.S. that people write. I had to go through an evolutionary period to do that, but "plaintiff alleges" says all you need to say.

The same is true in contracts–you can do the same thing quite often without getting bogged down in legalese, and that was always one of my goals. I didn't succeed to the extent that I would have liked, because it is harder to practice this way. (You know the saying: "I am sorry to write you such a long letter, but I did not have time to write a short one.")

There were three or four key people in my professional development. Of course, Frank McNamee, the judge in Las Vegas, was a very key person, because he took me into his chambers and used me as a law clerk when I wasn't even qualified; but the most significant was Bruce Thompson, who taught me more about the practice of law and the analysis of cases than anybody else I ever dealt with. One of the things that Bruce taught me was that every case rests on a theory. You must find the theory on which you are going to handle the case, and then everything you do must be aimed at that theory. Never get sidetracked. Cut out the excrescence.

Another key person, of course, was George Vargas. Bill Harrah used to call him King George. George was a spectacular person–spectacular in his dress and in the way he tried cases. He was totally different than Bruce Thompson, but George was key to me in the sense that no matter how dazzling or brilliant he was, he was like Bruce Thompson or George Springmeyer: he was a person of total integrity, total honesty. George never once had a thought about representing a client that wasn't aboveboard and honest. I learned some of George's weaknesses, too–that George did not have the patience to maintain long-standing relationships with boring clients. He liked to work at the top of the spectrum; he was a lawyer who had primarily case-by-case relationships, rather than long, ongoing relationships.

George was very good in his lobbying efforts, and he taught me a lot about the legislature. His reputation in the Nevada legislature was such that if he told a senator or an assemblyman something, they believed him. George carried the imprimatur of integrity–the longer you knew him the more certain you were that he would tell you things the way they were, and he helped me understand the value of being honest and straightforward. I always thought I was, but I could really see it in George, and it helped reinforce my belief in my associates and myself. Really, honesty is the best policy! You don't come to that conclusion by lecturing yourself–you simply *are* or are not that kind of person.

Throughout my legal career, I had a problem with whether attorneys should take advantage of the system, or live with the system as it was taught. At the University of Missouri we were on the honor system, and we had courses in legal ethics. And when I came to Reno I met competent lawyers like John Belford, Tom Cooke, H. R. Cooke, Sam Platt, and Miles Pike, who drummed the hell out of me on legal ethics. I even remember Sam Platt having been disciplined because his picture appeared in *Life* magazine–we were trained to bend over backwards to avoid publicity, and I was told by people like Bert Goldwater and Clark Guild not to allow my name to appear in the newspaper. So I tried to be an ethical practitioner with the highest of standards, and nobody could ever criticize Dixon for going over the line.

Pete Echeverria was a very successful practitioner who taught me something to the contrary . . . but it took me a long time to learn it, and by that time my practice was headed in a different direction. Echeverria said, "Mead, when I walk into a courtroom, I want to be in charge. I'm going to go just as far as I can," which means that Pete would go, as aviators say, balls to the wall. (All of the controls in piston aircraft are in the form of balls on the tops of levers. When you have an emergency, you shove everything forward to the fire wall, so you say, "Balls to the wall," which means you are going all out. It has nothing to do with sex.) [laughter] Echeverria would go balls to the wall in a courtroom, and you had to stop him if you could. The judge might say, "Mr. Echeverria, that question is improper," but it didn't bother Pete at all. He'd go as far as he could with the next question, and then come back to the old, improper question. His goal was to win his cases.

Pete marked a generational change in the practice of law in Nevada, and he was one of the successful innovators of the personal injury practice. (That practice really started in Nevada with Gordon Rice, who was one of the first, if not the first, to develop a personal injury practice in Reno and to help establish a chapter of NACCA [National Association of Claimant's Compensation Attorneys] here.) Pete's technique was simply to win. Pete was not only skilled as an examiner, he was fluent! He would ask a question knowing that the answer might give the wrong impression, which was absolutely of no consequence to him–it was up to *you* to take care of your side of the case, because he's going to take care of his side. Pete taught a lot of people how to practice law. In Nevada he was more effective than Melvin Belli, the king of torts.

I had the misfortune of being diagnosed on September 9, 1987 (my birthday) with a metastatic prostate cancer. The discovery was by the old-fashioned method–that is, during a routine physical examination, there was felt to be a small growth or lesion on the prostate gland, and then a bone scan gave the indication that it might have metastasized. A biopsy showed that it was malignant. At that time in Reno, there was no blood test for PSA–prostate specific antigen. (It has since become the most common marker for determining the existence of potential prostate cancer.) I was extremely depressed about having cancer, of course. I asked my urologist what I should do, and he said, "Well, if I were you, I wouldn't do anything. Just let nature take its course. But if you want to do something, then you better consider looking at a major cancer center." Well, that [laughter] gave me *one* choice: I tried to find a major cancer center, and hurry was the name of my game; I wanted to get on top of it.

My son, Sherwood, is a vascular surgeon in Reno, and I asked him for help. I also called Mickey Rudin, who has reasonable knowledge of what goes on in the Los Angeles area. (He's a lawyer friend of mine.) It turned out that I would have to go to Los Angeles, San Francisco, New York, or perhaps the Mayo Clinic. I called my retired Mayo physician, Dr. David G. Hanlon, and asked him if he could schedule an appointment with someone at the Mayo who specialized in my kind of case. He called me back and said, "You have an appointment at eight o'clock Wednesday. Can you make it?" (This was Monday afternoon.)

I said, "You bet I'll make it." So I traveled all day Tuesday and kept my eight o'clock Wednesday meeting at the Mayo Clinic. They had a staff of physicians in various specialties present; my medical records were there. A series of examinations were ordered, and in a period of two or three days I had a number of consultations. Things moved quite rapidly. I said, "I want surgery; I want to get rid of the cancer."

They said, "It's too late for that. We'll see if we can do it with radiation. We'll not only radiate your prostate, but we'll try to include in the radiation process the bone in your hip where the cancer has metastasized, in the chance that may help." To make a long story short, I underwent about three months of radiation, and I got some very serious injuries out of that radiation. (That was when I decided to get involved with computers. I had always wondered about computers, so while I was at the Mayo I purchased a computer and began to learn all I could about computers and DOS and so forth . . . in the meantime taking radiation treatments.) My radiation burns were pretty bad: it ruined my urethra; it ruined my bladder; it ruined my lymph glands. The radiation really crippled me and made me a pretty sick kid.

I returned to Reno late in December of that year, and eventually I began follow-up treatments at Mayo. Everything went pretty well until September of 1990, when it was concluded that

I had to go on chemotherapy . . . so I started a regimen of chemotherapy that might last three to five months, depending on how well my body tolerated it. I was able to maintain that course of chemotherapy from September 1990 until December 1991, but I soon found myself getting sicker and sicker. I would be pretty sick after the chemo, and would have to spend a lot of time in bed–initially, maybe two or three hours a day . . . then I found I had to spend four or five days in bed. Then between treatments I began to spend time in St. Mary's Hospital in Reno, largely because I was becoming so weakened from the chemotherapy that I was susceptible to just about anything that came down the street, and I had some close brushes with death.

My son told me in January of 1992 that I was so weak that I should not go back for more chemotherapy. (I had been taking one week of chemotherapy, five weeks off; one week of chemotherapy, and five weeks off.) When Sherwood told me I shouldn't go, I said, "I am going to go," and I went back to the Mayo Clinic and said, "Here I am. I'm ready for more. It's my schedule." They ran some examinations and told me I was too weak, I was no longer a candidate for chemotherapy. So we spent about a week in various tests, and I could barely walk at that time because my left hip had become so involved that I was basically crippled.

They said, "We'll radiate your left hip; that's going to take several weeks." Well, I debated whether to spend those weeks in a hotel room in Mayo or have it done in Reno. You see, my body is tattooed where Mayo set it up for radiation. They had their machinery and their tattoo marks and so forth, and I concluded that I could get the most accurate radiation with minimum setup time with my old three-point system: the three tattoos and the lasers and so forth. So I decided instead of coming to Reno and starting afresh, I'd tough it out in the hotel room and try to decide where I was going.

In January of 1992, Dr. John Earle, who was chairman of radiation oncology at Mayo said, "There may be something else. There is a study on strontium 89, and there may be something we can do for you."

Later, I went in to see my principal oncologist, Dr. R. G. Hahn, as my radiation was winding up. I said, "I'll be through with my radiation in a couple of days. What about strontium?" Hahn wouldn't answer me. I felt like getting out a Browning automatic and forcing him to . . . but I could not get him to discuss strontium. So I got hold of Dr. Earle, and he said, "Well, I can't discuss strontium with you either, because the FDA hasn't approved it for treatment." (At least he used the word; Hahn wouldn't.) He said, "But whatever future course of treatment you have will be up to your principal oncologist, Dr. Hahn."

Dr. Hahn gave me friendly advice, such as, "I don't want you to think about tomorrow; think only about today. And remember, you might outlive me. I might get hit by a car on the way home." I've heard that odds game before, and his advice wasn't comforting. I think his last words were, "If you get in pain, call me."

I came home to Reno and I talked with Sherwood. After a couple of days, Sherwood got hold of Dr. Hahn, and Dr. Hahn told him he would get my name on the list for strontium as soon as the FDA approved it. But waiting for FDA approval is like waiting for the second coming of Christ, so I talked to Mickey Rudin again (he lives in Beverly Hills). It wasn't long before Mickey called Sherwood and said, "I want you to speak to Dr. Peter Kennedy." Through that contact I was able to go to Los Angeles to St. Vincent Medical Center. They could administer strontium. When I met Dr. Kennedy, he had already reviewed some of my records, and he had what patient history Sherwood was able to give him. Kennedy had no hesitancy–or damn little–in getting me into a strontium study program after I had some pre-examinations, such as a bone scan and a metastatic survey. I started in early March of 1992.

I'd had terrible side effects from steroids I was taking–my hands would bleed; I would bleed in bed; my arms would bleed; and my skin was like wet Kleenex. I was even suffering atrophy of the leg muscles and some other muscles because of the steroids, so I asked Dr. Kennedy if he would help me get off them. Mayo had declined to help me get off them, because they said I could not withdraw, but Dr. Kennedy said, "Well, let's see if we can handle withdrawal." So we've started a withdrawal program. Now, I am too early into this to say anything except that I am now down to 25 percent of my usual steroid dose. I still feel fatigue because the steroids suppress your adrenal glands, and the question is whether my adrenal glands can recover enough to give me strength. On the other hand, my skin isn't tearing or bleeding quite as easily as it was. My legs are getting stronger, too, and I'm able to walk up stairs a little better, and to walk down the street a little better than before.

I've got some pains that I can't account for, but a lot of my cancer pains have diminished as a result of the strontium program. It's too early for me to know what's happening, but if I were to judge based upon the last thirty to sixty days, I would say . . . I'm afraid to say that I feel better. I don't know whether this is a simple remission or whether there will be a long-term result.

The disease has two characteristics: It attacks the bones, and the bones eventually will become so weak that they break. It also attacks the internal organs, the soft tissues. The strontium program that I am on is primarily aimed at reducing the effect cancer has on the bones. If I'm lucky and don't have any soft tissue involvement, then I've got a reasonable chance of hanging on for a while. But if I get soft tissue involvement, there is not much left that can be done except rather harsh chemotherapy. That's a bridge that the doctors don't want to talk about and I don't want to cross. The difficulty that I have as a patient is that I can't perceive the soft tissue involvement by feel–it has to be analyzed by medical examination. I've had some soft tissue involvement in the past, which the prior chemotherapy that I undertook backed down. Whether that's going to start up again since I'm off chemo, I don't know.

This struggle with cancer has been depressing, but I made the decision to live; I was going to try to succeed . . . but it changed my career a bit. I kind of lost enthusiasm to do more work for the law firm, and I have minimized some activities and tried to do things that might be a little more important with my children and my personal life. I also tried to become more active physically and to do some of the outdoor things that I had done in the past. The illness for the last couple of years has really been tough on me, but I am happy that I beat the projected twenty-eight months life expectancy.

So that's cancer. It's been hard to live with the pain, the soft tissue bleeding, the swelling of my legs and having to be bandaged and wrapped up. (It takes me longer to dress or undress than the average person, because I have to use Jobst stockings, bandages and other paraphernalia to keep the edema in my legs down.) I think I've lived with it pretty well. I've sure challenged it, and I've really tried to challenge the medical profession. I don't know where to look for more help than I'm getting at present.

My brother, John Brown Dixon, is four years younger than me. We have been close all our lives, and our relationship is an easy one. All I have to do is pick up the phone and say, "John, I've got a problem," and he'll help me. My children and I have that same kind of relationship, both ways. I mean we don't have any talks and palaver and baloney about anything, but we have an inherent relationship and an inherent trust, and it's easy—no fuss. They don't have to worry about my being on their side, and I don't have to worry about their being on my side.

Beyond my brother and children, I would just as soon not get into family relations. I've had a lot of personal problems, and there is no use in me commenting on that . . . if I did, I would bring sorrow to some people; maybe even sorrow to myself. I have not been as successful in family life as I would have liked to be. I haven't been the grandfather who can sit down and smoke a pipe in front of the fireplace, and pick up grandchildren and hold them on my knee and have nice Christmases and all of those traditional American things. Somehow my life has denied me those particular pleasures . . . or perhaps I've denied myself those particular pleasures.

However, my son Sherwood and I have grown increasingly closer over the years. He lives in Reno with his wife and two children. His wife, Trudy Larson, is prominent in the medical field, and she's involved with the University of Nevada. While Sherwood is a source of comfort to me in being so close, I have been very conscious of the fact that he must lead his life and I must not be the kind of guy to interfere with it. Our relationship is a good one, which is true of all of my children . . . but it's not been the Norman Rockwell traditional family life.

As for career high points, I felt I had a high point every time I won a case, (and I won some tough cases that didn't have very much money in them); and I had a high point every time I did a project that came off well. I suspect that the single greatest achievement of my career was my ability to take the Harrah estate and get on top of it. I was able to turn it around from the unsatisfactory condition it was in when Bill died, and make it into something that had a good outcome for the heirs as well as for Harrah's as a company. That was *the* single high point in all of my career.

Druthers means what you would druther. And maybe I'druther have been the president of the United States, or worked for the state department, or had a wonderful education at Harvard or another Ivy League school, or that sort of thing. But you don't have those druthers in real life–you have to play the cards that are dealt.

Index

A

Adair, Carlton, 83-84, 86, 88-89
Adams, Everett, 99, 155
Adler, Sanford "Sandy," 94, 95
Aladdin hotel-casino (Las Vegas), 230-231
Alexander Grant & Co., 187
American Federation of Musicians, 106
Anderson, Arthur, 187
Andreotti, Rome, 106-107, 108-109, 114-115, 119, 121, 125, 126-127, 137-138, 169, 172, 190, 191, 192, 205, 208
Ansett, Reginald, 196
Archer, Bill, 176
Armstrong, Bryn, 73
Arthur Little report, 127-128
Association of Aviation Underwriters (AAU), 58

B

Babcock, Howard, 45
Baer, Eddie, 10
Bahan, Jimmy, 56
Bahan, Tom, 56
Bally slot machine, 190, 191, 192
Baring, Walter, 76
Barnes, Miss, 10-11
Bartlett, John, 48, 63, 67
Bayley, Warren "Doc," 84, 87, 88, 90, 92
Beck, Jessie, 90
Belford, John, 47, 48, 53, 240
Benninger, Fred, 209, 211, 222
Berry, Bill, 73
Bible, Alan, 74, 77
Biltz, Norman, 45, 46, 75, 76, 220
Booz Allen and Hamilton, Inc., 139, 192
Boulder Dam (Nevada), 39
Bounty replica, 210

Photo Credits

Mead Dixon: *Courtesy Harrah's Archives*; Mead Dixon's parents: *Courtesy John Brown Dixon*; Brown Family: *Courtesy John Brown Dixon*; John Brown, Mead Dixon: *Courtesy John Brown Dixon*; Christmas Day, 1926: *Courtesy John Brown Dixon*; In the Military, 1942: *Courtesy John Brown Dixon*; Dixon Family Portrait: *Courtesy Mead Dixon*; Judges Thompson, Foley, and Thompson: *Courtesy Ellen C. Thompson*; Showboat Hotel-Casino: *Courtesy Showboat, Inc.*; Reno's "Strip": *Courtesy Harrah's Archives*; Harrah's Tower: *Courtesy Harrah's Archives*; Rome Andreotti: *Courtesy Harrah's Archives*; Bill Harrah, Maurice Sheppard: *Courtesy Harrah's Archives*; Bill Harrah, Robert Ring: *Courtesy Harrah's Archives*; Lloyd Dyer: *Courtesy Harrah's Archives*; Ed Berg, Mead Dixon: *Courtesy Harrah's Archives*; J.K. Houssels, Sr. and Jr.: *Courtesy Showboat, Inc.*; Barron Hilton: *Courtesy Hilton Hotels Corporation*; Robert Maheu: *Courtesy Las Vegas News Bureau*; Howard Hughes: *Courtesy Las Vegas News Bureau*; Mead and Gwendolyn Dixon and James Santini: *Courtesy Gwendolyn Dixon*; Goeglein, Dixon, Rose: *Courtesy Harrah's Archives*; Philip G. Satre: *Courtesy Harrah's Archives*; John Sande: Courtesy Vargas and Bartlett.

Playing the Cards That Are Dealt

Text and photo mechanicals designed by Helen M. Blue.
Camera-ready master composed and printed
at the University of Nevada Oral History program
in Caslon 224 Book and Caslon Open Face
using WordPerfect for Windows
and a Hewlett Packard LaserJet IIISi postscript printer.